List of Contributors

Tom Bottomore, MSc(Econ), Professor of Sociology, The University of Sussex School of Social Sciences, Arts Building, Falmer, Brighton BN1 9QN, Sussex, UK.

William Fellner, PhD, Resident Scholar, American Enterprise Institute for Public Policy Research, 1150 17th Street NW, Washington, DC 20036, USA; Sterling Professor of Economics, Emeritus, Yale University, USA.

Gottfried Haberler, PhD, Resident Scholar, American Enterprise Institute for Public Policy Research, 1150 17th Street NW, Washington, DC 20036, USA; Galen L. Stone Professor of International Trade, Emeritus, Harvard University, USA.

Arnold Heertje, PhD, Professor of Economics, University of Amsterdam; 1412 ER Naarden, Laegieskampweg 17, Holland 2.

Robert L. Heilbroner, PhD, Norman Thomas Professor of Economics, Graduate Faculty, New School for Social Research, 66 West 12th Street, New York, NY 10011, USA.

Hendrik Wilm Lambers, ec.drs, Professor of Economics, Economic Faculty of the Erasmus University, Rotterdam (formerly Netherlands School of Economics), The Netherlands.

Paul A. Samuelson, PhD, Professor, Massachusetts Institute of Technology, Cambridge, MA 02139, USA.

Arthur Smithies, PhD, Nathaniel Ropes Professor of Political Economy, Emeritus, Department of Economics, Harvard University, 229 Littauer Center, Cambridge, MA 02138, USA.

Peter J. D. Wiles, MA(Oxon), Professor of Russian Social and Economic Studies, The London School of Economics, University of London, Houghton Street, London WC2A 2AE, UK.

Herbert K. Zassenhaus, Dipl.rer.pol, Dr.rer.pol, 4446 Reservoir Road NW, Washington, DC 20007, USA; formerly Deputy Director, International Monetary Fund.

Jelle Zijlstra, PhD, President, De Nederlandsche Bank NV, Amsterdam, The Netherlands.

Schumpeter's Vision

Schumpeter's Vision

Capitalism, Socialism and Democracy
after 40 years

EDITED BY
Arnold Heertje

PRAEGER

PRAEGER SPECIAL STUDIES • PRAEGER SCIENTIFIC

Published in 1981 by Praeger Publishers
CBS Educational and Professional Publishing
A Division of CBS, Inc.
1 St Anne's Road, Eastbourne, East Sussex BN21 3UN, UK
and 521 Fifth Avenue, New York, New York 10017, USA

Copyright © 1981 Praeger Publishers

British Library Cataloguing in Publication Data

Heertje, Arnold
Schumpeter's vision.
1. Capitalism—History
I. Title
330.12′2′09   HB501
ISBN 0–03–060276–9

Photoset, printed & bound in Great Britain by
Redwood Burn Limited, Trowbridge, Wiltshire.

CONTENTS

Preface

This book is the outcome of an initiative by the Dutch private bank *Insinger, Willems & Cie* to celebrate its bicentenary with a tribute to the world of economics. The idea of a review of Schumpeter's expectations for the development of capitalism suggested itself as a timely theme for evaluation. In his book *Capitalism, Socialism and Democracy*,★ published nearly 40 years ago, he gave a negative answer to the question 'Can capitalism survive?' But have Schumpeter's predictions been realized in any way, and what is to be expected in the future? I approached a number of scholars in different countries to consider this theme and was delighted to find that these distinguished economists, who combine profound theoretical knowledge with a lifetime's practical experience, were willing to take part in the project.

It gives me great pleasure to present the final outcome of the work done by Professors Tom Bottomore, William Fellner, Gottfried Haberler, Robert L. Heilbroner, Hendrik W. Lambers, Arthur Smithies, Paul A. Samuelson, Peter Wiles and Herbert K. Zassenhaus. I believe that this will attract the attention not only of economists but also of other social scientists, indeed of anyone concerned with the development of modern societies, not least the bankers who play such a prominent role in Schumpeter's conception of capitalism.

The book opens with a brilliant contribution by Nobel Prize winner Paul A. Samuelson. The other illuminating articles are placed in alphabetical

---

★ All references to *Capitalism, Socialism and Democracy* in this book are to the fifth edition by Professor Tom Bottomore, London, 1976, George Allen and Unwin.

ix

order according to the names of the authors. The reader will notice that authors from different countries, sometimes for different and sometimes for the same reasons, have come to the conclusion that they must disagree with Schumpeter's main thesis, although they share admiration and esteem for his observations and insights.

In the present climate of economic recession and general pessimism about the future of our capitalistic society, the rejection of Schumpeter's vision is a remarkable outcome of our inquiry. The entrepreneur, as the driving force of the capitalistic engine, is often viewed as a diminishing resource, not least by himself, and encroachment by the public sector is often blamed for this development. Against this background it is striking that nine economists, differing in important respects, reach conclusions opposite to what one would expect from a simple extrapolation from day-to-day experiences. The elimination of the socio-economic function of the entrepreneur, especially in large corporations where technical change is routinized and management is bureaucratized, reinforced by the growing influence of the public sector, is one of Schumpeter's main themes.

This theme, in particular, has been taken up by Bottomore, Haberler, Smithies and Zassenhaus. Putting aside subtle differences, these authors— although acknowledging, at least partly, the truth in Schumpeter's reasoning—share the opinion that Schumpeter was rather pessimistic in the short run and probably too pessimistic in the long run. There has been more room for dynamic entrepreneurial activity than Schumpeter foresaw, especially in smaller scale operations.

Some contributors agree to a certain extent with Schumpeter's point that capitalism itself destroys its essential social strata, but others have a tendency to argue against it. The well-known Schumpeterian view, that capitalism produces an army of critical and frustrated intellectuals who by their nega-tive attitude contribute to the decline of capitalism, is touched upon by nearly all authors. Such intellectuals help to establish an atmosphere in which private property and bourgeois values are daily subjected to attack by journalists and public opinion. Looking back to the general political atmos-phere in the sixties and seventies, the contributors acknowledge without hesitation the element of truth in Schumpeter's vision. Not one of them, however, considers it a decisive ground for the decay of capitalism. Most authors point out that socialism seems to show an increasing lack of attrac-tion as an alternative.

The ultimate refutation of Schumpeter's main thesis does not imply an overall rejection of the arguments Schumpeter put forward to structure his case. The contributors to this volume have carefully examined the pros and cons of these arguments.

The outcome of our survey may be projected against the background of a growing awareness of the empirical significance of the theory of public choice. The well-established approach in economic theory, which takes individual behaviour as its starting-point, is today no longer restricted to the market, but is also applied to the behaviour of politicians and bureaucrats in the public sector. The insight that these individuals, too, aim at some specification of their *own* interest may help to revalue the market sector and the entire entrepreneurial system.

The common root may be the third component in Schumpeter's book, viz. democracy. The need for individual expression, the call for participation at all levels, may be conceived of as an attempt to express preferences about the optimal allocation of resources outside the market sphere. Is it too bold to suggest that, of all possible economic systems, capitalism is the best equipped to absorb the shocks of modern democracy? If this is the case, there is less reason to be surprised about the rejection of Schumpeter's prophecy of doomed capitalism.

It is a great honour that Dr Jelle Zijlstra has written the introduction to this book. I am also grateful to Professor Dr P. Hennipman, my lifelong teacher, who helped me with his stimulating advice and criticism.

Finally, I should like to express my gratitude to the management of Insinger, Willems & Cie and my confidence that the theme put forward in this volume will remain relevant for a long time to come.

ARNOLD HEERTJE

Introduction

JELLE ZIJLSTRA

This is an excellent collection of essays about a unique book by an exceptional man. *Capitalism, Socialism and Democracy*, the first edition of which appeared in 1942, is one of the books which has earned itself a lasting place in economic, social and political science. Insinger, Willems & Cie NV deserve great praise for their commendable initiative in publishing *Schumpeter's Vision: Capitalism, Socialism and Democracy after 40 years*, and of this praise no small part is due to Professor Arnold Heertje.

The authors of the various essays require no introduction. Nor does it seem necessary to give a summary of their contributions. The mere fact that after nearly 40 years these authors still consider Schumpeter's book to be of great value is significant enough. After all, in the world of science, obsolescence is a ruthless and rapid process. It is only the very greatest who succeed in holding their own; Smith, Ricardo, Marx and Keynes are cases in point. I will not attempt a classification of Schumpeter, but it is clear that his *Capitalism, Socialism and Democracy* still holds the same fascination today that it had at the time of first reading. When, after the end of the Second World War, the flow of publications reached the countries of Western Europe which had been cut off for so long from the Atlantic world, Schumpeter's was one of the books which delighted us with a feeling of rediscovery. I have read it, re-read it, read it to pieces. Why, what is the secret it holds? It is as if one hears a piece of music composed around such a haunting theme that one continues to hear it being unfolded in endless variation, sometimes almost hidden in the accompaniment but never drowned. This is the theme: 'Can capitalism survive? No, it cannot. Can socialism work? Of course it can'.

Preceded by a brilliant analysis of Karl Marx and followed by profound reflections about such subjects as the history of the socialist parties, this theme is at the heart of Schumpeter's music. Capitalism is on the wane and must disintegrate and socialism is coming, and indeed must come. Capitalism will die not from its failure but from its inordinate success. As one of the authors puts it, it will die not from a cancer in the body but from an incurable neurosis (meaning a prosperity neurosis). The sublime chapter 'Crumbling Walls', dealing with the intellectuals gone haywire, evokes startling pictures of a prophecy come true: May 1968 in Paris, the campus revolts in the United States, the unrest among the youth of Western Europe. It is thus that the birth of socialism becomes inevitable. Socialism can work, it is not against logic, as Ludwig von Mises held, convinced as he was that a centrally planned economy is impossible. Schumpeter says: 'There is nothing wrong with the pure logic of socialism'.

Viewed thus, the analysis would seem to be largely in accord with the teachings of Marx. After all, the inevitable transition from capitalism to socialism was the bearded prophet's main theme. Schumpeter undoubtedly had a high regard for the monumental works of Marx. It is—and this is not limited to the book under discussion here—as if he wishes to match his strength with Marx's, to join battle with him. This is also clear if one compares his view of Marx with his attitude towards John Maynard Keynes. True, he also held the latter in great esteem, witness his biographical essay contained in the collection *Ten Great Economists from Marx to Keynes*. But after having praised Keynes's qualities effusively, Schumpeter places him in a well-nigh disconcerting perspective: 'He was childless, his vision was essentially a short-run philosophy', and later, '. . . practical Keynesianism is a seedling which cannot be transplanted into foreign soil: it dies there and becomes poisonous before it dies'.

His grand struggle with Marx is of another order, for despite the superficial impression that he travels on parallel tracks with Marx, there is a fundamental difference. In the thinking of Marx the historic causality runs from the material substructure (the relationship between the factors of production) to the intellectual, spiritual superstructure of society. In the case of Schumpeter, it is the other way round. The crumbling walls begin with the cogitations of the prosperous upper stratum of society. The undermining neurosis in the spiritual superstructure destroys the material substructure. From socialism, sure to come, he does not expect Utopia. In its practical political form, the socialist structure of production could well end in a system with fascist traits. 'That would be a strange answer to Marx's prayer. But history sometimes indulges in jokes of questionable taste'. Again, lively pictures are evoked, now of the existing self-styled socialist states.

But if this is the essence of Schumpeter's thinking, why is it still so enthralling? For it must be admitted that his expositions are not beyond challenge. Before answering this question, let us select a few of the problems raised by Schumpeter's line of argument.

Schumpeter postulates that capitalism will inevitably pass into socialism. That, of course, gives rise to the question: what exactly are capitalism and socialism? True, he provides an answer himself: the decisive criterion is the ownership and control of the means of production. Private and public ownership of the means of production are characteristic of capitalism and socialism respectively (he himself defines this in a somewhat more circuitous manner, but that is not the point here). This division into two categories is, however, too strict and is inadequate for a true characterization of the various forms which the economic, social and hence political order may take. It is too strict because, with regard to the ownership and control of the means of production and the related actual influence over production, many variants are not only conceivable but are also realities, so that a black-and-white classification is well-nigh unworkable. It is inadequate because the question as to the political context of one or the other type of economic order is even more important. Schumpeter doubts whether it will be possible to combine socialism as an economic system with political democracy. But what does that mean for the inescapable transition from capitalism to socialism? Will not the people living under a socialist economic system be likely to attempt to free themselves from political dictatorship and enforce a transition to political democracy, even if this should have far-reaching consequences for the economic system? Phrased differently, should not Schumpeter's mighty theme be modulated in the following manner (additions and changes are shown in italics)? 'Can *dictatorship* survive? No, it cannot. Can *democracy* survive? Of course it can'. Or, put in yet another way, is the Schumpeterian monocausality in the transition from private to public ownership of the means of production, with the implicit acceptance of the attendant social and political context as a dependent variable, still acceptable in, let me stress it, the year 1981? In today's world, cannot a different causality be perceived? In the communist countries, which in large measure conform to Schumpeter's social and economic model, we can see forces acting in the opposite direction. Why, in the course of history, could that social and economic model, too, not exhibit those phenomena which Schumpeter so compellingly describes as signs of the waning of capitalism? Let me repeat them, with small changes in italics: 'Crumbling Walls', notably 'the obsolescence of the entrepreneurial function of *the State*, the destruction of the protective strata, the destruction of the institutional framework of *socialist society*'.

Has Schumpeter failed to see all this? It is characteristic of a book bearing the mark of genius that it conveys a distinctly recognizable message, but also that it reduces things to their true proportions, takes up side issues in a brilliant manner, thus offering starting-points for other reflections, without, however, muting the main theme. This reduction of things to their true proportions is brought about forcibly and impressively in an almost casual remark. In what time scale is one to think, Schumpeter asks, with respect to the transition from capitalism to socialism? Seemingly in passing, he notes that a century is a relatively brief span of time in the course of history. If that is so, the following question is obvious. Is it self-evident, from the situation prevailing in, say, the 1930s and 1940s, to predict, in such a monocausal fashion, the development of society in the next one or two hundred years? No, it is certainly not, but I presume that the author would have been the first to agree.

Why, then, is *Capitalism, Socialism and Democracy* still so incredibly captivating and intriguing after 40 years? In history it has always been the greatest thinkers who have pondered over the forces which govern the evolution of human society, economically, socially and politically. Definitive answers can probably never be given, but if we in the present time contemplate this fascinating problem we can benefit from what these thinkers have taught the world in the past. We may be able to see somewhat further ahead, standing as we can on the shoulders of our predecessors. When reading and re-reading Schumpeter's work discussed in the present volume, we cannot but realize that we are indeed standing on the shoulders of a giant.

Chapter One

Schumpeter's Capitalism, Socialism and Democracy

PAUL A. SAMUELSON

THE MAN

These are impressionistic reflections about my old teacher, Joseph Schumpeter. He deserves a more coherent analysis but alas I lack the free time to attempt that here. Nor shall I confine my attention to his last book alone.

It is a great book. Somewhere I wrote that the books Schumpeter toiled over longest turned out to be less important than those that gushed out in the heat of inspiration. Probably I was wrong. Perhaps I had in mind the contrast between his 1914 little gem on historical doctrines and the stillborn treatise on money to which he devoted the 1920s in self-styled competition with John Maynard Keynes; or the contrast between the pedantic two-volume 1939 *Business Cycles* and the 1942 *Capitalism, Socialism and Democracy*.

But, from the text of *CSD* one learns that part of it goes back to the mid-1930s, even though we graduate students thought that 'Schumpie'—what we called him, at first behind his back, and only later to his face—was solely engaged then on his *Business Cycles*. The great Mozart arias may seem to have soared out of the composer's quill but that is not cogent evidence of their comparative gestation periods.

One of Schumpeter's poses was that he did not work hard. He always had time for a cup of coffee at the disreputable Merle Cafe across from the Harvard Yard, and a spare hour in which to suffer fools gladly. Demand creates a responsive supply in the lonely barnyard of the graduate school, and the anteroom to Schumpeter's office was as crowded as Freud's must

1

have been. Nights and weekends Schumpeter wrote.

He was a driven man. Driven by the ambition for accomplishment, by the itch for lasting scholarly fame, Schumpeter below the surface of theatrical gallantry was daily grading himself—and daily finding himself wanting. Since his standards were high and his aspirations insatiable, no scratching could assuage his itch.

When did Schumpeter have time between the tasks of teaching and writing to do the reading needed to build up the erudition displayed in his works? He must have been a fast reader with a remarkable memory for whatever was once read.

Even so, by choice Schumpeter died early from overwork. When the adrenalin is always running, you burn up 500 days each year and are allotted proportionally fewer years. No doubt this was a Faustian gamble, willingly entered into and happy in its net outcome.

THE MESSAGE

A 400-page book contains many messages. The thesis in *CSD* that principally interests me can be indicated, to use Schumpeter's description, 'in one short and imperfect sentence':

> Capitalism, whilst economically stable, and even gaining in stability, creates, by rationalizing the human mind, a mentality and style of life incompatible with its own fundamental conditions, motives and social institutions, and will be changed, although not by economic necessity and probably even at some sacrifice of economic welfare, into an order of things which it will be merely a matter of taste and terminology to call Socialism or not.

These words have the Schumpeterian flavour, even though a 70-word sentence is not 'short' and occurs more commonly in his German than in his English prose. Granted, many of the ideas we associate with Schumpeter's name had antecedents in the past; this thesis seems peculiarly his own. What are its objective merits?

Firstly, if it is true, it is important. The more successful Peter the Great is in effectuating for Mother Russia an industrial revolution, the nearer comes the death of that new capitalistic order and the nearer in time the onset of the socialist order that is next in turn. Such is the allegation.

Secondly, there are some facts that Schumpeter's paradigm does seem to fit. Observing the behaviour of New Left students at the end of the 1960s in Berkeley, Harvard, Heidelberg and Paris, I was impelled to write in the course of a 1970 *Newsweek* column:

It is just twenty years since Joseph Schumpeter died. Although it is not my practice to tout profitable speculations, today I'd like to suggest that Schumpeter's diagnosis of the probable decay of capitalism deserves a new reading in our own time. The general reader cannot do better than begin with his 1942 *Capitalism, Socialism and Democracy*.

Sour Smell of Success

Nothing that has happened in recent years at Berkeley or Harvard would have come as a surprise to those who have absorbed this work. And if there are good clubs in the great beyond, one can picture Schumpeter—a spry 87-year-old by this time, martini glass in hand—reading the New York Review of Books and chuckling in clinical amusement. Only his Viennese veneer keeps him from saying, 'I told you so.' The successes and rationalism of bourgeois capitalism will breed a swarm of discontented intellectuals—to fan the flames of hostility toward an efficient but unlovable system with no mystique to protect it.

THESIS AND ANTITHESIS

Joseph Schumpeter was long dead when I wrote those words. The prophecies implicit in *CSD* were formulated a quarter of a century *before* their fulfilment occurred. This adds to our admiration for Schumpeter's acumen. For, in science, it is somehow more impressive when an Einstein tells you in 1915 that observations during a *future* 1919 eclipse will reveal a shift of light's path as it passes near the sun's gravitational field, than if he tells you only in 1920 that what you *did* observe does indeed accord with his theory. If I or Schumpeter were to develop in 1970 or 1980 the quoted thesis to explain the 1968 happenings, that would be less impressive than for Schumpeter to have done so in 1942, prior to the fact itself. You will remind me, however:

Scientific inference is a tandem chicken–egg–chicken . . . sequence. From earlier inductive observations, we formulate our theoretical hypotheses, testing them and modifying them on later observations that we are lucky enough to make or that we contrive to observe because our provisional hypotheses suggested such observations would be of peculiar interest. Einstein already knew of *past* observations on the anomaly of the planet Mercury's aphelion and had framed his relativity theory in accordance . . . And Schumpeter, already in 1942, had observed the post-1929 withering away of capitalist democracy as the Great Depression made it vulnerable to the onslaughts of Hitlerism and Stalinism . . .

Precisely. One can always benefit from a sermon on the hypotheticological methods of 20th-century scientists. But my point concerning how remarkably early Schumpeter arrived at his fundamental insight remains untouched by these caveats. There is still something to wonder at—which means there is an interesting puzzle here that deserves to be studied in depth.

Let me make my case.

Yes indeed, Joseph Schumpeter did by 1942 know about the Great Depression. He could not have been unaware of the popular thesis that Franklin Roosevelt saved capitalism, whose existence in many countries had been threatened by fascist and communist movements that thrived on the mass unemployment and bankruptcies engendered by the Great Depression. Having been threatened by death once—you will go on to argue—capitalism might well be deemed to be subject to similar threats in the period after the Second World War. From which you will infer that a prophecy to that effect by Schumpeter in 1942 is not all that remarkable.

If you argue in that way, you quite miss the point. That capitalism will die because of its economic malperformance is a possible hypothesis to submit to testing at the bar of History. But it is not Schumpeter's hypothesis! Instead it is almost the negation of *his* hypothesis. For Schumpeter, capitalism is to be killed by its *successes*, not its failures; by its *good* performance, not its bad.

That Russia should turn communist in the wake of a disastrous war Schumpeter would take as obvious. That a long period of depression or of stagnation after the Second World War could undermine capitalism and usher in socialism is a proposition Schumpeter would not have sought to make his own. It was the implausibility of this proposition's antecedent— the implausibility that capitalism would *economically breed its own bad performance*—that constituted his contention. And Schumpeter shared this complacent contention with many who professed optimism about the postwar cyclical outlook, either out of conservative wishful thinking or careful analysis of accumulating wartime liquidity and consumption needs.

What distinguishes Schumpeter from others hopeful about postwar economic conditions is his assertion that capitalism's success will not protect it from dying, but *instead will be the very cause of its demise.*

That I am faithfully stating his position is attested by Schumpeter's own summary, at the beginning of *CSD*'s section entitled 'Can Capitalism Survive?' On page 61, he writes: 'The thesis I shall endeavor to establish is that

[T]he actual and prospective performance of the capitalistic system is such as to negative the idea of its breaking down under the weight of economic failure, but that its very success undermines the social institutions which protect it, and "inevitably" creates conditions in which it will not be able to live and which strongly point to socialism as the heir apparent.'

If you will compare this passage with the 70-word 'short and imperfect sentence' that I earlier quoted to encapsulate Schumpeter's basic vision, you will see that they are essentially the same (albeit this last passage covers less of the ground).

Fatal to the notion that Joseph Schumpeter arrived at his vision of how the capitalist order was to generate its own demise *by empirical induction from the unrest of the 1930s* is the fact, which I have until now artfully concealed, that Schumpeter's 70-word enunciation of his schemata is not taken from his 1942 book but instead dates back to his 1928 *Economic Journal* article, 'The instability of capitalism'.

In the palmy days of the 1920s' new epoch of perpetual prosperity Schumpeter had already announced his prophecy.[1]

The Great Depression is rather a refutation than a confirmation of Schumpeter's thesis. The events from 1928 to 1942 surely mock Schumpeter's 1928 guess that capitalism is 'economically stable, and even gaining in stability.'

We are left in the end with a more remarkable phenomenon. Even *before* the world's most capitalistic society, that of the United States, showed any signs of age or decay, Schumpeter had already, in 1928, arrived at his prediction of its psychosomatic demise as a result of self-induced will not to resist dying.

This is almost too much of a good thing. To predict from a few facts already seen many new facts yet to come is the apex of good science. But to predict something about a domain before you have seen anything of it smacks of superhuman powers or of chance serendipity. (It is like the case of de Tocqueville, who correctly foresaw in the 1830s the weakness of future American presidents. But he did so while lacking recognition that the American presidents before his time—Washington, Jefferson, Madison, Jackson—averaged out as remarkably strong presidents!)

A RED HERRING

It is well, I think, to differentiate the thesis that is characteristically Schumpeter's and which is what I am engaged in appraising here from a somewhat

---

[1] Since so many of Schumpeter's seminal ideas go back to the 1903 to 1913 period, his third decade of life—the epoch for scholars he glorified as 'that sacred period of fertility'—a pre-1928 formulation cannot be ruled out.

I fell into the trap of believing that Schumpeter generated his thesis out of the observations of the post-1929 collapse. In my World Economic Congress speech in Mexico City, August 1980, I wrote: 'The Great Depression showed Schumpeter how prone the political systems of Europe and North America were to depart from the conventional patterns and practices of constitutional democracy.'

different thesis popular with certain historians. The late Crane Brinton, expert in French history at Harvard, used to make the point that revolutions do not come when a region is at its poorest. When people are down and out, they do not have the energy to burst out of their lethargy. Therefore, Brinton asserted, revolutions are more likely to occur after a regime has begun to make some progress towards raising the standard of life. The French Revolution broke out in the most prosperous region of Europe, not in the poorest. (There is evidence, however, of French agricultural distress in the decades prior to the 1789 Revolution. To this degree, the simple Brinton thesis of progress as conducing towards instability is contradicted or at least is laid open to the need for qualification and dilution.) Forcing the thesis and ignoring the more important factor of the Czar's army being defeated in the First World War, you might try to claim that it was the burst of industrial development in Russia early in this century that led to the 1917 February Revolution.

Whether Schumpeter would have agreed with this, I can't say. He did know Brinton at Harvard's Dunster House (but Brinton's name does not appear in *CSD*, nor does Brinton's explicit thesis). But even if Schumpeter would have concurred with Brinton, it is not the Brinton hypothesis that we associate with the name of Schumpeter. Here I confine my attention to the peculiarly Schumpeterian twist, which alleges that it is capitalism's economic success that leads to its political failure.

AD HOMINEM

How can we explain Schumpeter's early genesis—almost too early genesis—of his basic sociological–political paradigm? The effort to find an explanation is interesting for its own sake. In addition, that effort may help to clarify what the content of Schumpeter's thesis really is, and help suggest procedures by which we can hope to test, corroborate or refute its contention and perhaps improve upon its formulation and content.

I am on treacherous ground in studying a scholar's biography to illuminate his thought. My old friend, the economic historian Alexander Gerschenkron, who was also the Harvard colleague of Schumpeter in Schumpeter's last few years of life, was dead set against all biography of scholars. 'Let their works stand for themselves, and don't look for dirty underwear', was Gerschenkron's dictum. Schumpeter himself thought otherwise. In his 1948 Presidential Address to the American Economic Association, 'Science and Ideology', Schumpeter set out to 'look for ideological elements in three of the most influential structures of economic thought, the works of Adam Smith, of Marx, and of Keynes' (p. 353). To ascertain 'what kind of ideology we are to attribute to him [Adam Smith]', Schumpeter wrote: 'Proceeding on the Marxist principle we shall look to his social location, that is, to his personal and ancestral class applications and in addition to the class connotation of the influences that may have helped to form what we call his vision.'

Even if we bless the effort to apply psychobiography to Schumpeter, adding to the shaky methods of Marx the even more problematic methods of Freud, I am ill-equipped for the job. Children never know their parents. I knew Schumpeter for only the last 15 years of his 67-year life, and never had the intimate knowledge of him that Wolfgang Stolper or Paul Sweezy enjoyed. Gottfried Haberler, Wassily Leontief, Edward Mason and Arthur Smithies have told us much about their colleague, but the still more that they can bear witness to should be recorded while yet there is time.

If biography of class and personality cannot be done well, better not do it at all? That is a defensible rule. I violate it with the explicit warning that all my inferences are dubious. If I have little confidence in them, the reader should have less.

I begin by presenting a popular stereotype about Schumpeter, one that I myself fabricated in 1969. For the second time I quote from an earlier *Newsweek* column, this time in its entirety.

MEMORIES (June, 1969)

When Diaghilev revived his ballet company he had the original Bakst sets redone in even more vivid colors, explaining, 'so that they would be as brilliant as people remember them.' Recent events on college campuses have recalled to my inward eye one of the great happenings in my own lifetime.

It took place at Harvard back in the days when giants walked the earth and Harvard Yard.

Joseph Schumpeter, Harvard's brilliant economist and social prophet, was to debate with Paul Sweezy on 'The Future of Capitalism'. Wassily Leontief was in the chair as moderator, and the Littauer Auditorium could not accommodate the packed house.

Let me set the stage. Schumpeter was a scion of the aristocracy of Franz Josef's Austria. It was Schumpeter who had confessed to three wishes in life: to be the greatest lover in Vienna, the best horseman in Europe, and the greatest economist in the world. 'But, unfortunately,' as he used to say modestly, 'the seat I inherited was never of the topmost caliber.'

Half mountebank, half sage, Schumpeter had been the *enfant terrible* of the Austrian school of economists. Steward to an Egyptian princess, owner of a stable of race horses, onetime Finance Minister of Austria, Schumpeter could look at the prospects for bourgeois society with the objectivity of one whose feudal world had come to an end in 1914. His message and vision can be read in his classical work of a quarter century ago, *Capitalism, Socialism, and Democracy*.

Whom the Gods Envy

Opposed to the foxy Merlin was young Sir Galahad. Son of an executive of J.P.

Morgan's bank, Paul Sweezy was the best that Exeter and Harvard can produce. Tiring of the 'gentlemen's C' and of the good life at Locke-Ober's with Lucius Beebe, Sweezy had early established himself as among the most promising of the economists of his generation. But tiring of the conventional wisdom of his age, and spurred on by the events of the Great Depression, Sweezy became one of America's few Marxists. (As he used to say, you could count the noses of American academic economists who were Marxists on the thumbs of your two hands: the late Paul Baran of Stanford; and, in an occasional summer school of unwonted tolerance, Paul Sweezy.)

Unfairly, the gods had given Paul Sweezy, along with a brilliant mind, a beautiful face and wit. With what William Buckley would desperately wish to see in his mirror, Sweezy faced the world. If lightning had struck him that night, people would truly have said that he had incurred the envy of the gods.

So much for the cast. I would have to be William Hazlitt to recall for you the interchange of wit, the neat parrying and thrust, and all made the more pleasurable by the obvious affection that the two men had for each other despite the polar opposition of their views.

Meeting of Opposites

Great debaters deserve great moderators, and that night Leontief was in fine form. At the end he fairly summarized the viewpoints expressed.

'The patient is capitalism. What is to be his fate? Our speakers are in fact agreed that the patient is inevitably dying. But the bases of their diagnoses could not be more different.

'On the one hand there is Sweezy, who utilizes the analysis of Marx and of Lenin to deduce that the patient is dying of a malignant cancer. Absolutely no operation can help. The end is foreordained.

'On the other hand, there is Schumpeter. He, too, and rather cheerfully, admits that the patient is dying. (His sweetheart already died in 1914 and his bank of tears had long since run dry.) But to Schumpeter, the patient is dying of a psychosomatic ailment. Not cancer but neurosis is the patient's complaint. Filled with self-hate, he has lost the will to live.

'In this view capitalism is an unlovable system, and what is unlovable will not be loved. Paul Sweezy himself is a talisman and omen of that alienation which will seal the system's doom.'

All this I had long forgotten. And a few years ago when I reread Schumpeter's book, I graded him down for his gloomy views on the progress that would be made by the mixed economy—capitalism in an oxygen tent, as Schumpeter put it. His failure to predict the miraculous progress of the postwar years earned Schumpeter a C in my eyes.

However, 1969 university happenings reveal an alienation of privileged youth entitling Schumpeter to a report-card recount.[2]

---

[2] After that column appeared, several readers wrote nice notes to tell how much they had liked it. I was struck with the finding that all my correspondents seemed to be over 50, from which I concluded that such reminiscence had a limited audience. However, half a dozen years later, when I was making an informal luncheon talk in the Lowell House junior common room, a sophomore addressed me belligerently, saying: 'It was on account of you that I came to Harvard. Your column of memories of great debates enticed me, and I've not found it true that there are such bright memories to be had here.' My reply was, 'Wait 30 years for them to brighten up.' I also realized that Schumpeter's thought still held relevance for the present, and future.

SECOND THOUGHTS

The above analysis needs revision. It classifies too confidently Schumpeter as an aristocrat. Psychobiology has to do better than that. Even if I had been correct in type-casting Schumpeter as a fossil from a pre-capitalistic epoch, at best that could only explain his cheerful objectivity in uttering gloomy prophecies about the future of capitalism. It is easy to utter gloomy prophecies. Cranks do so all the time. My account failed to specify exactly how and why Schumpeter could cogently claim that capitalism would endogenously generate its own demise out of its very successes.

I did, however, specify one possible line of causation. You could call it the 'spoiled, rich dissident' syndrome. According to this special mechanism, as the Schumpeterian entrepreneur goes from shirt-sleeves to shirt-sleeves in three generations, the detailed stages of his dynasty run as follows: farmer or labourer; small merchant; tycoon; diplomat and public servant; and finally parlour-pink or terrorist.

How much truth is there in this strain of the argument? On reflection, I would say, only a little. It is not just that Paul Sweezy serves only imperfectly to exemplify this paradigm. For if that were all, we could supplement Sweezy with Samuel Bowles, son of the Chester Bowles who went from the highly successful advertising agency of Bowles and Benton to be Ambassador to India and Assistant Secretary of State. The fact that someone like Samuel Bowles was a leading radical economist at Harvard around 1970 could be used to give some plausibility to the model and still other confirmatory anecdotes could be marshalled in which Patty Hearst plays a bit part.

Affluent elite institutions like Harvard and Yale did display more campus unrest than was to be seen in landgrant universities of the Middle West. During the 1960s, when a more radical course competed with the mainstream introductory economics course, a census revealed that those who opted for the radical course came from families with incomes that on average were higher than those in the university at large. Other bits of like evidence can be supplied.

The reasons, though, why I think the thesis will not wash include the following: the most radical American college students come on the average from parents who already have themselves possessed ideologies somewhat critical of market capitalism. Sometimes these parents are successful capitalists. More often, such parents are professional people rather than businessmen or corporate executives. If you look at the children of Paul Sweezy's Harvard class of 1931, a class which predated the meritocracy democratization of Harvard and did contain many who were to be capitalists, I doubt that children of this affluent set showed much pinkness of ideology.

In any case, I doubt that Joseph Schumpeter himself put considerable weight on this particular straw.[3] Schumpeter took it for granted that intellectuals were a source of disaffection in any capitalist society. He recognized that the affluence characteristic of modern industrial economies made possible the existence of an intellectual class of some size. But would he have thought it more likely that the son of a successful entrepreneur would become a dissident than the son of an immigrant tailor would? No, according to my recollection.

When European capitalism seemed to be succeeding less well than American capitalism, as in the 1920s, did Schumpeter believe that dissident intellectuals were being recruited at a greater relative rate in America than in Europe? I doubt that he had any such unrealistic expectations. Furthermore, Schumpeter as cynic discounted heavily the political importance of the intelligentsia, both as scribblers and as chatterers. Had Schumpeter been alive these last 30 years, to observe in Japan the continued omnipresence of Marxist terminology among journalists and teachers, I doubt that he would have been astonished that alongside this there should be recurrent victories at the polls of the ruling conservative party. What I do think might cause in him some squirming and some need to recast his paradigm would be the following phenomenon that is virtually independent of the content of Japanese intellectuals' ideological leanings:

> The fantastic material success of Japan's mixed economy—its characteristic amalgam of capitalism and bureaucracy—far from undermining that mixed economy to the point of harakiri, instead did succeed in keeping the ruling powers in power despite a number of scandals and external shocks.

As I write these words, Ronald Reagan has been elected President on a conservative platform. Was it the successes of the mixed economy that led to this repudiation of New Dealism? Or was it the mixed economy's failure? Surely, it was a rational and not an irrational reaction to America's inflation and stagnation during the 1970s that led voters to repudiate Jimmy Carter, the heir to the Roosevelt–Truman–Kennedy tradition. Reagan may not be able to do better, but pragmatic voters are ready to try out new methods in the best tradition of scientific logic; and those of us who disagree with them do not do so primarily on logical grounds.

Am I denying any empirical triumphs for Schumpeter's thesis? That

---

[3] Opposite to the notion that intellectual dissidents are themselves rich is Ludwig von Mises's notion that those who can't hack it in the competitive commercial struggle for existence become the whiners and complainers who seek to subvert the capitalistic order.

would be unjust. At Mexico City in August 1980, I was able to say on his behalf:

> As *Capitalism, Socialism and Democracy* approaches its fortieth birthday, what stands up best in its analysis is this striking thesis of Schumpeter that capitalism's very success will be its undoing. Joseph Schumpeter, looking down from Valhalla on the Iranian revolution against the Shah, must be crowing, 'I told you so!' In his view the same fate would have been meted out to Peter the Great were it not that the feudal elements of superstition and religion conspired to protect Peter from the Shah's destiny.
> Schumpeter, like Thorstein Veblen, does not really document conclusively the interesting dogmas that he promulgates. Like Oliver Twist, we readers ask for, 'More'.

Against Schumpeter's favourable case of the Shah in Iran, we might have to balance Ataturk, who successfully modernized the Ottoman society, even altering its alphabet and secularizing its cultural life. Empirical science is a more tedious business than speculative brainstorming is.

After pondering over how Schumpeter arrived at his thesis, I am inclined to the view that it was not primarily a clever inference from empirical observations. So, to echo Max Planck's work, as an act of desperation we are led to dig deeper into Schumpeter's own biography.

UNDER THE MICROSCOPE

Firstly, Schumpeter was more than an aristocrat—*and less!* He was not born in Vienna, but rather in the province of Moravia (now Czechoslovakia), son of a textile manufacturer; his mother was the daughter of a physician. What evidence there is I do not know for von Beckerath's[4] assertion: 'Born to a fairly affluent family of Moravia, with aristocratic connections...' His mother, widowed when Joseph was four, did marry a Viennese general, when Schumpeter was ten. As a stepson, his years until 23 were spent on the fringe of higher Viennese society. Von Beckerath's appellation of Schumpeter as of the class 'gentleman-bourgeois' seems merited, but one would not say that the adult Schumpeter had the vacant good looks associated with

---

[4] When this paper was at the revision stage, I received a reprint of Frank Meissner's *The Schumpeters of Trieve*. It documents that he came from a Catholic family of textile entrepreneurs. (In my recollection Schumpeter considered himself a Lutheran in his later years; when he formally ceased being Catholic I do not know. The Meissner account refutes what was always a dubious rumour—that Joseph Schumpeter may have had some original Jewish connections. It also reveals no aristocratic 'connection'.)

court circles. There was always something of the outsider[5] about him. Except that Schumpeter was not Jewish, he shared some of the insecurities and strengths of those other Moravians, Freud and Mahler.

Many of Schumpeter's best friends—maybe most of them—were intellectuals. When I give him the label aristocrat–bourgeois–intellectual, the ordering is monotone increasing in weightiness.

To understand Schumpeter's Wagnerian vision of capitalistic self-death, I don't think we should look to the facts of economic history. Consider that Vienna was a dying culture even before 1914. Its brilliance was that of the feverish tubercular genius of the arts. That Ludwig Wittgenstein should have had five siblings who committed suicide was more than par for the course, but it is indicative.

I am not yet done. Ludwig von Mises, who was as different from the urbane and cynical Schumpeter as you could imagine, was already convinced before the First World War that capitalism was being killed from within by its enemies. He enunciated no Schumpeterian thesis, nor indeed any interesting thesis at all to explain that fact believed in with paranoid passion.

Moreover, we learn from von Mises why Carl Menger, the Abraham of the Austrian School, was so sterile as a scholar the last 25 years of his life. Already, when Schumpeter was still in knee pants, Menger was convinced that the liberal economic order was doomed to be succeeded by the interfering state. So in a sense the less interesting part of Schumpeter's thesis—the assertion that capitalism is dying—involves little mystery as to its genesis: it only reflects the conventional wisdom of Schumpeter's own teachers and colleagues.

What is impishly Schumpeter's personal twist is the part of his thesis that asserts that *success of capitalism is what constitutes its own undermining.* How did Schumpeter arrive at that notion? Did the facts in the Austrian–Hungarian Empire of 1870 to 1925 suggest that hypothesis? Did the facts in the England that Schumpeter admired call for it, or the facts in America of the first part of the 20th century?

---

[5] At the November 1980 Viennese symposium on Schumpeter, Professor Erich Streissler in his paper 'Schumpeter's Vienna and the Role of Credit in Innovation' confirmed my *a priori* surmise that the young Joseph Schumpeter was considered something of an unreliable upstart. Dr Streissler quotes 'the first society' in Vienna as considering him 'impossible'. So much the better for Schumpeter, we now say looking back on those old times: but my earlier thesis of Schumpeter as a secure feudal aristocrat, with no regrets over capitalism's possible demise, is contradicted.

SCHUMPETER'S INADEQUATE ARGUMENTATION

As I said in my Mexico City address one wants more in the way of argumentation from Schumpeter than he gives us. I shall review briefly some of his reasoning in *CSD* and then address the problem of whether we can cogently supply for Schumpeter the buttressing argument that he has not supplied for himself.

Schumpeter at different times reads different meanings into the expression 'capitalism'. It is a tricky word and most of us will be surprised to learn that the word itself goes back barely more than a hundred years.

At times Schumpeter gives *capitalism* a very narrow meaning, if anything too narrow. Capitalism is thus associated closely with the innovation process elaborated in Schumpeter's own scientific writings. Or, it is supposed to be intrinsically connected with the ability of a banking system to create new money for the purpose of financing innovational activity. Personally, I find it very easy to imagine a capitalistic order in which the total money supply is rigidly controlled à la Chicago and in which the Walrasian equilibrium is stably maintained over time, either without important innovation, or with innovation being provided by large corporations that are subject to the checks and balances of other large corporations. If Joseph Schumpeter cannot concede this to be capitalism, then that only shows his human weakness in succumbing to infatuation for his own special theories.

At other times Schumpeter uses capitalism in too broad a sense. Everything that you and I associate with post-Renaissance modernism—for example, the development of Newtonian science—Schumpeter's rhetorical pen tends to regard as part and parcel of capitalism. There is nothing startling in the statement that modernism of the last few centuries tends to disintegrate the cake of custom, tends to undermine reverence for established hierarchies of order and social stratification. Who would care to deny that? Part, therefore, of what seems paradoxical, perverse, startling and interesting in Schumpeter's thesis comes from verbal vagueness. If a translator explains to us that modernism undermines custom and historic order, we yawn. And we feel some element of anticlimax and disillusionment if the translator goes on to explain to us that such a banality is all that is substantively implied in Schumpeter's dictum that the very success of capitalism will undermine its political stability and continued existence.

Such a vague thesis is of little interest. So I move on to consider the more interesting thesis of whether the private-property market system, as it is understood by economists who do not accept Schumpeter's theory of zero-interest-rate equilibrium, is likely to be politically damaged by its own successful operation.

PERSONAL DOUBTS

My own studies of political economy began in 1932 when the American economy was in collapse. Under Herbert Hoover, hundreds of banks were closing down. Bankruptcies were rampant. One out of four workers was jobless, and this was a great depression that did not spare the middle class. In no sense could the years 1929 to 1932 be considered an epoch of capitalism's success. Whether or not Schumpeter would consider this era of capitalistic failure to be the result of *political* instability as against *economic* instability, the citizenry at large regarded the period as one of failure. If Schumpeter is right that capitalistic success jeopardizes continuation of capitalism, reversing the direction of movement along his regression we are entitled to attribute to him the paradoxical hypothesis: failure of capitalism ought to enhance the longevity of capitalism.

The subsequent facts, of course, quite contradict any such hypothesis. By the end of Hoover's term, more than half of the rural editors in the United States favoured nationalization of the banking system. The road was paved for the victory of Franklin Roosevelt's New Deal.

I would interpret the transition from the pre-1929 virtual laissez-faire order to the mixed economy of the welfare state less as a movement from 'capitalism towards socialism' than Schumpeter would. But let us grant Schumpeter the rope he needs for his argument. Certainly the facts of the 1930s, both in America and abroad, seem contradictory to Schumpeter's paradoxical thesis.

I realize that my example is slightly strained. A lawyer for Schumpeter might offer the following defence: when Schumpeter says 'an increase in A causes B to increase', he doesn't have to be regarding the relation as a *completely reversible* one. I bring up the example of the 1930s not in order to foreclose such a defence or settle the issue. Rather, the case is mentioned as relevant to my own autobiographical reason for querying the plausibility of the Schumpeter paradox.

REFORMULATING THE QUESTION

Let me go on to survey different times and different places. Successful functioning of a market system is neither a necessary nor a sufficient condition for promoting its longevity. Malfunctioning of a market system from whatever causes is neither a necessary nor a sufficient condition for its demise. Agreed. The question we should therefore want to address along with Schumpeter is the following. Given that capitalism may ultimately become extinct whatever be its failures or successes in operation, does experience and plausible analysis lend credence to the view that *the forces of mortality operating against capitalism*, and which will determine its expected longevity, will be intensified by successful performance of the system?

If Schumpeter still insists upon giving an affirmative answer to the question put in this way and if in the end we find ourselves having to agree with him, that would indeed be an important finding, all the more important in view of its element of paradox.

However, on reflection, I suspect that *the totality of the facts point away from Schumpeter's answer*. Since facts are rarely conclusive in economics, we must supplement them by examining which modes of logical analysis seem most plausibly relevant. Here too I find the prosaic paradigm more plausible than Schumpeter's paradoxical one. *It seems reasonable that governments which are in power during times of economic progress, other things being equal, have a greater probability of being re-elected to stay in power.* The fruits of this prosaic syllogism seem on the whole to be *corroborated* by cross-sectional and time-series surveys on how politics and economics interact.

Schumpeter's own Austria had an economy that worked out badly after the First World War. Its economy seems to have been working out much better after the Second World War. That should incline you to bet that the post-Second World War regime would have a longer life expectancy than that following the First World War. For once, economic history has been content to fulfil our expectations.

ACCOUNTING FOR SCHUMPETER'S VIEW

This leaves the reader with a question: how did Schumpeter come to form the thesis that I have been trying to test? If induction and deduction command such a thesis, we are confronted with no mystery. But if, as I have been arguing, neither facts nor theorizing suggest his thesis, we are left with a puzzle.

So let us look again into Schumpeter's biography. Just prior to 1928 when Schumpeter wrote the *Economic Journal* article containing the 70-word formulation of his thesis, many economists all over the world fell for the notion that we were then in a 'new era' of lasting prosperity. We should not censure Schumpeter if he succumbed at that time to the view that capitalism was becoming increasingly stable economically. Thus, even Alvin Hansen the stagnationist concluded his 1927 *Business Cycle Theory* with the surmise that '. . . the cycle phenomenon itself, at least in its extreme manifestations, will be seen to have been a disease which came and passed in the few swift centuries during which the world was made over from a rural, local economy to a highly industrialized world economy' (p. 206).

Although we can exculpate Schumpeter for having fallen into the complacency of the 1920s, what are we to think of his failure in 1942 to follow Hansen's example in changing his mind as a result of subsequent economic history? Here are my tentative explanations, based upon Schumpeter's biography, for his continued complacency concerning the *economic stability* of capitalism and indeed for his compulsion to insist upon a distinction between capitalism's *economic stability* in the face of its *political instability*.

From Schumpeter's early twenties, as we see in his very first 1908 book and again in the famous first chapter of his 1912 *Theory of Economic Development*, Schumpeter developed an inordinate admiration for circular-flow equilibrium. I believe he was right to consider Leon Walras the greatest of all economists; and in my view he awarded Walras the laurel wreath for the right reason, namely Walras's Newtonian accomplishment of formulating the system of general equilibrium.

But I think one should admire without being carried away. Schumpeter always showed resistance to any doubts that economic equilibrium, if only the system could be left alone to work out its destiny, would be stable. As an instance in point, I remember how bothered Schumpeter was when I showed him the complete set of Keynesian equations in Lawrence Klein's MIT thesis, *The Keynesian Revolution*. What bothered Schumpeter was that here was a complete equation system that somehow violated voluntary full employment. His instinct—not incorrect but not usefully relevant to policy dilemmas in, say, 1938—was to look for some price rigidity in the scenario and, having located it, to shrug off the phenomenon with the remark: 'Of course, if you introduce rigidities in your system, you can fabricate involuntary deviations from full employment for it.'

Schumpeter in *CSD* rejects the notion of Keynes and Hansen that laissez-faire capitalism might generate a tendency towards excessive unemployment. In a sense, 1945 to 1980 events have vindicated Schumpeter's hunch. But his discussion in *CSD* and elsewhere does not adequately provide reasons why we should agree with his rejection. According to my personal recollection, Schumpeter for many years after the 1936 appearance of Keynes's *General Theory* did not really understand its analysis and allegations. Alvin Hansen corroborated this impression when he told me that Schumpeter's questions at oral PhD examinations at Harvard revealed a lack of comprehension on Schumpeter's part of what 'hoarding' assumptions are involved in the *General Theory*. Hansen went on to say that by the 1940s Schumpeter's questions at such examinations betrayed some deepening of his understanding.[6] Signs of such deepening are not easy to find in *CSD*.

To sum up, an important source of Schumpeter's need to insist upon the economic stability of capitalism as distinct from its political instability I attribute to Schumpeter's excessive confidence in capitalism's purely-economic stability.

SCHUMPETER'S AMBIGUOUS VIEW OF MARX

There has always been a puzzle connected with Joseph Schumpeter's repeated praises of Karl Marx. In 1970 I wrote 'A foreword: Schumpeter and Marx' for Alexander Balinsky's book *Marx's Economics: Origin and Development*, an item that inadvertently seems to have been left out of the third volume of *The Collected Scientific Papers of Paul A. Samuelson*. I commented there on the mystery of Schumpeter's favourable opinion. Although Schumpeter admired Marx for the *pretension*(!) of his effort, how can a person who if anything exaggerates capitalism's stability honestly applaud Marx's efforts to deny that stability?

Part of the puzzle will disappear once we recognize that some of Schumpeter's praise of Marx is only patronizing and superficial, designed more to *épater la bourgeoisie* than intended as serious approbation. When you turn your attention from Schumpeter's broad florid praise of Marx to Schumpeter's actual detailed specific evaluations—as, for example, his rather contemptuous dismissal in *The History of Economic Analysis* of Marx's fear of technological unemployment—there is no admiration there to puzzle us.

Schumpeter regards Karl Marx as being learned, bold to speculate, and broad in his dynamic vision. Schumpeter himself was learned, bold to speculate, and broad in his dynamic vision. So perhaps we should leave it there and consider Schumpeter to be primarily awarding Marx the highest form of narcissistic praise—as a veritable chip off the new block. It still remains true that Schumpeter was of all my teachers the one whose *economics* was essentially farthest from Marx's: the labour theory of value he considered a joke; Marxian surplus value degenerated to zero in Schumpeter's stationary state; the poor grew richer along with the rich as a result of Schumpeterian

---

[6] After Schumpeter's *Business Cycles* appeared in 1939, Lloyd Metzler proposed at Harvard that graduate students hold a serious seminar to discuss it. Schumpeter agreed to attend. Although Metzler was the gentlest of critics, Schumpeter for once lost his temper under the barrage of critical questioning. To the persistent Keynesian question, 'Do you assume *full* employment?', Schumpeter never gave a serious answer, fobbing off his audience with the facetious remark: 'I'd never dream of wearing a waistcoat that is out of fashion, so of course I don't assume full employment.' But, frictions aside, didn't he?

development; business cycles had no Marxian tendency to worsen as Schumpeter's entrepreneurs checked each other by competition.

GAME-THEORETIC POLITICAL VULNERABILITY OF LAISSEZ FAIRE

I believe Schumpeter's intuition was correct that the relatively laissez-faire economy embodied in Walrasian general equilibrium (even when we allow it some Chamberlin–Galbraith deviations from perfect competition) is prone to be interfered with by the political process. What I am sceptical about is Schumpeter's claim that this proneness to interference is actually intensified by successful economic advance.[7]

I can agree with Schumpeter that we are each of us going to die; and, at the same time without inconsistency, disagree with him if he were to argue that exercise and weight-control paradoxically add to longevity. My Schumpeter critique will gain in plausibility if I can supply him with an alternative explanation for the vulnerability of pure capitalism to change—an alternative explanation, that is, to his view of capitalism's own success as the alleged cause of change.

People in the advanced economies of Western Europe, North America, Japan and Australia enjoy a high standard of living. They have a lot to lose, particularly those in the upper two-thirds of the income and wealth distribution. I see little reason to doubt that this does serve politically to limit the rate at which the state infringes on the market economy.

Firstly, there is the obvious point that capitalism has often been changed, democratically and by force, often because of its failures. Depressions and hyperinflations, whatever be our diagnoses of their peacetime or wartime

---

[7] Successful advance does, to be sure, involve disturbance by innovators of various established interests. One could imagine that Main Street shop-keepers who are displaced by innovating chainstores and mail-order houses might possibly form a political faction that leads to a displacement of conventional capitalism by some kind of a fascistic socialism. But Schumpeter is least in a position to advance this syndrome to rationalize his thesis of capitalist success as the predisposer of its demise. According to *his* characteristic *economic* theory, the fruits of innovation *soon* go to wage earners and landowners, the only groups in society who possess the *primary* factors of production who are the ultimate benefiters from innovation. Remember also that Schumpeter disbelieves in mass unemployment—at least prior to the point where government has already got into the act to interfere with capitalism. If he switches his argument—and instead alleges that government interferences will convert what would otherwise be *successful* capitalistic innovation into *unsuccessful* deadweight loss of unemployment and overcapacity— his interesting paradoxes disappear and with them our necessary scepticism. See my Mexico City paper, in which I argue that Schumpeter's exaggerated fears of the inefficiencies of 'capitalism in an oxygen tent' caused him to underestimate the miracle-growth performance in the *1950s and 1960s* of the *mixed economy*!

causes, have often unseated regimes.

Then too, if we broaden our definition of failure to go beyond the behaviour of broad real aggregates of output and income, if we include failure of a market system to provide what electors deem a fair and equitable *degree of equality* of income and opportunity—if we do this, we can assert with propriety and confidence that *often failure of capitalism is what can be expected to result in its demise.*

No one should know better than Joseph Schumpeter that the behaviour equations of Walrasian equilibrium never promised us a rose garden of egalitarianism. Bastiat, von Mises, Hayek and Friedman can emit purple prose to play down, or deny, laissez faire's *actual* degree of inequality; and they may urge readers to tolerate that outcome in preference to feasible alternatives. But their words are persuasive primarily to those who draw the prizes in the Darwinian competitive jungle, and are ignored by those who draw the blanks (or think they do).

My final point is offered to Schumpeter as a better explanation of why pure capitalism is indeed politically unstable. It is an explanation congenial to Schumpeter's self-interest theory of politics.

That same self interest which provides the gasoline to run the competitive machine of Adam Smith and Leon Walras, according to the theory of games, will inevitably in the broadened context of political democracy lead to group coalitions that use the state to alter the economic imputations of the laissez-faire regime.

John Adams, Alexander Hamilton and Thomas Babington Macaulay feared that, under universal suffrage, the poorer 51 per cent of the populace would use the state to gang up on the richest 49 per cent. John von Neumann shows that this is a correct theorem in the non-zero-sum theory of games. It is only (1) the ensuing deadweight loss, (2) the existence of non-economic sentiments and traditions, and (3) the power of money to defend politically the possessors of money that limit the degree to which capitalism is interfered with by the political state.

FINAL FOREBODING

In concluding, this needs to be said: what capitalism is succeeded by is not necessarily 'socialism' in any of the conventional senses of that word. There Schumpeter trod on uncertain ground.

Speaking for myself, what I find to wonder at is not that the considerable efficiencies of the market mode of organizing society have been interfered with in this century. What is to be wondered at is how restrained and orderly that process has been for the advanced nations in the mid 20th century. To say this is not to express optimism. On the contrary, as I look around the world at the recent developments in the mixed economies, I confess to some anxiety as to whether the combining of equity and progress may not be in jeopardy at the century's end.

That I have extended to my old teacher and friend bountiful criticisms is the highest form of praise. A century after Schumpeter's birth, we take his writings seriously and treat them as living contributions to contemporary debate.

ACKNOWLEDGEMENT

I owe thanks to the National Science Foundation for financial aid, and to Aase Huggins and Kate Crowley for editorial assistance.

REFERENCES

Hansen, A. (1927) *Business Cycle Theory*. Boston: The Ginn Co.
Harris, S.H. (Ed.) (1951) *Schumpeter, Social Scientist*. Cambridge: Harvard University Press.
Keynes, J.M. (1936) *The General Theory of Employment, Interest and Money*. London: Macmillan.
Klein, L. (1947) *The Keynesian Revolution*. New York: Macmillan.
Meissner, F. (1978) The Schumpeters and industrialization of Trieve. *Zeitschrift für die gesamte Staatswissenschaft*, **135**, 2.
Merton, R.C. (Ed.) (1972) *The Collected Scientific Papers of Paul A. Samuelson*. Cambridge, MA: MIT Press.
Samuelson, P.A. (1969) Memories. *Newsweek*, June. Reprinted in Samuelson, P.A. (1973) *The Samuelson Sampler*.
Samuelson, P.A. (1970) A foreword: Schumpeter and Marx. In *Marx's Economics: Origins and Development* (Ed.) Balinsky, A. Lexington, MA: D.C. Heath.
Samuelson, P.A. (1970) Joseph Schumpeter. *Newsweek*, April. Reprinted in Samuelson, P.A. (1973) *The Samuelson Sampler*.
Samuelson, P.A. (1973) *The Samuelson Sampler*. Esp. pp. 259–261 and 265–267. Glen Ridge, NJ: Thomas Horton.
Samuelson, P.A. (1980) *The World Economy at Century's End*. Mexico City, World Economics Congress (August).
Schumpeter, J.A. (1908) *Das Wesen und der Hauptinhalt der theoretischen Nationalökonomie (Nature and Main Content of Theoretical Economics)*. Leipzig: Verlag von Duncker und Humblot.
Schumpeter, J.A. (1912) *Theorie der wirtschaftlichen Entwicklung*. English translation (1934) *Theory of Economic Development*. Cambridge, MA: Harvard University Press.
Schumpeter, J.A. (1914) *Economic Doctrine and Method*. English translation (1967) Oxford: Oxford University Press.
Schumpeter, J.A. (1928) The instability of capitalism. *Economic Journal*, **38**, 361–386.
Schumpeter, J.A. (1939) *Business Cycles: A Theoretical, Historical and Statistical Analysis of the Capitalist Process* (2 volumes). New York: McGraw-Hill.
Schumpeter, J.A. (1942) *Capitalism, Socialism and Democracy*. (2nd edition, 1949.) New York: Harper and Row. 5th edition, 1976, London: Allen and Unwin.
Schumpeter, J.A. (1949) Science and ideology. Presidential Address to the American Economic Association. *American Economic Review* (March).

Schumpeter, J.A. (1954) *History of Economic Analysis* (Ed.) Schumpeter, E.B. 1260 pp. New York: Oxford University Press.

von Beckerath, H. (1951) Joseph A. Schumpeter as a sociologist. In *Schumpeter, Social Scientist* (Ed.) Harris, S.H. p. 110. Cambridge, MA: Harvard University Press.

von Neumann, J. & Morgenstern, O. (1944) *Theory of Games and Economic Behavior*. Princeton, NJ: Princeton University Press.

Chapter Two

The Decline of Capitalism,
Sociologically Considered

TOM BOTTOMORE

PRESENTATION OF THE PROBLEM

In this essay I propose to examine from a sociological perspective Schumpeter's predictions concerning the decline of capitalism and the advent of socialism. I use the term 'prediction' here in the highly qualified sense which Schumpeter himself gave to it in his paper 'The March into Socialism', which was appended to the third edition of *Capitalism, Socialism and Democracy* (1950): 'I do not advocate socialism... More important ... I do not "prophesy" or predict it. Any prediction is extrascientific prophecy that attempts to do more than to diagnose observable tendencies and to state what results would be, if these tendencies should work themselves out according to their logic. In itself, this does not amount to prognosis or prediction because factors external to the chosen range of observation may intervene to prevent that consummation; because, with phenomena so far removed as social phenomena are from the comfortable situation that astronomers have the good fortune of facing, observable tendencies, even if allowed to work themselves out, may be compatible with more than one outcome; and because existing tendencies, battling with resistances, may fail to work themselves out completely and may eventually "stick" at some halfway house' (*CSD*, 1950 and subsequent editions, p. 422).

Thus Schumpeter's general prognosis, which is also expressed in a qualified form in the third edition as a belief 'that the capitalist order tends to destroy itself and that centralist socialism is—with the qualifications mentioned above—a likely heir apparent' (p. 423), has to be considered from two

22

aspects. First, is his diagnosis of the 'observable tendencies' sound? And if so, have any new countervailing tendencies emerged, during the 30 years since the third edition of his book was published, which suggest a different outcome, and possibly some kind of 'sticking' at a halfway house?

Schumpeter made clear that he did not think capitalism would disappear as a result of economic failure or breakdown. On the contrary, he claimed that it would be destroyed by its economic success, which was bringing about social and cultural conditions inimical to its own survival. These conditions were, in his view, the obsolescence of the entrepreneurial function; the destruction of the protecting strata constituted by pre-capitalist social groups; the destruction of the institutional framework of individual proprietorship; and a growing hostility to the social system and culture of capitalism, which is widely diffused by a large stratum of critical intellectuals. Let us consider these various tendencies in turn.

THE VANISHING ENTREPRENEUR

Schumpeter argued that the social function of the entrepreneur is being steadily undermined, as 'economic progress tends to become depersonalized and automatized', and 'bureau and committee work tends to replace individual action' (p. 133), and that this process 'affects the position of the entire bourgeois stratum ... Economically and sociologically, directly and indirectly, the bourgeoisie therefore depends on the entrepreneur and, as a class, lives and will die with him ... The perfectly bureaucratized giant industrial unit not only ousts the small or medium-sized firm and "expropriates" its owners, but in the end it also ousts the entrepreneur and expropriates the bourgeoisie as a class' (p. 134).

This process of eliminating the entrepreneur, through the growth of large corporations in which management and administration are bureaucratized, while scientific and technological progress is routinized, is reinforced by the increasing intervention of the state in economic life. Schumpeter summed up the latter tendency by noting the extent to which, in the years immediately following the Second World War, the business class, as well as many economists, accepted approvingly a large amount of public management of business situations, redistributive taxation, price regulation, public control over the labour and money markets, indefinite growth of the sphere of wants to be satisfied by public enterprise, and extensive social security legislation (p. 424).

Hence, in Schumpeter's view, the economic process tends to socialize itself, and the development of the Western industrial societies can be regarded as passing through the three stages of entrepreneurial capitalism, organized or bureaucratic capitalism, and socialism. This view is not unlike that of the Austro-Marxist thinkers, with whom Schumpeter was acquainted in his student days (Smithies, 1951, p. 11) and whose work influenced him in several respects. Karl Renner, for example, drew attention during the First World War to the significance of what he called the 'state penetration' of the economy: 'The epoch of the individual entrepreneur operating in a situation of completely free competition is already farther away than we think. Here I am not so much concerned with the fact of the numerous nationalizations, which only make the state a private owner and change little or nothing in its social character. It is a question rather of the penetration of the private economy down to its elementary cells by the state; not the nationalization of a few factories, but the control of the whole private sector of the economy by willed and conscious regulation and direction... The enterprise takes the place of the entrepreneur and becomes semi-public' (Renner, 1916). Similarly, Rudolf Hilferding, in *Finance Capital* (1910) and in subsequent writings (Hilferding, 1915, 1924), analysed in detail the concentration of capital in large corporations, and the changing economic role of the state, which were bringing into existence a new kind of economic and social order, namely 'organized capitalism'.

The growth of corporations and the increasing state regulation of the economy have continued unabated over the past 30 years. In the 1950s and 1960s there was a wave of mergers, comparable with that which took place around the turn of the century when the early trusts and cartels were formed (Hannah, 1975), and large corporations have become increasingly dominant in the economy as a whole (for the United States of America see Miller, 1975). At the same time, state intervention has continued to grow, in the provision of infrastructural services (welfare and the education and training of the labour force), in the management of demand, intended to maintain economic growth and a high level of employment, and in a more general planning of the economy. State expenditure has increased in all the Western capitalist countries and now represents between 40 and 50 per cent of gross national product in most of them. It is evident that the health of the economy now depends overwhelmingly not upon entrepreneurship but upon regular, efficient activity in the major spheres of industry, food production, distribution, transport, communication, and finance, which is assured by large corporations—both public and private—and by state regulation. Innovation and economic development now result much more from scientific research programmes, largely sponsored and financed by the state, and from a massive investment of public funds, than from the activities of individual inventors and entrepreneurs.

The question is how far this socialization is likely to proceed in the next few decades. Schumpeter, as we have seen, thought that the decline of the entrepreneur would weaken the position of the whole bourgeois class, and presumably lead to the social and political dominance of new social groups. I shall consider the situation and role of various classes more fully later, but first it should be observed that in the present day 'mixed economies' the power of private capital is still very great and there is a close relation between business and the state (Domhoff, 1967; Johnson, 1973). It is indeed the contradiction between the private appropriation of profits and the socialization of costs (of unemployment, research and development, unprofitable or excessively risky undertakings) which is considered by some writers to be the main cause of the 'fiscal crisis of the state' (O'Connor, 1973) or of a more general 'legitimation crisis' (Habermas, 1973). Since it is very doubtful that a modern economy could continue to function effectively without this 'socialization of costs'—that is to say, if public expenditure were substantially, or perhaps even marginally, reduced—the most likely outcome of the present economic crisis is a further extension of public control and planning of the economy. Undoubtedly, one major way out of the fiscal crisis would be for the state to socialize profits as well as costs, and thus to derive a larger proportion of its revenues from profit-generating activities—in the oil industry, automobiles, insurance, banking—as against taxation. However, this postulated tendency towards an extension of public control depends for its actualization upon a great many other social and cultural factors, and in the first place upon the orientation and strength of various economic and political interests, which we now need to consider.

THE CHANGING CLASS STRUCTURE

Although Schumpeter himself wrote an original and illuminating study of social classes (Schumpeter, 1927)—concerning which he observed that ' . . . the subject . . . poses a wealth of new questions, offers outlooks on untilled fields, foreshadows sciences of the future. Roaming it, one often has a strange feeling, as though the social sciences of today, almost on purpose, were dealing with relative side-issues . . .'—he did not in fact assign a very large place to the actions of classes in his analysis of the developmental tendencies of modern capitalist society in *Capitalism, Socialism and Democracy*. To be sure, he discussed briefly, as we have seen, the disappearance of the entrepreneur, and what he took to be its consequences for the whole bourgeois class (pp. 131–134); and he went on to note (pp. 134–142) the 'destruction of the protecting strata', that is to say, of those social groups surviving from feudal society—aristocracy and gentry, small traders, artisans and peasants—which had provided a political protective framework for the bourgeoisie, as well as the decline of the bourgeoisie as a cohesive and distinctive property-owning class with the growth of the joint stock company and the emergence of a more diffuse pattern of ownership which, he argued, 'takes the life out of the idea of property'.

But Schumpeter did not examine in any detail the changes in the class structure, and in particular he did not associate the advent of socialism with the politics of a class. The development of capitalism, as he portrayed it here, is conceived as a purely economic and impersonal process, and socialism—defined only in economic terms, as a system in which 'the economic affairs of society belong to the public and not to the private sphere'—is represented as the most probable outcome of that process. In short, the economy socializes itself. There is expressed here an implicit economic determinism—qualified by Schumpeter's remarks on prediction in the social sciences[1]—which has a close kinship with those deterministic forms of Marxist theory that envisaged an inevitable economic breakdown of capitalism; above all in its disregard of the mediating influence of ideological and political struggles among classes and other groups. On the other side, this view contrasts strongly with another form of Marxist theory, well represented by Hilferding who also worked out, as I have indicated, a conception of 'organized capitalism', but regarded the transition from capitalism to socialism as being a question of political struggle between classes, not an ineluctable outcome of economic development.

Even a brief consideration of the changing class structure in advanced capitalist societies will provide a vantage point from which to criticize much of Schumpeter's argument about the necessary, or probable, transition to socialism. Let us consider, first, the position of the bourgeoisie. Schumpeter envisaged its demise ensuing from the disappearance of the entrepreneur; but what has occurred can more plausibly be interpreted as a change in its composition, and in the specific manner in which it dominates the economic system, while at the same time a historical continuity is maintained. We need to examine two aspects of these changes. One is the emergence, in the period of organized capitalism, of much larger and more influential groups of technologists, managers and officials, who play a major part in the control and planning of the economy, whether in the public or the private sphere. The rise to prominence of these social groups was analysed several decades ago in terms of a 'managerial revolution' (Burnham, 1941); and since that time it has been frequently discussed as an indication of the formation of a 'new class', comprising technocrats and bureaucrats, in both capitalist and socialist societies (Gurvitch, 1949, 1966; Djilas, 1957; Meynaud, 1964).

---

[1] See p. 22 above. In the preface to the first edition of the book this deterministic view was more forthrightly expressed: 'I have tried to show that a socialist form of society will inevitably emerge from an equally inevitable decomposition of capitalist society.'

More recently, the same theme has assumed a central importance in various conceptions of 'post-industrial society'. Thus Touraine writes, in a discussion of 'old and new social classes', that 'The new ruling class can no longer be those who are in charge of and profit from private investment; it can only be all those who identify themselves with collective investment and who enter into conflict with those who demand increased consumption or whose private life resists change'; and further, 'If property was the criterion of membership in the former dominant classes, the new dominant class is defined by knowledge and a certain level of education' (Touraine, 1969).

What is common to these studies is the idea that a new dominant class has emerged, or is emerging, in the advanced industrial societies. Thus in the case of the Western countries the most likely path of social development is no longer visualized, at least in the medium-term future, as a transition from capitalism to socialism, in the sense of the advent of a classless society, or even in Schumpeter's narrower sense of the more or less complete substitution of public for private ownership and control of production (although the enhanced role of the state in the economy is recognized), but rather as a consolidation of 'organized capitalism' or 'state capitalism'. Where the analyses differ is in the account they give of the relation between the new dominant class and the traditional bourgeoisie. Touraine asserts a more or less total separation when he claims that property is no longer a criterion for membership of the dominant class. Marxist writers, on the other hand, emphasize the continued dominance of private capital—and indeed its increasing power, with the concentration of capital in giant corporations, including the transnational corporations[2]—and conceive the Western economies as being still essentially capitalist market economies. At the same time they recognize the changing character of 'late capitalism' (Mandel, 1972), and some Marxist interpretations come close to those proffered by social scientists who, while acknowledging the significance of the 'techno-bureaucracy' (Gurvitch, 1949), see these new social groups as being largely assimilated to, or merging with, the old bourgeoisie.

The second aspect of this question, therefore, concerns the extent to which there is a historical continuity between the traditional bourgeoisie and the dominant class in the present-day Western societies. My own view is that the element of continuity is very great, being sustained both by the considerable overlapping of ownership and management of productive capital and by the ideological commitment of a large proportion of those managers, technocrats and bureaucrats who are not substantial owners of capital to the bourgeois conception of a capitalist market economy, although this does not exclude the possibility of diverse, and even contradictory, interests and

---

[2] See p. 23 above.

values within the dominant class, or the existence, for example, of important similarities between Western and Soviet societies in the functions, and to some extent in the outlook, of techno-bureaucratic groups. I conclude, therefore, that Schumpeter was mistaken in arguing that the decline of the entrepreneur would necessarily entail the decline of the whole bourgeois class.

This criticism of Schumpeter is strengthened, I believe, by consideration of another feature of the class structure in present-day Western societies; namely, the growth of the 'new middle class'. This has been seen as a major factor in the development of Western capitalist societies ever since Bernstein (1899), in his reassessment of Marxist theory and social democratic politics in Germany, drew attention to the fact—among other things—that the middle class was not disappearing, and that the polarization of modern society into two great classes, which Marx had envisaged, was therefore not taking place. During the present century, and especially in the past three decades, sociologists of all persuasions have had to reckon, not simply with the non-disappearance of the middle class, but with its sustained expansion, as white-collar occupations of all kinds have proliferated; and to explore the social and political consequences of this development.

Broadly speaking, three different views have been adopted. The first suggests that the middle class, or at any rate large sections of it, align themselves ideologically and politically with the bourgeoisie; and one reason for this tendency was indicated by Hilferding (1910) in his analysis of the changes in class relations accompanying the development of 'organized capitalism', when he observed that the growth of salaried employment has created a new hierarchical system in which: 'The interest in a career, the drive for advancement which develops in every hierarchy, is thus kindled in each individual employee and triumphs over his feeling of solidarity. Everyone hopes to rise above the others and to work his way out of his semi-proletarian condition to the heights of capitalist income' (p. 347).

A second view conceives the middle class, notwithstanding its diversity, as possessing some common characteristics which give it a distinctive and independent political role, between the bourgeoisie and the working class.[3] The postwar expansion of the middle class has reinforced this idea, and has given rise to a conception of 'middle-class societies' in which the political conflict between bourgeoisie and working class is likely to abate, or even disappear, and to be replaced by a style of consensus politics based upon commitment to a mixed economy and the welfare state (Aron, 1968; Bell, 1973).[4]

---

[3] This view is discussed critically in Mills (1951). See also Lockwood (1958).
[4] See also the discussion of 'non-egalitarian classlessness' in Ossowski (1963), chapter VII.

Third, however, some social scientists, from a standpoint quite opposed to the foregoing, have conceived white-collar and professional workers in the present-day capitalist societies as constituting elements of a 'new working class' (Mallet, 1963; Touraine, 1968),[5] or at least as being potential allies of the working class and the socialist movement (Poulantzas, 1974). Such interpretations can be supported by some empirical evidence; notably the rapid expansion of white-collar trade unionism, the increasing militancy of white-collar unions, and on occasion (as in France in May 1968) some manifestations of political radicalism. Nevertheless, electoral data and surveys of political attitudes over longer periods indicate clearly that a very large part of the middle class, in spite of variations among different sections of it—small businessmen/women, shopkeepers, professional and technical employees, clerical workers, etc.—has maintained a political orientation which is much more favourable to parties of the right and the centre than to those of the left. This outlook might be encapsulated in the fairly obvious comment that an overwhelming majority of the middle class is much more strongly attracted by policies which would reduce taxation and diminish public expenditure than by any projects for extending public ownership or industrial democracy, or, in general, for bringing about greater equality.

Hence it may be claimed that the position of the bourgeoisie in present-day capitalist societies has been strengthened rather than weakened by the growth of the middle class. Concomitantly, the traditional working class has declined, both relatively (as a proportion of the employed population) and, in some cases, in absolute numbers; and these changes in its economic and social situation, which are likely to continue in the same direction with the further progress of technology and automation, must necessarily diminish its political influence. So far, this political decline has been counteracted to some extent by other factors, and in some countries, for example, labour and socialist parties have been more successful in gaining working-class votes since the war than they were in earlier periods, or have regained their electoral strength after a period of decline. In effect, such parties have gained

---

[5] Mallet argues that the 'new working class' comprises technically-trained manual workers, technicians and some cadres of managers and engineers in the technologically advanced and automated industries, while Touraine observes that in the May 1968 movement in France '... sensibility to the new themes of social conflict was not most pronounced in the most highly organized sectors of the working class. The railroad workers, dockers and miners were not the ones who most clearly grasped its most radical objectives. The most radical and creative movements appeared in the economically advanced groups, the research agencies, the technicians with skills but no authority, and, of course, in the university community' (1968, p. 18). These views are critically examined in Mann (1973). In his later writing Touraine has somewhat modified his views, and he now conceives the main oppositional groups in the 'post-industrial societies' as being, not 'new classes', but the new social movements (e.g., the women's movement, the ecology movement). See Touraine (1980).

a greater degree of support from a smaller working class, and in this respect perhaps it can be argued that there has been a development of working class consciousness, and a more pronounced polarization of society, at least since the end of the 1950s.

But is the working-class vote a vote for socialism? The answer to this question is far from clear, but I think it may reasonably be argued that for most of the social democratic labour parties in Western Europe—and they are the pre-eminent political representatives of the Western working class— the goal of socialism has been relegated to a distant future, if it is seriously entertained at all, while the practical, effective political aim is to consolidate and improve the existing system of a mixed economy and a welfare state. Of course, there are considerable differences among countries even in Europe, and in Sweden, for example, where the social democratic movement has been a dominant force in politics for a much longer time than elsewhere, it has been suggested that the *political* levels of aspiration of wage earners are likely to rise in the medium-term future, extending increasingly to issues of control over work and production (Korpi, 1978). But changes in the opposite sense seem to have been taking place in some of the communist parties of Western Europe, and some observers have seen in the Eurocommunist movement a distinct trend towards a more reformist outlook, closer to that of the social democratic parties. Outside Europe, the socialist movement is particularly weak in North America; in the USA there is no independent labour or socialist party of any significance, and in Canada the labour party (the New Democratic Party) has nothing like the strength of similar parties in Europe.

If the commitment of working-class political parties to socialism is thus questionable, this is even more clearly the case with the mass organizations of workers, the trade unions. As I have argued elsewhere (Bottomore, 1979) the link between the trade unions and socialism seems, in the postwar period, to have become more tenuous, or at any rate ambiguous; though again there are important variations between countries. Undoubtedly, the economic power of trade unions (both working-class and white-collar unions) has increased considerably over the past few decades, but the exercise of this power takes place very largely in the context of an acceptance of the capitalist market economy, as modified and regulated by the present degree of state intervention. This is notably the case in Britain, where the enormous importance attached to 'free collective bargaining' by much of the trade-union leadership and membership represents both an accommodation to a market economy and an abandonment of wider political aims. More generally, the dominant tendency in the European trade-union movement— with some exceptions where unions or federations are still closely allied with more radical socialist parties—seems to be a development towards a form of 'business unionism' within the existing economic and social framework, and in this sense a 'depoliticization' of the unions.

From this brief account of the class structure, and of what appear to be the political orientations of the major classes, it may be concluded that the 'march into socialism' has been much less vigorous and rapid than Schumpeter expected. The development of the modern capitalist societies does indeed seem to have stuck at some kind of halfway house—or perhaps it would be more accurate to say, at a point which is a quarter or a third of the way—along the road to socialism. But this is not to claim that a position of stable equilibrium has been reached. Clearly, the present form of society is still contested—from both sides. In Britain at present a vigorous attempt is being made to reduce state intervention and augment the role of capitalist enterprises and the market economy. On the other side, the worsening economic crisis may well lead to an extension of public planning of the economy, and to a reanimation of the socialist movement, in many countries. Before considering these possibilities more fully, however, it is necessary to look at some other aspects of the decline of capitalism as Schumpeter envisaged it.

CAPITALIST VALUES

Just as Schumpeter saw the economic trend towards socialism as being facilitated by the destruction of the institutional framework of capitalism and the decline of the bourgeoisie as a class, so also he thought that the assault upon, and the decay of, capitalist values would give a further impetus to this trend. Capitalism, he argued, 'creates a critical frame of mind which, after having destroyed the moral authority of so many other institutions, in the end turns against its own; the bourgeois finds to his amazement that the rationalist attitude does not stop at the credentials of kings and popes but goes on to attack private property and the whole scheme of bourgeois values. The bourgeois fortress thus becomes politically defenceless' (p. 143).

But Schumpeter devotes only a few pages to this issue, and his analysis is quite inadequate. Let us, therefore, examine more closely the capitalist ideology, and the counter-ideology of socialism, and try to assess their development in the postwar period. By an ideology I mean here the body of ideas in which the values and aspirations of a social class (or other social group) are expressed in a more or less systematic and coherent way.[6] In the case of a

---

[6] I am not concerned here with the specifically Marxist concept of ideology, in which ideology is seen as a distorted world view, arising from a 'false consciousness', strictly related to social classes; and is contrasted with science. For an account of the different conceptions of ideology see Jorge Larrain (1979).

dominant class its ideology does not only serve to systematize its values, and in this way reinforce the cohesion of the class, but is also a means of legitimating—and is at least in part consciously intended to legitimate—its domination, by ensuring as far as possible the support or acquiescence of other classes.[7] For a subordinate class ideology also has this systematizing and unifying role, and it provides at the same time the ground for a critical assault upon the ideology of the dominant class. Clearly, it is this kind of ideological conflict which Schumpeter had in mind in discussing the cultural aspects of the decline of capitalism, but he referred to the capitalist ideology only in vague general terms as the 'scheme of bourgeois values', and largely ignored the role of a counter-ideology as expounded by representatives of a subordinate class. The dissolution of bourgeois values was presented by Schumpeter as the outcome of a purely intellectual process of rational criticism.

What then are the principal elements of the capitalist ideology, and how have they fared over the past few decades? The fundamental components—which may be related in diverse ways and have varying degrees of importance in particular formulations of the ideology—are, I would suggest, the ideas of private property, individualism, achievement and nation. When Schumpeter argued that corporate ownership 'takes the life out of private property' he expressed in a one-sided and inadequate form an important observation which has been more clearly and comprehensively formulated by socialist thinkers in their criticism of individualistic interpretations of property as applied to the modern system of industrial production.[8] The underlying theme of this criticism has been concisely stated as follows: 'Property rights can no longer be defined as a relation between the individual and the material objects which he has created; they must be defined as social rights which determine the relations of the various groups of owners and non-owners to the system of production, and prescribe what each group's share of the social product shall be' (Schlatter, 1951).

The important question to consider is whether the undoubted expansion of social or collective property—in the form either of capitalist corporate property or of public property—has actually weakened the idea of private property as an ideological influence. The answer, it seems to me, is that it has not done so to any significant degree. No doubt there is now a greater acceptance of fairly extensive public ownership, particularly in connection with the provision of infrastructural services, and even to a limited extent in

---

[7] In this respect 'ideology' has the same significance as what Mosca (1896) called the 'political formula', which represents the essential element of persuasion and legitimation, as against coercion, in the dominance of a ruling group.

[8] See, for an interpretation of the individualist theories, Macpherson (1978).

the sphere of production, but the idea of private ownership and control of productive resources is still pre-eminent. There is no evidence that share-holding, as distinct from the direct ownership of physical plant, has attenu-ated the sense of private property in the very small section of the population who actually own shares, as Schumpeter thought it would. On the other hand, those who run the large corporations as directors are still engaged, and know that they are engaged, in the productive use of private property, some of which they 'own' in the legal sense, while the rest of it they collectively 'possess' in the sense that they can effectively decide, within very wide limits, how, when and where to use the property in production, and upon the disposition of the profits.[9] In addition, it should be remembered that a large part of production in the most advanced economies is still carried on by businesses in which the capital is owned directly by individuals, families or partnerships. Finally, it is important to recognize that the socialist criticism of private property has evoked a powerful counter-criticism of collective, or public, property, based largely upon arguments about the inefficiency of state-owned enterprises and about the threat to individual freedom where property ownership becomes concentrated in the state. Hence, although property relations have certainly been modified, and have become more complex, in the advanced capitalist societies, I do not think there is any evi-dence to support the view that private property in the sphere of production, either as a fact or as an ideology, has been steadily and continuously eroded over the past few decades. In this case too, a halfway (or quarter-way) house seems to have been reached, where there is a precarious and contested balance between private and collective property, with conflicting move-ments to change the balance in one direction or the other.

Individualism, of course, has always been closely associated with the idea of private property in the bourgeois scheme of values, most evidently in the individualistic theories of property mentioned earlier. But this association, which was relevant at any time only to a minority of the population, has become increasingly anachronistic, as far as the ownership of industrial property is concerned, with the economic dominance of large corporations. As C. Wright Mills (1951) observed with respect to American society, the prevailing ideology, with its emphasis on independence, individualism and mobility, which may have been appropriate to the small-propertied world of the early 19th century, was only a mystification in the conditions of the mid-20th century when most Americans had become 'hired employees' (and still more so today, we might add). The persistence of this ideology, not only in the USA, although it has doubtless been strongest there, is due in

---

[9] On the various distinctions which need to be made in considering the sociological meaning of 'property', see especially Hegedus (1976).

large measure to a confusion between private property in the sense of ownership of means of production—which may be considered to confer a certain
economic, and hence political, independence—and 'personal' property. No
doubt, a sufficient amount of personal property, even without any direct
ownership of means of production, also makes possible a greater independence of the individual; but the notion then does not apply to the vast majority of people in any modern capitalist society, whose 'ownership' consists
for the most part of 'owning' a mortgage on their dwelling, in the case of
those (50 per cent or less) who are owner-occupiers, and a substantial
amount of hire-purchase debt.

Nonetheless, the ideology of individualism remains strong, and continues
to sustain the capitalist order. One important factor in addition to the confusion just considered is the widespread apprehension about the increasing
power of the state, the invasion of privacy (though this is by no means due
only to the activities of the state), and a general sense of living in 'over-
regulated' societies. Such views seem to reinforce the prevailing capitalist
version of individualism,[10] in spite of the fact that the extension of the state's
activities has not been primarily associated with the advance of socialism in
the Western capitalist countries, but may be regarded as essential to the functioning and continuance of modern capitalism itself, and also as a consequence of international rivalries and conflicts, including two world wars.
And oddly enough, the idea that a capitalist market economy (and hence
strict limits to state intervention) is essential for individual liberty to flourish
has remained very persuasive in spite of the fact that our 'over-regulated'
societies are at the same time characterized as 'permissive', and that the
'march into socialism' has actually been accompanied by greatly expanded
opportunities for large numbers of people to choose more freely their individual style of life.

The third element in the capitalist ideology, the idea of 'achievement', is
also quite closely related to individualism, and it has been regarded by some
socialist critics as the major factor which legitimates and sustains the
present-day capitalist order. Thus Claus Offe (1970) writes: 'In contemporary capitalist industrial societies, the system of official self-imagery and self-
explanation is dominated by the concept of the achieving society.' This
'achievement principle', he goes on to argue, legitimates differences of social
status and reward by attributing them to individual differences in achievement or 'merit', and represses alternatives to the existing arrangements. An
effective criticism of the prevailing ideology in modern capitalist societies
therefore requires above all a criticism of this particular principle, which he

---

[10] For a broader discussion, which brings out the diverse meanings of individualism, see
Lukes (1973).

attempts to provide, not by showing that it is incompletely realized in practice (as is evidently the case), but by demonstrating the consequences of its success, inasmuch as 'these consequences conflict with existing interests and values', and by pointing out 'the "costs" that a society must be prepared to pay if it accepts the achievement principle as a "just" mechanism by which to distribute status' (Offe, 1970, p. 137).

Finally, the 'nation' and nationalism play an important part in bourgeois ideology; both positively, in fostering a sense of unity and an attachment to traditional values, and negatively, in countering the divisiveness implied by ideas of class differences and class conflict, which are especially prominent in Marxist socialism. In some periods nationalism has been expressed with particular intensity, in the form of imperialism, by the dominant groups in capitalist countries.[11] Such nationalism contrasts sharply with the internationalism which has been an important feature of socialist ideology from the beginning, and has assumed a variety of institutional forms since the creation of the First International in 1864. The fact that internationalism has been relatively ineffectual in practice is in part an indication of the continuing strength of nationalist ideology, which remains one of the mainstays of the bourgeois scheme of values.

As I suggested earlier, the specific form taken by the capitalist ideology at any given time and place involves diverse combinations of the various elements which compose it. During the past three decades, rapid economic growth and increasing prosperity seem to have linked together the ideas of private property, individualism and achievement in a social outlook which can best be characterized as one of unrestrained acquisitiveness—as R.H. Tawney (1921) described it more than half a century ago in a work which has lost none of its relevance—notwithstanding the fact that there has also been, during the same period, some movement towards more extensive collective provision of basic social services. An analysis of present-day culture suggests, therefore, that the economic successes of capitalism—the 'managed capitalism' of the postwar period—far from killing it, as Schumpeter predicted, have greatly strengthened it. On the other side, its possible economic failures now loom larger again (as in the 1930s), not only because of the immediate crisis, with declining rates of growth and rising unemployment, but because of the longer-term problems associated with the natural and social limits to growth, and with the impact upon the whole labour process of advanced technology. These prospects have already given rise, since the late

---

[11] Schumpeter himself recognized this phenomenon in his monograph on imperialism (1919), although he did not accept the view that imperialism is a *necessary* stage in the development of capitalism. It should be added that a Marxist conception of the relation between modern capitalism and imperialism does not exclude the possibility that there are other sources and forms of imperialist expansion.

1960s, to new social movements, such as the ecology movement, which perhaps mark the beginning of a significant change in the cultural orientation of Western capitalist societies. Whether they also indicate a possible resumption of the 'march into socialism', a revival and renewal of the socialist movement, still needs to be considered in a wider context.

THE INTELLECTUALS AND SOCIAL CRITICISM

There was one social group to which Schumpeter attached particular importance in his account of the growing climate of hostility to capitalism; namely, the intellectuals. Capitalism, he argued, 'unlike any other type of society ... inevitably and by virtue of the very logic of its civilization creates, educates and subsidizes a vested interest in social unrest' (*CSD*, p. 146). But in this case Schumpeter was undoubtedly too greatly influenced by the particular circumstances of the 1930s; by the notoriety given to what were in fact relatively small groups of radical intellectuals in most countries, and by the phenomenon of 'intellectual unemployment' which produced, in his view, large numbers of discontented and resentful individuals. The intellectuals, he argued, had 'invaded labour politics' and radicalized it, 'eventually imparting a revolutionary bias to the most bourgeois trade union practices... Thus, though intellectuals have not created the labor movement, they have yet worked it up into something that differs substantially from what it would be without them' (p. 154).

This account exaggerates both the radicalism and the social influence of intellectuals in modern societies. If we take a longer historical view it soon becomes apparent that there are major fluctuations in the radicalism of intellectuals over time, as well as important differences among the various categories of intellectuals (for example, between social scientists and natural scientists, and between different intellectual professions, with university teachers probably being more radical, in general, than lawyers). One significant factor in the historical fluctuations is undoubtedly the degree of overproduction of educated persons (and hence intellectual unemployment), as Schumpeter suggested, and as a recent study largely confirms while introducing some important qualifications (Brym, 1980). But even in periods when intellectual radicalism appears to be flourishing, as in the 1930s and 1960s, it is hard to demonstrate that even a majority of intellectuals adopt a radical orientation; and there are certainly very great differences between countries.[12] Moreover, such periods have almost always been followed by a

---

[12] In the USA, for example, during the 1930s, radicalism, and in particular Marxism, seem to have had their greatest influence among small groups of literary intellectuals, while the social sciences, and still more other spheres of intellectual activity, remained largely unaffected (Bottomore, 1968, chapter 3).

conservative reaction among intellectuals (the 1950s, the 1970s), so that it would in any case be invalid to argue that a consistent and progressive radicalization of intellectuals has been taking place which, in itself, tends to undermine capitalism.

But Schumpeter also attributes too great an influence to intellectuals even when large numbers of them are radical. What is much more evident, I think, is the relative social isolation of intellectuals, and their incapacity to exercise any profound effect upon social and political life, though here too there are considerable differences between countries, with intellectuals having probably a greater political role in France than in Britain or the USA. The following comment on the American situation in the 1930s seems to me to present a more truthful picture than the one conveyed by Schumpeter: 'While novelists, in the main, fought shy of the proletarians, critics in some cases welcomed the new literary credo [the idea of 'proletarian literature'—TB]... In Greenwich Village the revolution seemed about to burst forth at any moment... After election day, when noses were counted, it was discovered that about one hundred thousand Americans had voted red—1/4 of 1 per cent of the electorate. The millions of unemployed, the dispirited of the breadlines and flophouses, had voted for either Hoover or Roosevelt. Even the mild Socialist programme suffered overwhelming defeat...' (Harrison, 1933). Similarly, in 1968 and again in 1972, after several years of intellectual ferment, and an apparent upsurge of radicalism, the American electorate voted for Richard Nixon as President, while in France, after an even more turbulent and dramatic display of intellectual radicalism, culminating in the events of May 1968, the electorate gave overwhelming support to the regime of General de Gaulle.

Against Schumpeter's conception of the more or less autonomous, and generally radical, social and political orientation of intellectuals, I think it is more convincing (i.e., better supported by empirical evidence) to argue that the politics of intellectuals are primarily determined by the direction of their 'ties with society's fundamental classes and groups' (Brym, 1980, p. 71), and that the rate and level of intellectual radicalism '... vary proportionately with the size, level of social organization and access to resources of both radical intellectual groups themselves, and other radical groups which can sustain them' (Brym, p. 72). It is not, therefore, intellectuals who radicalize the labour movement (or other social movements), but social movements which, in certain circumstances, radicalize the intellectuals. This enables us to explain why it is that the main elements of the culture of capitalism, as I indicated in the preceding section, have retained their vitality and their dominant position through the postwar period. Economic growth and the consequent changes in class structure and class relations have been the main factors restricting the growth and influence of intellectual radicalism;

although as we shall see there are also other forces at work, quite neglected by Schumpeter, in the continuing contest between capitalism and socialism.

SCHUMPETER'S CONCEPTION OF SOCIALISM

The major weakness in Schumpeter's account of the probable transition from capitalism to socialism is that the process itself, and the end result, are defined too exclusively in economic terms. By 'centralist' socialism Schumpeter understood '. . . that organization of society in which the means of production are controlled, and the decisions on how and what to produce and on who is to get what, are made by public authority instead of by privately-owned and privately-managed firms'; and by the 'march into socialism', '. . . the migration of people's economic affairs from the private into the public sphere' (*CSD*, p. 421). He deliberately excluded the idea of socialism as a class movement expressing broad political and cultural goals, among which the reorganization of the economy is only one, though a crucial, element; and while recognizing that for many people socialism '. . . means a new cultural world', he argued that its 'cultural indeterminateness' is so great that it cannot be given any precise definition in these terms (pp. 170–171). In practice Schumpeter took as his principal model of a centralist socialist society the USSR in the 1930s, although in a new chapter on 'the consequences of the Second World War', added to the second edition (1947), he also considered very briefly the kind of socialism which might emerge in Britain and elsewhere in Western Europe.

But the cultural 'indeterminateness' or diffuseness of socialism should not be exaggerated. In just the same way as bourgeois ideology, the socialist ideology incorporates various distinctive conceptions, which may be combined in different ways in specific formulations of the doctrine. Among the most important underlying conceptions are those of the collective ownership and use of the major physical productive resources of society; the emancipation of subordinate or oppressed groups; the eventual attainment of a classless society in which all individuals would be able to participate fully, on broadly equal terms, in social and cultural life, and more particularly in major decisions affecting work and community life;[13] and finally, internationalism.

---

[13] The idea of 'participatory democracy', which was formulated in some of the radical movements, and notably in the student movement, of the 1960s, is an important restatement of the socialist conception. It has also a close affinity with the idea of 'self-management' which is the most distinctive feature of Yugoslav socialism. There is not yet, I think, a comprehensive study of the development of this body of related ideas, but a useful introduction to the subject will be found in Carole Pateman (1970).

Whether or not there will be a sustained movement towards socialism in the above sense depends ultimately upon the extent to which the socialist scheme of values can establish its pre-eminence over the bourgeois scheme of values, and gain the support of large social groups for its realization in practice. The process in which, according to Schumpeter, the economy 'socializes itself'—through the growth of large corporations and increasing state regulation—is undoubtedly one very important element in this movement, establishing some of the essential preconditions for socialism, as Hilferding (1910) saw clearly; but by itself it may lead just as easily to some form of 'state capitalism' or a 'corporate state' in which the same social groups remain dominant, gross inequalities persist, and nationalism flourishes. In earlier sections of this chapter I have argued, against Schumpeter's view, that bourgeois values are still predominant in the present day 'organized' or 'managed' capitalist societies, and the principal question we have to consider is why it is that socialist values have made so little progress over the past three decades.

A part of the answer lies in the changes in class structure and class relations which I discussed earlier. From the outset socialism was the doctrine of a particular class, the industrial working class (most obviously when it was expressed in a Marxist form); and insofar as that class has become less powerful, especially in numerical terms, as an economic and political group, is less clearly delineated, and is more integrated into the existing society, the main social base of socialism has been attenuated. In consequence, the socialist ideology itself has become less sharply defined, less vigorous and challenging, more apt to be expressed in diverse, fragmented, and often sectarian views, as happens with all social doctrines which lose their connection with the interests of some major group in society which can claim at the same time to represent a general human interest. As Marx (1844) wrote, in the years which led up to the revolutions of 1848: 'No class in society can play this part [as the leader of a movement of emancipation—TB] unless it can arouse, in itself and in the masses, a moment of enthusiasm in which it associates and mingles with society at large, identifies itself with it, and is felt and recognized as the *general representative* of this society. Its aims and interests must genuinely be the aims and interests of society itself, of which it becomes in reality the social head and heart.'

It is all too evident that socialism and the working class are not now the 'social head and heart' of any such movement: evident in the reformism of the European social democratic and labour parties, which no longer look beyond an amelioration of conditions for the most deprived social groups within the existing, largely accepted, economic and social system; and in a different form, in the defensive and uninspiring outlook of the Eurocommunist movement. In Western Europe the socialist press has declined in readership and influence,[14] and the mass media as a whole are now more or less uniformly liberal or conservative in orientation. The expansion of the media, and especially television, has provided new careers for intellectuals, and the high levels of economic growth and more widespread prosperity of the 1950s and 1960s made it possible to assimilate them more fully into bourgeois society, with the result that the edge of radical social criticism has been blunted.

But it is not only these internal social changes which have diminished the appeal of socialism. One of the major blows to its intellectual and political influence has come from the experience of socialism in Eastern Europe, and above all in the USSR. There, 'centralist' socialism, in Schumpeter's sense, has produced regimes which were, in the Stalin period, despotic and have remained authoritarian. In no sense can these regimes be said to have achieved either the social equality or the emancipation of the individual which are essential aims of the socialist movement; yet they proclaim themselves socialist and they are widely regarded as models of what a socialist society would be like.[15] Their character and policies have unquestionably bred scepticism about socialism as a political goal, or in many cases outright rejection of it; and in this sense they have greatly strengthened the attachment to capitalism, and facilitated the task of its ideological defenders. It has become a matter of 'keep a-hold of nurse for fear of finding something worse.'

Even if we disregard the extreme authoritarianism of the regimes in Eastern Europe—which may be held to have developed in part, or even mainly, from particular historical conditions, and hence not to demonstrate a necessary connection with socialism—there are other problems in the functioning of a socialist society which have become more apparent as a result of the limited growth of a socialized economy within capitalism. One such problem, frequently raised by the opponents of socialism, is that of bureaucracy, but here Schumpeter seems to me to have taken a more realistic sociological view—clearly influenced by Max Weber's analysis of bureaucracy as a system of rational administration which is in fact inseparable from the development of capitalism—when he wrote that: 'I for one cannot visualize, in the conditions of modern society, a socialist organization in any form other than that of a huge and all-embracing bureaucratic apparatus . . . But surely

---

[14] It is worthy of note here that in the postwar period, when the British Labour Party substantially increased its electoral support, its daily newspaper eventually had to cease publication (in 1964).

[15] There exists in Yugoslavia a form of socialism which is much closer to the ideas embodied in socialist ideology, but it has been obscured by the prominence of the Soviet model and has had an influence only upon relatively small numbers of socialists.

this should not horrify anyone who realizes how far the bureaucratization of economic life—of life in general even—has gone already . . . We shall see in the next part that bureaucracy is not an obstacle to democracy but an inevitable complement to it. Similarly it is an inevitable complement to modern economic development and it will be more than ever essential in a socialist commonwealth' (p. 206). Nevertheless it may be argued that there are particular dangers to the liberty of the individual in the emergence of a huge, more or less unified, and omnicompetent *state* bureaucracy; and these dangers have been widely discussed by social critics in both capitalist and socialist societies.[16]

A second problem, related in certain aspects to that of bureaucracy, concerns the social and political consequences of centralized economic planning, which Schumpeter took to be the crucial feature of socialism (he always referred to 'centralist socialism'). Here two separate issues must be distinguished: that of economic efficiency and that of the concentration of power in the hands of a small elite who make all major decisions of economic and social policy without being subject to effective public democratic control. Both issues have been widely discussed in recent years, inside and outside the socialist countries, and the debates have become largely focused upon the idea of a 'socialist market economy'. The principal model for such an economy has been the Yugoslav system of self-managed enterprises and institutions within the framework of an overall plan, involving a considerable degree of decentralization of decision-making; and there has been a distinct movement towards such a system in other East European societies, although it has been limited by Soviet control, and sometimes arrested by direct intervention, as in Czechoslovakia in 1968. Some of the major issues involved have been well analysed by Wlodzimierz Brus (1961, 1973) who examines carefully the difficulties which emerge in the process of socialization of ownership and argues that, in the socialist countries, ' . . . the system for the exercise of state power must evolve so that there is a constant real growth in the influence of society on politico-economic decisions at all levels and an increase in social self-government in all areas of life, especially in economic activities' (1973, p. 99).

The experiences of the socialist countries in respect of the effective implementation of social ownership and of self-management in relation to central planning lend some support to the arguments (which I discussed earlier) of those sociologists who see in the development of advanced industrial societies a trend towards the formation of a new ruling group of technocrats and bureaucrats, and a probable transition, not from capitalism to socialism, but from 'organized capitalism' to some still more organized and regulated

---

[16] On the latter see especially Andras Hegedus (1976).

form of society, clearly differentiated into dominant and subordinate groups and highly inegalitarian, for which no better name has yet been invented than 'post-industrial society'. Whatever judgement may be made on the plausibility of these interpretations it is certainly the case that no serious student of society can any longer envisage a possible transition from capitalism to socialism in terms of a sudden and dramatic leap from a 'realm of necessity' into a 'realm of freedom'. The contrast between social ownership in practice, as the implementation of a central economic plan, and the ideas of 'classlessness', participation, and self-determination or self-government; the complex difficulties which the achievement of socialism in the latter sphere can now be seen to confront; these have contributed greatly, together with the other tendencies in the development of present-day societies that I described earlier, to diminishing the vigour of the drive towards socialism.

My own evaluation of the situation in the Western capitalist countries, 40 years on, is therefore just the opposite of that which Schumpeter expressed. He thought that the 'march into socialism' was well-nigh irresistible, and deplored the fact. I, on the contrary, think that this 'march' has come to an untimely halt, and regret the eclipse of the highest ideal that has emerged in modern Western culture. With this eclipse the prospect for Western capitalism has become more opaque than it was when Schumpeter embarked on his analysis. Two main possibilities present themselves: one is that the Western societies will continue to drift aimlessly and dully within the confines of the present status quo; the other that nationalist fervour (by no means only in the West) and the struggle for the world's limited resources will end in a nuclear conflict and the extinction of any kind of civilized society. Finally, there is a more remote and speculative chance that the economic crisis, and the tedium of our culture, will eventually provoke a revival of socialism, or some new form of radicalism, and with it a new conviction of the possibilities for human progress.

REFERENCES

Aron, R. (1968) *Progress and Disillusion*. London: Pall Mall Press.
Bell, D. (1973) *The Coming of Post-Industrial Society*. New York: Basic Books.
Bernstein, E. (1899) *Evolutionary Socialism*. English translation (1909) New York: Huebsch.
Bottomore, T.B. (1968) *Critics of Society*. London: Allen and Unwin.
Bottomore, T.B. (1979) *Political Sociology*. London: Hutchinson.
Brus, W. (1961). *The Market in a Socialist Economy*. English translation (1972) London: Routledge and Kegan Paul.
Brus, W. (1973) *The Economics and Politics of Socialism*. London: Routledge and Kegan Paul.
Brym, R. (1980) *Intellectuals and Politics*. London: Allen and Unwin.
Burnham, J. (1941) *The Managerial Revolution*. New York: John Day.
Djilas, M. (1957) *The New Class*. London: Thames and Hudson.
Domhoff, G.W. (1967) *Who Rules America?* Englewood Cliffs, NJ: Prentice-Hall.

Gurvitch, G. (Ed.) (1949) *Industrialisation et technocratie.* Paris: Armand Colin.
Gurvitch, G. (1966) *The Social Frameworks of Knowledge.* English translation (1971) Oxford: Basil Blackwell.
Habermas, J. (1973) *Legitimation Crisis.* English translation (1976) London: Heinemann.
Hannah, L. (1975) *The Rise of the Corporate Economy.* London: Methuen.
Harrison, C.Y. (1933) In *The Nation*, 22 March.
Hegedus, A. (1976) *Socialism and Bureaucracy.* London: Allison and Busby.
Hilferding, R. (1910) *Finance Capital.* English translation (1981) London: Routledge and Kegan Paul.
Hilferding, R. (1915) Arbeitsgemeinschaft der Klassen? *Der Kampf,* **VIII.**
Hilferding, R. (1924) Probleme der Zeit. *Die Gesellschaft,* **I.**
Johnson, R.W. (1973) The British political elite 1955–1972. *European Journal of Sociology,* **XIV,** 2.
Korpi, W. (1978) *The Working Class in Welfare Capitalism.* London: Routledge and Kegan Paul.
Larrain, J. (1979) *The Concept of Ideology.* London: Hutchinson.
Lockwood, D. (1958) *The Blackcoated Worker.* London: Allen and Unwin.
Lukes, S. (1973) *Individualism.* Oxford: Basil Blackwell.
Macpherson, C.B. (1962) *The Political Theory of Possessive Individualism.* Oxford: Oxford University Press.
Macpherson, C.B. (Ed.) (1978) *Property: Mainstream and Critical Positions.* Oxford: Basil Blackwell.
Mallet, S. (1963) *The New Working Class.* English translation (1975) Nottingham: Spokesman Books.
Mandel, E. (1972) *Late Capitalism.* English translation (1975) London: New Left Books.
Mann, M. (1973) *Consciousness and Action Among the Western Working Class.* London: Macmillan.
Marx, K. (1844) Contribution to the Critique of Hegel's Philosophy of Right. Introduction. English translation in Bottomore, T.B. (Ed.) (1963) *Karl Marx: Early Writings.* London: C.A. Watts.
Meynaud, J. (1964) *Technocracy.* English translation (1968) London: Faber and Faber.
Miller, S.M. (1975) Notes on neo-capitalism. *Theory and Society,* **II,** 1.
Mills, C.W. (1951) *White Collar.* New York: Oxford University Press.
Mosca, G. (1896) *The Ruling Class.* English version, compiled from the original edition and the 2nd edition (1923), by Livingston, A. (Ed.) (1939) New York: McGraw-Hill.
O'Connor, J. (1973) *The Fiscal Crisis of the State.* New York: St Martins Press.
Offe, C. (1970) *Industry and Inequality.* English translation (1976) London: Edward Arnold.
Ossowski, S. (1963) *Class Structure in the Social Consciousness.* London: Routledge and Kegan Paul.
Pateman, C. (1970) *Participation and Democratic Theory.* Cambridge: Cambridge University Press.
Poulantzas, N. (1974) *Classes in Contemporary Capitalism.* English translation (1975) London: New Left Books.
Renner, K. (1916) Probleme des Marxismus. *Der Kampf,* **IX.** Excerpts translated in Bottomore, T. & Goode, P. (Ed.) (1978) *Austro-Marxism.* pp. 91–101. Oxford: Oxford University Press.
Schlatter, R. (1951) *Private Property: The History of an Idea.* London: Allen and Unwin.
Schumpeter, J.A. (1919) *The Sociology of Imperialisms.* English translation (1951) in *Imperialism and Social Classes.* Oxford: Basil Blackwell.
Schumpeter, J.A. (1927) *Social Classes in an Ethnically Homogeneous Environment.* English translation (1951) in *Imperialism and Social Classes.* Oxford: Basil Blackwell.
Schumpeter, J.A. (1942) *Capitalism, Socialism and Democracy.* 3rd enlarged edition, 1950. 5th edition, 1976, with a new introduction. London: Allen and Unwin.
Smithies, A. (1951) Memorial: Joseph Alois Schumpeter, 1883–1950. In Harris, S.E. (Ed.)

Schumpeter, Social Scientist. Cambridge, MA: Harvard University Press.

Tawney, R.H. (1921) *The Acquisitive Society*. London: Bell.

Touraine, A. (1968) *The May Movement*. English translation (1971) New York: Random House.

Touraine, A. (1969) *The Post-Industrial Society*. English translation (1971) London: Wildwood House.

Touraine, A. (1980) *L'Après-Socialisme*. Paris: Bernard Grasset.

Chapter Three

March into Socialism, or Viable Postwar Stage of Capitalism?

WILLIAM FELLNER

SCHUMPETER AND MARX: SAME 'FINAL CONCLUSION'
FOR DIFFERENT REASONS AND WITH DIFFERENT VALUE
JUDGEMENTS

'J.A.S. (Joseph A. Schumpeter) had finished his monumental *Business Cycles* in 1938 and sought relaxation in *Capitalism, Socialism and Democracy*, which he regarded as a distinctly "popular" offering that he expected to finish in a few months. He completed it some time in 1941.'[1] We learn this from the Editor's introduction which Elizabeth Boody Schumpeter wrote to her husband's posthumously published *History of Economic Analysis*, in which

---

[1] The date is that of the completion of the first edition which appeared in 1942. The second edition seems to have been completed in 1946 and it appeared in 1947. It differs from the first edition only in that a chapter, 'The Consequences of the Second World War', was added and in that a preface to the second edition was added to the initial preface. The third American edition (1950) was published shortly after Schumpeter's death and it includes additionally a reprinting of his address at the American Economic Association, delivered in December 1949, on 'The March into Socialism'. Most page numbers to which references will be made are the same in all editions of the book. This is, of course, not true of a few references to passages which were added after the first edition, but in those few references I will make clear to which edition or editions they relate.

In my footnotes and other references I will abbreviate the title of the book to *CSD*. *The editions of other works referred to in the text are listed on p. 68.*

45

she gave a brief account of his activities prior to the close of the ten-year period he spent largely on the *History*.

The book which Schumpeter regarded as distinctly popular would, I think, be better described as semi-popular: a very lucidly written book, most of which a reader untrained in economics can also follow but without appreciating the meaning of a good many sections requiring a professional background. Elizabeth Schumpeter, herself an economist, who died not many years after her husband, and did not live to see the *History*'s appearance in print (1954), must have known what she was saying when she told us that Schumpeter had 'sought relaxation' in *Capitalism, Socialism and Democracy*. But whatever its author sought, it is a book of major importance, a book that needs to be taken very seriously.

Schumpeter felt convinced that capitalism, the achievements of which he held very high, was doomed. The capitalist system, he concluded, will be succeeded by socialism in the sense of a system in which the essential decisions concerning the production and the distribution of goods are made by the political authority. The decomposition of capitalism and the advent of socialism he regarded as the final conclusion of the analysis developed in this book. Yet, as will be stressed in the later sections of this chapter, the book has the rare quality of having made a significant contribution to the understanding of social and economic processes even if this final conclusion should prove wrong. Given the high value he placed on capitalist achievements, Schumpeter undoubtedly hoped that his final conclusion would not prove realistic, but to this possibility he assigned a very low probability—a much smaller probability than, I will suggest, may reasonably be assigned to it. In a peculiar sense Karl Marx also had been an 'admirer' of the achievements of capitalism and he, of course, also had predicted the doom of the system and its succession by socialism. But the Schumpeterian view differs sharply from the Marxian in what is to be meant by the admiration of capitalist achievements and in what will bring about the system's downfall.

As concerns the value judgements behind the admiration of the capitalist performance, Marx felt that the system's achievements, enormous though they were, were made by the exploitation of the working classes and that they were associated with a decline of the living standard of the workers into a state of increasing misery. It is the ownership of capital, and thereby of the means of production, that enables the exploiting class—the 'bourgeoisie'—to practise this exploitation. Through the exploitation of the working class the 'bourgeoisie' has—in Marx's words, or rather in those of Marx and Engels in the *Communist Manifesto* (1848)—'accomplished wonders far exceeding Egyptian pyramids, Roman aqueducts and Gothic cathedrals' (pp. 6–7) and 'during its rule of scarce one hundred years, [the bourgeoisie] has created more massive and more colossal productive forces than have all preceding generations together' (p. 10). All social systems preceding capitalism had also worked through the exploitation of the oppressed by oppressing social classes, but they had not produced 'wonders' comparable to those of capitalism. The unprecedented achievements of capitalism result from a particularly efficient method of oppressing and exploiting the workers, described by Marx as the 'proletariat'.

In Schumpeter's conception capitalism has indeed achieved wonders, though even he would not attribute them *exclusively* to the social stratum Marx meant by the 'bourgeoisie', but the capitalist system had not accomplished these wonders through the exploitation of the workers. Quite the contrary; capitalism, inherently a system of *mass production*, has brought about an exceedingly steep rise in the workers' standard of living, a rise the steepness of which would have seemed entirely unbelievable in any preceding era (*CSD*, pp. 64–68).

As Schumpeter saw it, the superiority of capitalist performance has had a great deal to do with the fact that the success of those who have proved most successful under the system, particularly the success of the founders of industrial positions, has in almost all cases resulted from 'supernormal intelligence and energy' (*CSD*, p. 16). By the workings of the system 'the man who rises first *into* the business class, and then *within* it, is also an able businessman and he is likely to rise exactly as far as his ability goes—simply because in that scheme rising to a position and doing well *is or was* one and the same thing' (p. 74; three words near the end of the quote in my italics).

As concerns the ending of this sentence, we shall see that the 'was' in the 'is or was' probably expresses not only doubts about how well it is possible at all to perform in the recent environment of growing hostility to capitalism but also a negative judgement about how well the business community, especially in its contemporary composition, is suited to *coping with* the social and political difficulties created by this hostility. But this reservation does not contradict Schumpeter's emphasis on high ability and supernormal energy as the qualities by which business success has typically been achieved, nor his emphasis on how greatly this system of mass production has contributed to the welfare of the workers. It is true, Schumpeter adds, that the system cannot wipe out unemployment but, as long as its efficiency is maintained, it can produce amply enough goods to avoid substantial hardship for unemployed persons—a proposition which the author does, however, qualify to some extent by noting that ample provision for the unemployed runs the risk of reducing work incentives and efficiency (*CSD*, p. 70).

So much for the contrast between, on the one hand, Marx's 'admiration' for capitalist achievement in creating colossal productive forces by means of the exploitation of the increasingly poverty-stricken masses, and, on the other hand, Schumpeter's conception of a system that, by creating these forces, has raised the standard of living of the masses to levels that would earlier have overtaxed the imagination. There is a corresponding contrast between the two conceptions of how capitalism is destroying itself, though both Marx and Schumpeter predicted that it would.

In Marx's view the concentration of production into increasingly large units—the ownership of the existing capital by an increasingly small fraction of the population—will make the exploitation of the ever-growing proletariat unworkable. This is why the system will collapse. At some stage of this process the proletariat will take over and, since in the preceding phase all classes other than the exploiting bourgeoisie and the exploited proletariat will have been eliminated by the process, the takeover by the proletariat will result in the establishment of the classless socialist society. In the *Critique of Political Economy* (1859) Marx states: 'The bourgeois mode of production is the last antagonistic form of the social process of production—antagonistic not in the sense of individual antagonism but of an antagonism that emanates from the individual's social conditions of existence'. To this he adds: 'but the forces developing within bourgeois society create also the material conditions for a solution of this antagonism. The prehistory of human society accordingly closes with this social formation' (pp. 21–27). That is, capitalism is indeed raising the productive powers of the economy enormously, but it will become increasingly incapable of making use of these powers in a framework based on the exploitation of the population. Hence, the victorious proletariat, by then making up practically the entire population, will take possession of society's enormously risen productive forces.

Schumpeter saw it differently. In his view capitalism will not suffer the failure of an exploitative system that has over-exploited its victims. It will suffer the fate of a system that, largely because it has increased the productive capacity of society so greatly to the benefit of practically all social strata, is becoming increasingly defenceless against hostile social and political elements belonging among the beneficiaries.

Schumpeter reminds us that the business community, with its 'rationalistic' and 'anti-heroic' orientation (*CSD*, p. 127ff),[2] was never particularly well suited to inspiring in the population deep loyalty to the basic outlook of the type of civilization it represents. In most countries the business world lived in alliance with remnants of pre-capitalistic social strata which an older tradition made much better suited to exercising power directly and to com-

---

[2] Later in the book Schumpeter uses the word 'unheroic' instead of anti-heroic but, I think, anti-heroic expresses his meaning better. Essentially he is contrasting the 'absoluteness' of the outlook expressed in the motto *navigare necesse est, vivere non necesse est* with the rationalistic 'weighing' (calculating) outlook of capitalism (*CSD*, p. 160).

manding dedication. In most capitalistic countries these strata with a pre-capitalist tradition wielded large influence in military, political and top administrative positions (*CSD*, p. 134). There had developed a successful symbiosis of these elements with business leaders who in an earlier phase of capitalist developments were typically *founders* of enterprises and of family fortunes and, as such, were themselves more long-run oriented than their successors. The first part of this proposition, relating to the symbiosis with earlier social strata, has little relevance to the special case of the United States; the second half, relating to the change of the composition of the business leadership, is relevant also in the American context.

The success of the capitalist process has everywhere practically destroyed the protecting strata of pre-capitalist origin. At the same time, the success of the process has led to the routinization of many of the tasks that remain to be performed (*CSD*, p. 141). In this environment business leadership has passed largely into the hands of salaried executives of giant corporations, who have a more perfunctory and shorter-run relationship to the enterprises they serve than had the earlier business leaders. These new leaders are unpromising candidates for inspiring loyalty to the basic values of capitalist civilization and for defending those values against hostile forces. Businessmen in leading positions have become less effective representatives of these values even if we limit ourselves to comparing these men with their predecessors in the business world, leaving aside, as we presumably should in the case of the United States, the results of the earlier successful alliance with other social strata. One may perhaps express this more pointedly by saying that, compared with an earlier era, it has become much easier to visualize the type of person of whom the new business leadership is made up in the role of managing socialized enterprises. In their present capacities they are unpromising 'defenders of the faith'.

The need to defend the values of a civilization against hostility must be taken for granted under any system, not only because of the existence of unsuccessful individuals under all systems, but particularly because of the ubiquitous existence of groups whose tastes and attitudes are unconducive to the preservation of the values of the existing system. Such groups have always included individuals capable of articulating their dissent effectively. But with the passage of time various major achievements of successful capitalism, such as a printing press and mass media of great efficiency, have very greatly increased the effectiveness of hostile movements originating in good part in intellectual circles (*CSD*, p. 145ff). This has been happening along with the reduction of the ability of the 'anti-heroic' and by now largely short-run oriented leading strata to put up resistance.

In such circumstances capitalism will not survive. For some time it will become increasingly *fettered* by hostile government policies, including steep taxation and regulations, and its performance will deteriorate. Subsequently, the so-fettered capitalist systems will be succeeded by centralized socialism. This system, by which capitalism will be succeeded, is defined by Schumpeter specifically as one in which the supreme economic authority is exercised by a political agency in the nature of a Board or Ministry (*CSD*, pp. 167–168), and later the system is described as one in which orders are carried out by a 'huge and all-embracing bureaucracy' (p. 206).

Essentially, capitalism will thus have destroyed itself by the creation of a prosperous environment in which hostile elements find it easy to sustain themselves without participating in a constructive economic effort, and in which these same elements have the benefit of very efficient technical devices—all this in circumstances in which the industrial process has successfully routinized many of the tasks to be performed, mostly with salaried employees in charge of large-scale bureaucratic business organizations even before the socialist takeover.

In the chapter which he wrote immediately after the Second World War for inclusion in the second edition of *Capitalism, Socialism and Democracy*, Schumpeter stressed the system's inability to cope with *external* as well as internal hostility. He had already pointed out at that time that the West had proved incapable of preventing 'Russia's victory over her allies' (p. 398), and that this has created the prospect that in the years to come communist Russia will construct 'by far the greatest war machine, absolutely and relatively'.[3]

In Schumpeter's appraisal, the coming system of centralized socialism with a political agency representing the top authority for output and distribution decisions might function with reasonable efficiency as concerns the allocation of given resources. The authorities directing the system might pay the needed attention to rational pricing practices (pp. 173–177) which, by the way, implies that in performing these functions they would not be guided by the Marxian or any other version of the labour theory of value. Schumpeter explains in some detail that under socialism rational resource allocation with reliance on what are essentially neoclassical pricing principles is a possibility—we now may add: so far an unrealized possibility in socialist countries—yet he qualifies substantially his judgement concerning the prospective efficiency of socialism in another respect. He expresses scepticism about that system's ability to keep innovating activity at a high level, and in view of Schumpeter's path-breaking contribution to the understanding of the central role of innovation and of technological change in the process of economic development, this is a significant reservation. He considered it 'important for the success of a socialist society that it should enter upon its career not only as richly endowed as possible by its capitalist

---

[3] *CSD*, p. 403 in the second and third edition.

predecessor—with experience and techniques as well as with resources [inherited from capitalism]—but after the latter has sown its wild oats and is approaching the stationary state' (p. 178).[4] At a stage at which capitalism that is becoming increasingly fettered has already moved close to the stationary state, there is, according to the author, no reason why socialism should not function well, compared with the system which it will succeed.

It needs to be added that Schumpeter's emphatic rejection of the theory of 'vanishing investment opportunities' as an explanation of the difficulties into which capitalist economies had run in the 1930s (pp. 111ff) gives the impression that in his appraisal an approach of *unfettered* capitalism to the stationary state would be in the very distant future. He is comparing the future socialism with fettered capitalism which he expected to become increasingly inefficient and which, for this reason, may well be approaching the stationary state very much faster than would otherwise be the case.

The author leaves the question open whether his centralized socialism will prove compatible with democracy. The definition of democracy, with which he starts the analysis of this aspect of the problem, is formalistic: democracy is defined as a set of arrangements by which individuals acquire political power through competition for the people's vote. Yet he obviously has a more essential concept in mind when stating that democracy cannot function *satisfactorily* unless the bulk of the population agrees on the fundamentals of the existing institutional structure (p. 301). Schumpeter argues that, given the growing hostility to capitalism, this condition can hardly be met during the remaining lifetime of capitalism. He believed that after the socialist takeover a time might conceivably come at which the then prevailing institutional structure will be sufficiently taken for granted to meet the basic condition of the satisfactory functioning of democracy (p. 301). I think if he were still with us he would by now greatly discount this possibility, in view of the large tensions, sometimes overt but often wholly suppressed and latent, between those who govern and those who are governed under centralized socialism.

It is worth noting in this context that in a brief side-remark Schumpeter calls all systems in which political power is monopolized by any specific group 'fascist',[5] so that a sufficiently undemocratic socialist government— one in which the process of acquiring and sustaining central political power lacks the essential features of competition for the vote of the people—is

---

[4] I interpret this strong statement as superseding an earlier tangential one on p. 132, the connotations of which are different. The earlier tangential statement says that the success of capitalism tends to reduce innovation itself to a matter of routine.

[5] *CSD*, p. 404, in second and third editions, particularly footnote 37. See also p. 150 in all editions.

'fascist' as well as socialist. It follows also that full centralization of non-competitively acquired political power *with* private ownership of the means of production describes a type of 'fascism' that is not socialist in the sense relevant to Schumpeter's analysis. Considering the author's emphasis on lack of discipline (p. 215) and on increasing vulnerability to hostility under capitalism, this leaves the question open why the decomposition of Western-type systems could not lead to a non-socialist variety of 'fascism'. That possibility is not considered in Schumpeter's analysis.

Failure to attribute significance to this possibility could conceivably be justified by recognizing that a non-socialist 'fascist' government finds it more difficult to keep discipline than what Schumpeter calls a 'fascist' government of socialist type, because for the socialist variety the inevitable task of protecting itself against hostility is identical with protecting those in charge of production. On the other hand, if a 'fascist' government is non-socialist, thus permitting private ownership of the means of production, it has the more complex and more diversified task of protecting other groups as well as itself against hostility. This could, I think, be argued, but it is not in fact argued in the book.

What was said so far in this essay supports Schumpeter's own brief characterization of his position: 'My final conclusion therefore does not differ, however much my argument may, from that of most socialist writers and in particular from that of all Marxists. But in order to accept it one does not need to be a Marxist. Prognosis does not imply anything about the desirability of the course of events one predicts. If a doctor predicts that his patient will die presently, this does not mean that he desires it. One may hate socialism or at least look upon it with cool criticism, and yet foresee its advent' (p. 61).

Yet there is, of course, more to the relationship of Schumpeterian to Marxian thinking than such a brief passage could convey. In the first place, as for the asserted identity of Schumpeter's 'final conclusion' with that of Marx, there is a difference—perhaps only a shade of a difference—between the degree of confidence placed in it by the authors. Schumpeter does, while Marx does not, show awareness of the need to add at least a few qualifying sentences to a prognosis involving as high a degree of 'determinism' as does the announcement of the coming collapse of capitalism and the advent of socialism. The methodological qualification for which such a degree of determinism calls is stated clearly and eloquently in the book. 'Analysis, whether economic or other, never yields more than a statement about the tendencies present in an observable pattern. And these never tell us what *will* happen to the pattern but only what *would* happen if they continued to act as they have been acting in the time interval covered by our observation and if no other factors intruded. "Inevitability" or "necessity" can never mean more than this' (p. 61). This passage is already found in the first edition of the book. We shall see later that in the preface to the second edition essentially the same qualification became focused on how the behaviour of the public *could* change the underlying tendencies. Schumpeter's own personal appraisal of the outlook was not influenced by his qualifying sentences, but that is a different question.

So much for the asserted identity of Schumpeter's with Marx's final conclusion. As for Schumpeter's added hint 'however much my argument may [differ from Marx's]', enough was said about this in the foregoing pages to take it for granted that the reader will not overlook significant differences between the Schumpeterian and the Marxian line of reasoning. These differences add up to a sharp contrast. Yet it would be a mistake to disregard some overlaps in the argument. Two of these overlaps will be explained merely briefly in the next section while a third will call for more detailed analysis in the section that follows thereafter.

SCHUMPETER AND MARX: BRIEF OBSERVATIONS ON TWO OVERLAPS IN THE ANALYSIS

The two overlaps to be commented upon here merely in passing relate to the significance of technological change and to that of economies of scale. These two overlaps exist among the views of a large number of authors, including Marx and Schumpeter, although they fit very differently into the theories of various authors, again including Marx on the one hand and Schumpeter on the other. A similar statement could perhaps be made even of the third overlap—the economic interpretation of history to be discussed in the next section—but evaluating that overlap will require more detailed analysis because it provides a clue to the relationship between Marxian and Schumpeterian views of the nature of their respective approaches.

As for the first of those two overlapping elements which will be considered only briefly here, in the *Communist Manifesto* Marx and Engels say of the role of technological change under capitalism: 'The bourgeoisie cannot exist without constantly revolutionizing the instruments of production, and thereby the relations of production, and with them the whole relations of society. Conservation of the old modes of production in unaltered form was, on the contrary, the first condition of existence for all earlier classes' (p. 7). Except for the language used, this sounds like an expression of the Schumpeterian vision of the role of innovation in the capitalist process. Yet, in Schumpeter's conception, innovation—his process of Creative Destruction to which we shall return—is the main vehicle of increasingly efficient mass production to the benefit of all strata of the population and particularly

to that of the initially poor; in the Marxian conception the ongoing transformations of the available apparatus greatly raise the productive capacity of
society from which, however, during the remaining lifetime of capitalism,
merely the exploiting class will benefit to the detriment of the workers.

There is another overlap between elements of analysis of which no more
need to be said here than that these elements fit very differently into Schumpeter's than into Marx's reasoning. In chapter XXIII of the first volume of
Das Kapital[6] we find a discussion of economies of scale, and thus of the
observed growth of the size of efficient enterprise. In the Marxian view this
leads to the growing polarization of society into a smaller and smaller proportion of the population made up of the exploiters and an ever-increasing
proportion consisting of the exploited proletariat, a class structure that will
at the end prove untenable. In Schumpeter's view it is also important to recognize that the growth of the scale of operation of efficient enterprise creates
a threat to the system but, according to Schumpeter, the reason is different
from that given by Marx. The growth of the scale of operation of enterprise
meets the requirements of efficiency because the problems that need to be
solved by the enterprises are becoming increasingly routinized and, while in
the changed environment the resulting bureaucratic structures serve their
purpose well, these structures are far less resistant to the social–political
forces that move the system towards centralized socialism.

AN INTRIGUING MAJOR OVERLAP:
THE ECONOMIC INTERPRETATION OF HISTORY

Problems of greater complexity are raised by Schumpeter's strong endorse-
ment of the economic interpretation of history. This view of history represents a very major common element of Marxian and Schumpeterian
reasoning at a vital point of the analysis. Yet Schumpeter's version of the
economic interpretation omits an essential component of the Marxian. I
wonder whether in this book, in contrast to the *History of Economic Analysis*,
it is made clear enough to the reader that that omission is of crucial importance for a major link in the Schumpeterian analysis of economic and social
change. Marx would have passionately disapproved of that omission.

What in *Capitalism, Socialism and Democracy* is said to be the main and 'invaluable' content of the economic interpretation of history is that 'the forms
or conditions of production are the fundamental determinant of social structures which in turn breed attitudes, actions and civilizations' and that 'the

---

[6] In *CSD* the number of the relevant chapter of the first volume of *Das Kapital* is given as
XXV.

forms of production themselves have a logic of their own, that is, they change according to necessities inherent in them so as to produce their successors merely by their own working' (p. 12). Reduced to an even more straightforward and perhaps overly down-to-earth statement, we may say that Schumpeter viewed it as exceedingly useful to circumvent a chicken-and-egg dilemma by the appropriate choice of an initial state as the point of departure. Given any initial technology, and given the economic and social relations—'structural' relations—consistent with it, he suggested placing the emphasis on the very large influence exerted by these structural relations on the ideas that are apt to become influential in that technological, economic and social environment, and on the direction of further technological, economic and social transformation. At each stage of these transformations the new forms of production, and the economic and social 'structural relations' corresponding to these, again exert a large influence on ideas, tastes and, thus, on the general characteristics of civilization at that new stage.

Schumpeter has reason to credit Marx with the hypothesis so sketched. The attribution to Marx is, indeed, justified, and yet it requires making it clear that Schumpeter's version excludes an essential Marxian component. The omission of a component is pointed out a few pages after the presentation of Schumpeter's purified version (p. 18ff), but, I would say, more *tangentially* than is the case in the *History of Economic Analysis* where Schumpeter stresses from the outset that the Marxian original includes that component which, he suggests, needs to be appraised separately and in a highly critical vein (p. 439ff). We shall see that the omitted component collides *head on* with one of the main Schumpeterian propositions.

Let us look first at the Schumpeterian purified version of the economic interpretation of history, as sketched above. My own reaction to it is that there do exist many problems that can be fruitfully explored along those lines but that there exist many other problems the analysis of which would be hopelessly obscured by this choice of emphasis. Indeed, Schumpeter admits somewhat half-heartedly the validity of this qualification by specific historic illustrations and most of his readers could add to these several others. Let us, for example, remind ourselves that it is possible to make a case for the thesis that something like the economic and social structure of the ancient Greek and Hellenistic societies was very conducive to (or perhaps even 'necessary' for) the intellectual achievements that have proved so enormously significant over the millennia for shaping our civilization in *all* of its dimensions, including technological, economic, social and artistic. And yet it would be a thoroughly misguided effort to 'explain' that blooming of ideas by hypothesizing that in the then existing economic and social environment those ideas could be expected to develop as a corollary of things economic and social. Such a proposition would have to be confirmed by convincing historical analogies, which obviously cannot be done. Moreover, one does not have to be bigoted to feel that this particular unconvincing proposition has an especially repelling quality.

Marx, who in the *Critique of Political Economy* called the economic interpretation his 'guiding principle' (p. 20), would clearly not have approved of detecting in it 'merely' a circumvention of a chicken-and-egg dilemma for the sake of obtaining a working hypothesis useful for many purposes, though not for all. While Schumpeter also abstains from terminology quite as pointed as mine is here, he does suggest that this *is* at the heart of the matter. He does suggest this in spite of his high praise of the particular working hypothesis, as he calls it. But the main point which will turn out to have a bearing on the present appraisal of Schumpeter's thinking is that purging a major element from the original Marxian hypothesis was quite essential for developing Schumpeter's reasoning.

In the Marxian view *class relations* and the *struggle between classes* were at each stage of technology at the heart of the economic and social relations that had such a decisive influence on the intellectual developments of successive eras and also on the further course of technological, economic and social events.[7] It is these class relations and their intellectual superstructure that had to become transformed again and again, from one epoch to the next, when the basic technological, economic and social structure had changed sufficiently under its own momentum. Now, Schumpeter did not deny the existence of a relevant problem of social classes, but he did not believe that much had as yet been accomplished in attempts to define that concept usefully, and he was rightly convinced that Marx had badly misled himself and his followers in constructing his own concept of social classes.

The Marxian concept of social classes is based on a distinction between the oppressors and the oppressed—the exploiters and the exploited—and under capitalism this becomes a distinction between the 'bourgeoisie' and the 'proletariat'. The capitalist process is said gradually to reduce all hard-to-place intermediate groups to utter insignificance. The 'proletariat' consists of wage earners who are represented as being 'without property' (having 'nothing of their own'); the 'bourgeoisie' owns all the property and is in charge of the business enterprises. Its ownership of capital enables it to exploit the workers by hiring them at wages in the neighbourhood of mere subsistence level, and thus by depriving them of the remaining part of the

---

[7] This conception is not only present but it is 'hammered in' by the statement of the economic interpretation found in the *Communist Manifesto*. The statement of the economic interpretation in the preface to the *Critique of Political Economy* is, of course, written in a much less propagandistic style, but the same conception of the crucial role of class relations and of class 'antagonisms' is clearly present also in that statement.

value they create (that is, of the 'surplus value'). Yet even a superficial look at the social structure of a highly-developed Western economy makes it clear that this is an unsuccessful attempt to define social classes meaningfully.

Quite aside from the obviously important facts that by now a great many wage earners own property of non-negligible size, and that a clearly untenable (tautological) concept of 'subsistence' would be involved in identifying their real-wage level with mere 'subsistence', the Marxian classification leaves open the question how to place the top executives of modern corporations in this social map. This group simply does not fit in any social map in which the crucial dividing line for identifying 'antagonisms' is supposed to be the Marxian line between owners of the means of production and hired workers. The top executives of large corporations are mostly salaried employees in charge of these business organizations, and it would be unrevealing to define their function by focusing not on their being in charge of the enterprises but on the fact that, in addition to being salary recipients, they typically acquire a minute proportion of the stock of the corporations they direct. Nor would it be revealing to try to draw a sharp distinction between 'salary recipients' and 'wage earners'.

Marx might find it possible to place these executives in the category of the 'oppressors' or 'exploiters' with reference to the fact that they serve the interests of the stockholders (owners); he might add that they usually also receive bonuses the size of which depends on the profits (ownership income) earned by stockholders. But this would obviously open Pandora's box. At what level should the line be drawn in each business organization? From what level upward do these employees belong among the exploiters, and from what level downward among the exploited? Which of them belongs, jointly with the proverbial low-income widow who owns a few shares of the company, in the 'bourgeoisie' that is oppressing or exploiting all other wage and salary recipients in the organization who then would have to be said to belong in the 'proletariat'? This leads nowhere.

Yet, as Marx saw it, the economic and social relations which are at the core of his economic interpretation of history reflect themselves in a class structure as he defined it, and this structure results at each stage of economic development in a continuing class struggle or class warfare. There certainly exist social tensions within all modern societies but the groups among which these tensions develop are not 'classes' by the Marxian definition. Groups owning more property or earning more income do, indeed, have conflicts with groups owning or earning less, even if all of these groups also have important interests in common. However, it would be a hopeless effort to explain the economic and social process of a modern society, and the conflicts developing in it, by dividing such a society into two groups, of which one (the 'bourgeoisie') earns its income from the ownership of property and the other (the 'proletariat') earns wages or salaries. Small stockholders, and even depositors in a bank lending funds to corporations, would then be oppressing and exploiting the proletarian recipients of high salaries in the business world.

Consequently, Marx's proposition that the next stage of transformation of economic and social relations, as he described that transformation, would establish a classless society is merely a tautology that repeats his definition of classes. He predicted that the next stage would bring the elimination of the 'bourgeoisie' by the 'proletariat', consistently with the requirements of a process which will have reduced the 'oppressors' or 'exploiters' to a small number of crisis-prone large-scale producers and will have left the masses of 'proletarians' in worse poverty than that which they had suffered before. But while an institutional transformation that abolishes the private ownership of means of production, thereby turning the whole population into wage and salary recipients, would establish a one-class (hence classless) society by Marx's definition, it would not thereby abolish social groups among which large tensions are apt to develop. What such a transformation would abolish is a Marxian 'class' of property owners, including all stockholding individuals; thereby the transformation would put an end to the 'exploitation' which this 'class' practises at the expense of the wage and salary recipients including, among others, the top corporate executives—hardly a meaningful proposition.

As for Schumpeter, it is not enough to say that he was clearly aware of the inapplicability of the Marxian class concept to modern conditions. What needs to be said about this is that a distinctive feature of Schumpeter's analysis of capitalism's self-destruction—emphasis on the significant rise in the weight of hired managers in the business leadership even before the advent of socialism—*hinges* on the inapplicability of the Marxian class concept. This is why it is advisable to keep in mind that what Schumpeter omitted from the original version of the economic interpretation of history—that is, the elements based on Marx's concept of classes and on warfare among the classes as he defines them—is a component the *inclusion of which* is basic to Marxian theory but the *rejection of which* is equally basic to Schumpeter's analysis.

SIGNIFICANCE OF THE ANALYSIS REGARDLESS OF THE VALIDITY OF THE 'FINAL CONCLUSION'

If centralized socialism, as Schumpeter defines it, should become established in the advanced industrial countries, this will lend itself far better to an explanation along Schumpeterian than along Marxian lines. It would be very difficult to make sense of such an outcome in terms of the proposition that an exploitative system collapses if exploiters over-exploit, or if too few exploiters are trying to exploit too many victims. The outcome would make much better sense in terms of the proposition that in a system that has brought about an extraordinarily steep increase in practically the entire population's standard of living, the leading strata have proved unable to cope with hostility the existence of which must be taken for granted under any system but the growth of which has in this case been promoted by various adverse factors.

Among these factors it *is* convincing to include changes in the environment that are likely to have made the system more vulnerable, such as greater routinization of tasks and more advanced bureaucratization, as well as a change of the guards towards employee–executives in the business leadership; and it *is* convincing to include the increased ease of making hostility effective in circumstances in which the critics can better afford to do so and can rely on modern technological devices. Further, in the event of establishment of centralized socialism in the advanced industrialized countries, this might well have to do with a continued weakening of the West's international position, a theme on which, as we have seen, Schumpeter elaborated in the chapter he added to his book when publishing its second edition in 1947. This would be found to fit in well with the Schumpeterian conception of the inherent weaknesses of a 'rationalistic' and 'anti-heroic' civilization.

A paradoxical feature of that outcome would be that Schumpeter's interpretation of the events, successful though it would have proved, would presumably be suppressed by the authorities of centralized socialism. The new system would probably do what it can to impose on the mind the Marxian interpretation of the collapse of capitalism, or at least some closely related interpretation. It seems to me impossible to inspire loyalty to a system by allowing the view to spread that the other system in opposition to which it became established had the characteristics so highly praised by Schumpeter, but was unable to cope with hostile attitudes spread efficiently. Compare this with imposing the official interpretation that the old system was based on exploitation of a large social class by a class including a small fraction of the population, while the new bureaucracy represents a classless population as a whole and (needless to say) exploits no one!

However, I consider it essential that an appraisal of Schumpeter's analysis should not limit itself to the hypothetical case in which his centralized socialism would become established in the West with the top economic decision-making authority represented by a government agency. If that should *not* turn out to be the case, would we nevertheless have reason to conclude that, in a somewhat adjusted form, Schumpeter's analysis has greatly contributed to the understanding of the actual course of events? I think the answer is *yes*.

This needs to be stressed, not because Schumpeter would have failed to recognize that his conclusions concerning the final outcome may have to be
qualified, but because the qualifications he added to the entire package of his
conclusions amount merely to reminders that a strictly 'deterministic'
outlook, such as that characteristic of his book, can always turn out to have
misled an author and his readers. By now, however, we can say that in some
essential respects he has surely not misled us, not even if centralized socialism should never become established in the West, that is, not even if I am
right in suggesting that the qualification he added to his final conclusion deserves much more attention than he gave it.

It is possible to find at least two statements in the book in which Schumpeter introduces a safety valve—essentially the same safety valve—against
his going wrong on the West's predicted landing in centralized socialism. I
quoted earlier one of these, explaining why an assertion concerning the *inevitability* of such an outcome should never be taken quite literally (see p. 52).
Another statement in the book has essentially the same content, but with the
emphasis placed in such a way as to make that statement a particularly suitable point of departure for the remaining part of this essay.

This second statement was made five years after the publication of the first
edition of *Capitalism, Socialism and Democracy*. In the preface to the second
edition (1947), Schumpeter rejects the charge of defeatism which had evidently been voiced against him. 'The report that a given ship is sinking is not
defeatist. Only the spirit in which this report is received can be defeatist: The
crew can sit down and drink. But it can also rush to the pumps.'[8] This is a
significant qualification, and it is that despite the fact that Schumpeter's own
'betting odds' do not seem to have been much influenced by it.

What Schumpeter says in the passage just quoted (and essentially also in
that quoted earlier) requires elaboration, particularly because the ship which
the crew might rescue would obviously not be the ship that was sailing
during the heyday of capitalism. Hence two closely related questions need to
be raised here. One of these is: if the crew should 'rush to the
pumps'—which Schumpeter seems to have regarded as improbable but as a
possibility to be kept in mind—would not his analysis then nevertheless significantly contribute to the understanding of the process by which the economic, social and cultural relations of the heyday have changed into the
relations that the crew would defend and rescue? The other question, closely
related to the first, is: what would be involved in regarding these newer
structural relations as describing a stage of development in its own right—
one that has succeeded the stage of the heyday—rather than as part of a
decomposition process? Would such a reinterpretation not also bring out the

---

[8] Preface to the second edition of *CSD*, p. 413.

importance of Schumpeterian concepts and insights?

I suggest that the answers to these questions come out favourably for essential parts of Schumpeter's analysis. Until now the Schumpeterian 'fettering' and other hostile tendencies *have* generally continued, and this contributes significantly to the understanding of changes in the basic characteristics of the environment over a period of two or three generations. To have articulated this insight has already proved a great merit of the book. What our author has probably underestimated, however, is the efficiency with which many Western-type advanced economies continued to function until not long ago despite the Schumpeterian tendencies. This is one of the reasons that make one wonder whether the structural relations that have evolved in the postwar world need really to be viewed as representing a series of milestones on the road to centralized socialism. The facts do not so far contradict the interpretation that these structural relations describe a 'system' in its own right that may prove viable for an extended period and the further evolution of which may just as well lead towards less as towards more governmental power. Indeed, if the present essay had been written prior to the late 1960s, my suggestion would have been that the facts strongly support the hypothesis of the crystallization of a new set of structural relations, though even then I would have expressed the reservation that a further growth of the tendencies stressed by Schumpeter would threaten the viability of these relations—of this 'system'—significantly.

The recent weakening of the Western performance in its domestic and international dimensions does, indeed, raise the suspicion that we may live in a period of decomposition rather than in that of the crystallization of a system. This does have to do with Schumpeterian tendencies, including what he calls the fettering of market processes, but in many countries this weakening is of very recent origin. Moreover, signs are observable of spreading discontent with the results to which the further progress of these tendencies has recently led. There does seem to be a growing inclination to move to the pumps, and this leaves the question wide open whether the ship that was sailing during the greater part of the postwar period—not the ship of the 'heyday of capitalism'—will be rescued. These are the propositions which I would like to develop further, partly with numerical references to the United States, and I will end by stressing the value of Schumpeterian concepts regardless of whether rescue operations of the crew will or will not prove successful.

REDUCED EFFICIENCY AFTER MANY YEARS OF SCHUMPETERIAN FETTERING

In 1929 the fiscal expenditures of the United States at the three governmental levels, Federal, State and local, amounted to 11 per cent of the net national product. I will not list tax revenues in addition to listing expenditures because, when expressed in relation to the national product, the deficits or surpluses have not been large enough to make the revenues different from the expenditures by a margin sufficient to justify burdening the reader with a separate set of numbers. From 1929 to 1965 the 11 per cent ratio of total fiscal expenditures to the net national product had risen to 29.8 per cent; by 1973 it had further risen to 34.1 per cent; and by 1979 to 36.3 per cent. Meanwhile, a steeply rising share of the expenditures has come to be made up of government transfer payments now consisting of social security benefits, government employees' pensions, unemployment compensation, veterans' benefits, and various 'welfare' payments. The share of these transfer payments in total fiscal expenditures was 0.8 per cent in 1929, 20 per cent in 1965, 28 per cent in 1973 and 32 per cent in 1979. Thus, aside from the transfer payments, the ratio of fiscal expenditures and of the tax burden to the total national product would have been just about the same in 1979 as in 1965. As was just said, in reality the ratio rose, however, from roughly 30 to 36 per cent between these two years.

The recent weakening of the performance of the American economy came after many years of strong performance during which the trends surveyed above had already been progressing. Whether the weakening should be said to have started in the mid-1960s or in the first half of the 1970s is very much a matter of judgement. I would opt for the mid-1960s, both in view of the slackening of the productivity trends (in which there occurred, however, a very pronounced *further* deterioration a few years later) and in view of observable signs of orienting policies increasingly to short-run objectives with the result that the mid-1960s mark the beginning of a new inflationary era in the United States. As for the productivity trends, from 1948 to 1966 the average yearly increase in output per worker-hour in the private non-farm sector was 2.6 per cent; from 1966 to 1973 the yearly increase was 2.1 per cent; and from 1973 to 1979 it was 0.6 per cent.

At any rate, after about 20 years of very efficient postwar performance, there started roughly 15 (or 10 to 15) years ago a deterioration, and the *further growth* of 'Schumpeterian factors' has played an important role in this recent deterioration. The trend towards larger budgets and higher taxation has progressed further. Domestically the prevalence of short-run objectives has started manifesting itself in inflationary demand policies; internationally it has started resulting in a substantial weakening of our influence; regulatory policies have generally been made much more burdensome to producers; and when a cartel abroad took control of the bulk of our foreign oil supply regulations have been used to keep prices low instead of allowing the price system to reduce the energy demand and to create supply incentives. All this fits in well with Schumpeter's analysis.

However, discontent with the policies that have had these results has been spreading noticeably, and it would be premature to write off the possibility that the ship that was sailing during the first 20 years of the postwar period will again be put in good working order. After all, historically it has not been unusual for systems to go through 10 to 15 years of difficult readjustment. If this should happen, what adjustment would Schumpeter's analysis require? As I said, I think these adjustments could be made in a Schumpeterian spirit and would leave much of his analysis intact.

HOW TO ADJUST THE ANALYSIS IF POSTWAR CAPITALISM REMAINS VIABLE

In the first place it would in this case have to be recognized that, up to a point, market economies have shown a considerable ability to adjust to what Schumpeter describes as fettering. Despite the substantial advance of this process of fettering, it would be highly unconvincing to grade down the performance of many Western-type market economies during the first 20 or so postwar years. The performance was spectacular in some of the countries that had lost the war, and it was a high performance also in the United States. This is a fact of major importance. The extent of fettering in the Schumpeterian sense was not the same in different countries, but compared with the heyday of capitalism there was much fettering across the board.

As for the growing extent of this fettering in the United States, we have seen, for example, that from the end of the 1920s to the mid-1960s the ratio of American fiscal expenditures and of the tax burden to the net national product rose from little more than 10 per cent to about 30 per cent. Thus, by 1965 most of the rise to the recent level of roughly 36 per cent had already taken place. The presumption that Schumpeter underestimated the efficiency with which this rise remained compatible until relatively recently—say, into the second half of the 1960s—can be supported by a numerical illustration he presents.

He tells us, in a somewhat sceptical tone, what some of the essential achievements of the American economy *would be* over the period 1928–78 *if* the fettering of capitalism were not to interfere with the continuation of the trend observed for the preceding 50 years; yet the actual result has turned out better in spite of the fact that the 1928–78 period includes the recent 10 or 15 years of substantially weakened performance. In the event that the system could be kept well functioning—a questionable assumption, as he saw it— Schumpeter expected for 1928–78 a doubling of *per capita* real national product (p. 65); actually we obtained a rise in this measure of performance to about 2.5 times its 1928 level, and a rise in the real product *per employee* to 2.1 times the level of 1928.

Restoring the American economy's performance to the neighbourhood of that shown in the earlier part of the postwar era would, of course, call for stressing the limits of tolerance of market economies to the Schumpeterian tendencies and, particularly, their limits of tolerance of economies to policies oriented to short-run objectives. In view of the acute discontent with the recent past, excesses would have to be corrected, but whether this will or will not happen in fact depends not on whether the economic and social relations of capitalism's heyday command sufficient loyalty to be defended, but on whether a different set of economic and social relations will pass this test. If the structural relations of the postwar era *will* pass this loyalty test, then it will be possible to attribute the recent poor performance to deviations from 'normal' caused largely by temporary deviations from the policy course suitable to the basic structural relations of the era. In the contrary case the entire line of development will indeed have turned out to have been a phase of the slide into a much more highly centralized type of society. Further, in that case Schumpeter's 'conditions of the satisfactory functioning of democracy' would have a very poor chance of being met.

If the more recent structural relations will prove viable rather than merely a phase of a slide into centralized socialism, they could be regarded as describing the type of market economy which in West Germany was named *Soziale Marktwirtschaft* (social market economy). The characteristics of such a 'system' include a number of those which Schumpeter regards as symptoms of capitalism's decomposition, but I am considering the possibility that social relations with those traits will become crystallized.

I will not try my hand at a complete listing of these characteristics. However, we should be able to respond to the challenge to list at least some of these traits coherently because to call these systems 'mixed', as has recently become usual, is not only unrevealing but also singularly ahistorical in spirit. These systems are no more mixed than were most systems of the past. Further, by implying somewhat obliquely, as is usually done, that the new admixture has a generally socialist colouring, one would be misinterpreting a good deal of what Schumpeter was conveying in his discussion of how the system of the heyday of capitalism has become fettered. Believers in a socialist system may have reasons of strategy to favour carrying the fettering process further and further because, if carried far enough, the process makes the contemporary Western-type economies unworkable and hence is apt to land us in socialism. Yet many of these fetters are alien to the socialist blueprint itself which is supposed to describe a system not requiring them. In countries, not including the United States, in which government-owned enterprise has acquired a noteworthy weight, it is, to be sure, legitimate to speak of a socialist element being present in the mixture. Yet this shades over into important elements of the new mixture that are definitely not described on any page torn from the blueprint of a socialist economy as conceived of either by Marx or by Schumpeter. Prominent among these elements is the influence of labour unions, the leadership and bureaucracy of which form no part of the government apparatus. The graduated income tax also belongs among these elements.

On the assumption of the crystallization of economic and social relations describing the postwar stage of capitalism, one would have to include among its characteristics the predominantly private ownership of the means of production but mostly with salaried executives in charge of the important enterprises; the dominant role of large and often 'multinational' enterprises in the major industries, but mostly also a substantial degree of partly domestic and partly foreign competition among these in markets in which the products are usually differentiated; collective bargaining of employees with labour unions whose sense of responsibility for a reasonable degree of cost and price flexibility, and thus for the efficient functioning of the 'system', has so far been very different in different countries; the 'rise to middle-class status' of the bulk of the industrial workers, that is, the spread among them of attitudes and of an outlook usually associated with the 'middle class'; wide access to educational opportunities which it is not always easy to reconcile with the quality of education (an unresolved problem in several countries); a reduction of hardships by means of complex systems of transfer payments which, if not kept within reasonable limits and if not financed by a tax structure safeguarding incentives, can obviously become the undoing of the system; and an administrative apparatus, the complexities as well as the powers and costs of which would also have to be kept within reasonable limits if these systems are to remain workable.

The political processes of the most important countries living in this type of setting are based on the 'one person, one vote' principle, and they permit free criticism of the political and administrative authorities. An important question to be faced in such an environment is whether the political leadership will have the quality needed for resisting pressures to orient the process towards short-run objectives with inflationary consequences and with the consequence of a weakened international posture.

Even a brief sketch of these structural relations suggests rightly that their viability is constantly exposed to dangers, but this is almost necessarily true of any set of structural relations developing in an environment of rapid technological and organizational change. It is clear also that no set of structural relations—no 'system'—is here to stay for ever, but that piece of truism does not answer the question whether future changes will move us towards centralized socialism under a political authority operating through a 'huge and all-embracing bureaucracy' or will move us in the opposite direction.

To illustrate with merely one of the outstanding success stories of recent decades: giant corporations and their salaried executives have indeed played a crucial role in the achievements of the electronics 'revolution'; and in developing one's thoughts about this, one may well want to keep in mind the Schumpeterian dictum (essentially credited to Marx) that 'the forms of production have a logic of their own, that is, they change according to the necessities inherent in them.' Yet a peculiar jump would be involved in inferring from this that the 'inherent logic' of the observed results in electronics, as well as in other rapidly advancing industries, favours relying in the next such phase of development on a 'huge and all-embracing bureaucracy' of the government. That bureaucracy would have an excellent chance of making a complete mess of what the existing structure has accomplished with flying colours.

If the sketch of structural relations presented above should turn out to be that of a viable 'system' rather than a listing of capitalism's decomposition symptoms, then Schumpeter would still have correctly identified the factors which led to the decline of *that* particular 'system' under which the West lived at an earlier stage of capitalism. In this case, Schumpeter's analysis would still greatly contribute to the understanding of how the fettering of the older system has led to this newer 'system', which, one would then conclude, *can* remain workable by an adjustment of the market economy to the fettering if the latter does not exceed limits of tolerance (or if excesses are corrected soon enough).

There would be quite a bit of Schumpeterism in this as well as in his original presentation. There is even a sense in which there would be more Schumpeterism in this adjusted presentation than in the original. There is a sense in which the adjusted version could be placed with greater ease in the characteristically Schumpeterian framework for the analysis of the capitalist process, with the role of innovation in the centre of that framework.

Ever since his major early contribution published in *The Theory of Economic Development* (1911), Schumpeter associated the concept of capitalism closely with a continuing and highly effective innovational process. This process was leading to the application of new knowledge, and thus to a continuing displacement of existing technological and organizational methods by more efficient ones and to the substitution of improved products for the existing types. The entrepreneurial activity producing this result was in his conception the essential trait of capitalism. All along he considered the competition reflected in this Creative Destruction the main condition of the workability of capitalism. He felt that traditional theory had greatly over-stressed the importance of price competition in the allocation of resources to alternative productive processes, defined as implying given technological and organizational methods. If the capitalist process evolves along the Schumpeterian lines through the process of Creative Destruction, however, should we then expect it to imply unchanging economic and social relations as long as it is not replaced by centralized socialism?

It might have come naturally to the author of *The Theory of Economic Development* to present the evolution of the capitalist process as involving changing economic and social relations, and to associate these changes with changes in the cultural environment. It might have come naturally to him to recognize that time and again these cumulating changes accompanying the innovational process may become large enough to describe a succession of 'systems', or, if one feels uncomfortable about the vagueness of that concept, a succession of substantially different types of economic and social organization with different manifestations in the cultural lives of societies. The postwar type of organization has indeed been substantially different from that of earlier times, though for some of the most important market economies *that* difference is not capable of being captured by contrasting forms of organization in which production decisions are made by private individuals with forms of organization in which a government agency is the top authority in making these decisions.

What was just said lends itself to being condensed into a one-paragraph summary of the present essay. If by a system we mean a set of economic and social relations that remain characteristic of a period of reasonable length, and if one places oneself in Schumpeter's world, as it was first described in his *Theory of Economic Development*, then capitalism should be expected to include a succession of systems rather than to be a single system. Whether in *Capitalism, Socialism and Democracy* Schumpeter has explained the transformation of a system in this sense into another variety of capitalism or, as he believed, a decomposition process leading into centralized socialism, is a question which his reasoning does not decide. The answer will depend on the relative strength of several currents, all of which clearly possess significance on the contemporary Western scene. It would be at least premature, and it may prove a source of grave error, to write off the prospective strength of currents that have been generated in wide circles of the population of advanced industrial nations and that are directed at preventing the outcome Schumpeter predicted in the later part of his life. After all, it is difficult to take a good look at the contemporary world without arriving at the conclusion that the bulk of the population has a vital interest in preventing that outcome.

REFERENCES

Marx, K. *Das Kapital,* Volume 1 (1st edition published in 1867). Hamburg: O. Meisner.

Marx, K. (1859) *Critique of Political Economy.* English edition, with an introduction by Dobb, M. (1970) New York: International Publishers.

Marx, K. & Engels, F. (1848) *The Communist Manifesto.* English edition, with a foreword by Huberman, L. & Sweezy, P.M. (1964) New York: Monthly Review Press.

Schumpeter, J.A. (1911) *Theorie der wirtschaftlichen Entwicklung.* English translation (1934) *The Theory of Economic Development.* Cambridge, MA: Harvard University Press.

Schumpeter, J.A. (1950) The march into socialism. *American Economic Review,* May.

Schumpeter, J.A. (1954) *The History of Economic Analysis* (Ed.) Schumpeter, E.B. 1260 pp. New York: Oxford University Press.

Chapter Four

Schumpeter's Capitalism, Socialism and Democracy *after Forty Years*

GOTTFRIED HABERLER

INTRODUCTION

The contributors to the present book have been asked to give their assessment of how the messages of Schumpeter's famous tract *Capitalism, Socialism and Democracy*[1] have stood the test of time. Much has happened in the 40 years since Schumpeter wrote the book. Is it possible to say that events have tended to confirm or refute the author's provocative prognoses?

This is not an easy task, despite the fact that Schumpeter formulates his main conclusions with great clarity and boldness. On the first page of the preface to the first edition he states 'that a socialist form of society will inevitably emerge from an equally inevitable decomposition of capitalism' (p. 409) and again, on page 61: 'Can capitalism survive? No. I do not think so.' On this he agrees with Marx and other socialists. But the reasons for the breakdown of capitalism according to Schumpeter are entirely different from those given by Marxists and other socialists. It is not any failure of the capitalist system, neither declining productivity, increasing monopolization, or vanishing investment opportunities. Nor is it a tendency towards an inequitable or in any other way undesirable income distribution, a

---

[1] Cited as *CSD* from now on. Page references are to the fifth edition (London: Allen & Unwin, 1976).

polarization of society between the rich and the poor. On the contrary, according to Schumpeter it is the virtues of capitalism, 'its very success', especially the increasing general wealth and affluence, that 'undermine the social institutions which protect it', and 'inevitably' lead to socialism (p. 61).

Schumpeter was never a Marxist or a socialist. Although he again and again states emphatically that he does not want either to advocate or to criticize capitalism or socialism, occasional remarks in the book and elsewhere make it quite clear that he had no sympathy whatsoever for a socialist society, but he leaned over backward to do justice to the socialist cause. Not only is socialism perfectly feasible—a thesis contested by many economic liberals,[2] such as L. v. Mises and F.A. v. Hayek and their recent followers (the so-called 'Neo-Austrian' school)—but Schumpeter also argues at length that a socialist regime can be quite efficient and that, in some respects and under certain circumstances, the efficiency of socialism compares well with, or even exceeds, that of capitalism. 'There is a strong case for believing in its [socialism's] superior economic efficiency' (p. 188); socialism is quite compatible with democracy—propositions hotly denied by most liberals.

If stated without qualification, as Schumpeter himself sometimes states them, these propositions are indeed controversial and potentially misleading. They have in fact misled many people. Thus the editor of the German edition of CSD, Edgar Salin, refers in his introduction to Schumpeter as 'that socialist'. In the preface to the second edition Schumpeter rejects the criticism 'of defeatism' that was made by defenders of the free enterprise system: 'I deny entirely that this term [defeatism] is applicable to a piece of analysis... The report that a certain ship [capitalism] is sinking, is not defeatist. Only the spirit in which this report is received can be defeatist. The crew can sit down and drink. But it can also rush to the pumps' (p. 413). He does not say in so many words that the crew, the beneficiaries and advocates of capitalism, should rush to the pumps. But it is pretty clear that this was his real feeling; in other words, that capitalism or the 'bourgeois' society is very much worth fighting for.

I cite another remark which reveals Schumpeter's personal feelings about socialism. In a chapter entitled 'Transition' (from capitalism to socialism), there is a section 'Socialist policy before the act; the English example', in which he discusses the industries and sectors of a modern economy that 'could be socialized without serious loss of efficiency' (p. 229). At the bottom of the list is agriculture. 'If he [the socialist] insists also on nationalizing land—leaving, I suppose, the farmer's status as it is—i.e., transferring to the state all that remains of ground rents and royalties, I have no objection to

---

[2] I use the words 'liberal' and 'liberalism' in the original European sense of laissez-faire liberalism, not in the modern American sense which means the exact opposite.

make as an economist.' To this statement the following revealing footnote is appended: 'This is no place for airing personal preferences. Nevertheless I wish it to be understood that the above statement is made as a matter of professional duty and does not imply that I am in love with that proposal which, were I an Englishman, I should on the contrary oppose to the best of my ability' (p. 231). This remark refers to a special case, agriculture, but it clearly expresses his general attitude towards socialism and collectivism.

Before going into a detailed discussion of the precise meaning and interpretation of the broad conclusions stated above, some general remarks on Schumpeter's style of writing and theorizing and on the genesis of the book are in order.

SCHUMPETER'S STYLE AND THE GENESIS OF THE BOOK

Schumpeter's rather complicated style of writing and theorizing makes the interpretation of his findings difficult. His style is characterized, if I may repeat what I said on another occasion (Haberler, 1950), by long sentences, numerous qualifying phrases, qualification of qualifications, careful or even pedantic definition of terms, and casuistic distinctions of meanings.[3] His style of writing reflects his style of theorizing, especially on a subject that extends far beyond economics into sociology and political science and that needs the historical underpinning which Schumpeter provides in profusion.

CSD was written during the Second World War. It is important to visualize the intellectual and political atmosphere in the United States at the time. Schumpeter's strong negative reaction thereto must have had some influence on the general tone of the book, contributing to the air of pessimism and gloom that pervades the whole work. At the same time it should be kept in mind that the subject of capitalism and socialism had occupied Schumpeter all his life. His theory—or model, to use a word now in vogue—of capitalist development was worked out in his second theoretical book, *The Theory of Economic Development. An Inquiry into Profits, Capital, Credit, Interest and the Business Cycle* (1912).[4] He had also written several important articles on

---

[3] These qualities of style are especially pronounced in his German writings, because the German language offers more freedom for complicated sentence construction and because in one's mother tongue one can take certain liberties which one does not dare in a foreign language. Paul M. Sweezy, in his brilliant introduction (p. xiv) to *Imperialism and Social Classes* by J. A. Schumpeter (1951) an English translation of two German essays written in 1919 and 1920 respectively, gives an example of a sentence in German that stretches over almost half a page and had to be broken up in the English translation into no fewer than four sentences.

[4] The main ideas were already sketched in Schumpeter's first book, *Das Wesen und der Haupt-tinhalt der theoretischen Nationalökonomie* (1908).

socialism and Marxism in the 1920s (see below). Furthermore, there is the massive monograph, *Business Cycles. A Theoretical, Historical and Statistical Analysis of the Capitalist Process* (1939). Thus the book under consideration sums up, brings up to date and slightly modifies the results of Schumpeter's life-long work and study, much of which goes back to the early 1920s.

The war years were the most unhappy and depressing period in Schumpeter's life. Out of sympathy with the political and intellectual atmosphere then prevailing in the United States, he was appalled by the wartime chauvinism; he was dismayed by the anti-German (as distinguished from anti-Nazi) policy and propaganda; and he foresaw grave dangers for Western civilization from the rising power of Soviet communism.[5] True, Schumpeter's (and other observers') gloomy forebodings of an imminent Russian takeover of large chunks of Western Europe turned out to be unfounded, at least in the short run (which has to be interpreted for a problem like that under consideration as extending over several decades). This relatively favourable outcome was mainly due, I believe, to three factors: first, Soviet Russia's economic and military exhaustion at the end of the victorious war, which was much greater than Western experts realized; second, Russian truculence and repeated aggressive moves,[6] which forced the West to take counter-measures such as the adoption of the Marshall Plan, the inclusion of the defeated countries in that plan and in other global economic recovery measures, and the creation of NATO; third, the unexpectedly fast economic recovery of Western Europe and Japan (see below), which would not have been possible without the immediate inclusion of Germany in the Marshall Plan.

The fact that Schumpeter's gloomy forebodings proved to be unfounded does not deny that they were distinctly plausible in the political atmosphere of wartime Washington. I offer two illustrations of that atmosphere. The first is the Morgenthau plan for the de-industrialization of Germany. I can do no better than quote the impressions of a prominent foreign observer. In

---

[5] In Austria during the First World War, Schumpeter was an outspoken dissenter of the policies and propaganda of the Central Powers. He openly displayed his pro-British sentiments while official propaganda in Austria (and especially in Germany) pictured Britain as the arch-enemy. *Gott Strafe England* (God Punish England) was the chauvinist slogan. In the 1940s his Harvard friends cautioned him to restrain himself, because in times of war American democracy might be less tolerant of dissent than the Austro-Hungarian monarchy had been.

[6] The great Soviet expert Adam Ulam has argued (1980), convincingly in my opinion, that Stalin's aggressive gestures and threats in the immediate postwar period were largely a façade, a conscious attempt to camouflage Russian weakness. If this is accepted, Schumpeter's remark that the Western allies should not have stopped at the demarcation line was not so far-fetched. He said: 'Surely this is a case where a job half done is worse than nothing. Moreover, the other half would have been not only possible but relatively easy' (*CSD*, p. 401). However, politically and psychologically it would have been out of the question.

a confidential official report to Sir John Anderson, the British Chancellor of the Exchequer, dated 4 October 1944 (and published for the first time in 1980), J.M. Keynes wrote from Washington: 'I must now mention that, just as I feared would be the case, both Morgenthau and Harry White were considerably more interested in their plan for de-industrializing Germany than in anything else. Morgenthau started off with this before coming to our main business... He said that he would like ... to have a round table talk with me about it. I asked White how the inhabitants of the Ruhr were to be kept from starvation; he said that there would have to be bread lines but on a very low level of subsistence. When I asked if the British, as being responsible for the area, would also be responsible for the bread, he said the US Treasury would if necessary pay for the bread, provided always it was on a very low level of subsistence. So whilst the hills in the Ruhr are being turned into a sheep run, the valleys will be filled for some years to come with a closely packed bread line on a very low level of subsistence at American expense. How I am to keep a straight face when it comes to the round table talk I cannot imagine' (p. 134).[7]

The Morgenthau plan was opposed by Cordell Hull and Henry Stimson, but Roosevelt accepted it and at a conference in Quebec put pressure on Winston Churchill to endorse it. It did enormous damage. Joseph Goebbels, Hitler's propaganda chief, picked it up: he told the German people what they had to expect in defeat. The German will to continue a hopeless fight was strengthened and so the war was prolonged. After the surrender the economic absurdity of the plan quickly became apparent, and Russian truculence and threats speeded its abandonment.

The other illustration of the political atmosphere prevailing in Washington during the war is an entry in Morgenthau's diary reported by J.M. Blum (1970), the Yale University historian who edited the Morgenthau diaries. I quote from Blum: 'In his Diary, the Secretary reported his conversation of August 23, 1944, with Henry Stimson and John McCloy: ... "He [Stimson] was also very much interested evidently in a proposal made by Jean Monnet to internationalize the Saar Basin and have joint control by some international body and permit the Germans to work there but not run it. They thought if we could control the Saar we could keep the Germans from going to war again." So I [Morgenthau] said, "Well, if you let the young [German] children of today be brought up by SS Troopers who are

---

[7] Keynes added: 'I try to prepare and sustain myself by repeating every night the three vows which I always make before a visit to America, namely, one that I will drink no cocktails, two that I will obey my wife, and three that I will never allow myself to be betrayed into speaking the truth; loyally striving, as a rule without much success, to deserve Sir Henry Wotton's epigram "An Ambassador is a man sent to lie abroad for the good of his country".' See Moggridge (1980) *The Collected Writings of John Maynard Keynes*.

indoctrinated with Hitlerism, aren't you simply going to raise another generation of Germans who will want to wage war? . . . Don't you think the thing to do is to take a leaf from Hitler's book and completely remove these children from their parents and make them wards of the state, and have ex-US Army officers, English Army officers and Russian Army officers run these schools and have these children learn the true spirit of democracy?"' (pp. 573–574). Such were the views of one of the most influential members of the Roosevelt administration!

Schumpeter was extremely critical of Roosevelt and his New Deal. In 1944, when Roosevelt was running for his fourth term as president, a lady who was unaware of Schumpeter's intense aversion asked him at a cocktail party whether he would vote for Roosevelt. He answered: 'My dear lady, if Hitler runs for President and Stalin for Vice President, I shall be happy to vote for that ticket against Roosevelt.'

Two comments are in order. First, as already mentioned, Schumpeter was appalled by Roosevelt's foreign policy. As far as the economic policies are concerned, it was not the social welfare measures of the New Deal that drew Schumpeter's criticism; it was, rather, the anti-capitalistic spirit, especially as evidenced in tax policies and price and wage boosting measures that produced inflation in the midst of continuing high unemployment and led to the extremely precipitous slump of 1937–9 (*CSD*, pp. 64–65). Roosevelt's recovery policy was, indeed, quite unsuccessful in eliminating unemployment. After seven years of the New Deal, unemployment was still very high (14.6 per cent in 1940), and full employment was reached only after the United States entered the war. (In 1941 unemployment was 9.9 per cent, in 1942 4.7 per cent and in 1943 1.9 per cent.) Many other industrial countries were much more successful in lifting their economies out of the Great Depression.[8]

Second, needless to say, Schumpeter had no sympathy at all for the Russian type of socialism; he was shocked by the horrors of the Stalinist era and appalled by the failure of most Western socialists and left-leaning intellectuals to recognize the true nature of Bolshevism. But unlike modern laissez-faire liberals, he attributed the ugly features of Bolshevism to special Russian factors and not to socialism as such. 'The trouble with Russia is not that she is Socialist but that she is Russia' (*CSD*, p. 404).

Schumpeter was curiously silent about Fascism and Nazism; Hitler and Mussolini are hardly mentioned. The reason is not, as some people suspected, that he had sneaking sympathies for the Fascist regimes, although he at first probably underestimated the horrors and aggressive power of the

---

[8] For details see Haberler (1976). Keynes, too, was critical of important parts of the New Deal (see below).

Hitler regime. The real reason for his silence on Fascism and Nazism probably was that the two regimes were so generally detested and abhorred in the West that it was not necessary to discuss them. He may also have been reluctant to associate himself with the anti-Nazi chorus in the press and in official statements, which he found repugnant because it tended to become a condemnation of all things German.

There is another, not incompatible, reason for Schumpeter's silence on Nazism: the enormity of the evil of Hitlerism simply may have left him speechless, like the great Austrian satirist, poet and critical commentator on current events, Karl Kraus.[9] This is suggested by a remark in a highly critical review (1944) of a book by Harold Laski: 'Socialism . . . we see lying ahead on a trendline which we think we can understand. Fascism . . . is for the analyst as yet a riddle' (p. 164). But in the same review Schumpeter indicates what in his opinion Fascism and Nazism are *not*: 'In fact, Professor Laski perfectly realizes two essential truths: first, that the German and Italian bourgeoisies submitted to a mass movement that was far from congenial to them as classes; and second, that much can be explained in terms of the foreign experience of both nations. A third truth it would not, perhaps, be fair to expect him to realize: the strong similarities in vital respects that exist between Fascism and Bolshevism, similarities that stand out the better the more we take into account the differences in the objective conditions of the respective countries' (p. 163).[10] Thus, he rejects the Marxist theory, disseminated by Russian propaganda and widely accepted by Western intellectuals, that Fascism and Nazism are essentially a late form of capitalism.[11]

---

[9] While many people eagerly were waiting for Kraus's flaming condemnation of Nazism, after Hitler's rise to power, *Die Fackel* (*The Torch*), the periodical that Kraus wrote almost single-handedly for 37 years, did not appear for several months. Then a slim issue was published with comments on some unrelated matters and a beautiful poem that gave expression to Kraus's speechless silence:

Man frage nicht, was all die Zeit ich machte.
Ich bleibe stumm;
und sage nicht, warum.
Und Stille gibt es, da die Erde krachte.
Kein Wort, das traf;
man spricht nur aus dem Schlaf.
Und träumt von einer Sonne, welche lachte.
Es geht vorbei;
Nachher war's einerlei.
Das Wort entschlief, als jene Welt erwachte.

[10] See also *CSD*, p. 404, where the strong similarity of the 'Stalinist regime' and 'fascism' is stressed.

[11] It is true that some German industrialists supported Hitler because they regarded him as a bulwark against communism and thought they could easily tame him. They soon realized their mistake, but it was too late.

I now come to the intellectual atmosphere. The war years and early postwar years saw the high tide of anti-capitalist and anti-liberal sentiments and economic planning. The Great Depression of the 1930s was widely interpreted, not only by Marxists, as a breakdown of the capitalist system. There was a confluence of Keynesian and Marxian thought. Keynes's radical followers, the Marxo-Keynesians, as Schumpeter used to call them,[12] dominated the scene.

The catastrophic slump in the West gave Soviet Russia a great boost. That the communist economy was immune to the deflation and depression that engulfed the West should not have surprised anyone. Why should a centrally planned economy drastically deflate itself?[13] The fact is, however, that it made an enormous impression on the large crowd of left-leaning intellectuals and even on many economists, especially but not only the numerous Marxo-Keynesians. The widely accepted view was that the Soviet regime had 'abolished' unemployment and so Russia was spared the horrors of mass unemployment in the midst of glaring poverty and unsatisfied private and public needs.[14]

The widespread admiration and sympathy for the Soviet regime were not dampened by the thought that the 1930s was the period when Stalin liquidated the kulaks—which produced widespread famine—and ordered mass purges. There may have been no unemployment in Russia, but many millions were killed in the purges or died in the famine produced by the regime's policies.

It goes without saying that Schumpeter's view of the Great Depression was entirely different. The Great Depression did not signal a breakdown of capitalism and a triumph of socialism or communism. 'The thirties may well turn out to have been the last gasp of capitalism—the likelihood of this is, of course, greatly increased by the current war. But ... there are no

---

[12] See, for example, Schumpeter's paper 'English economists and the state-managed economy' (1949), p. 376. It is needless to add that not all Keynesians were radicals or socialists. Keynes himself belonged to the conservative wing of his school and became more conservative in his later years (see below). The same is true of his biographer, Sir Roy Harrod.

[13] It is true, however, that in the post-Second World War period several socialist countries (for example, Yugoslavia and Poland) have been badly hurt by inflation. This suggests that they may manage to produce an inflationary recession. But a deflationary depression of the order of magnitude of the one that hit the West in the 1930s probably exceeds their capacity for mismanagement.

[14] Robert Skidelsky has drawn attention to the fact that this view is even now used to defend acts of treachery in high places during the 1930s which have recently come to light. He is referring to the case of Sir Anthony Blunt, the distinguished and much honoured art historian and curator of the Queen's art collection, who last year was unmasked as a Russian spy and stripped of his knighthood.

purely economic reasons why capitalism should not have another successful run' (*CSD*, p. 163).

The Great Depression of the 1930s was not a regular depression in the sense of Schumpeter's theory (or model) of the business cycle. Although he flirted (though not in *CSD*) with the idea that the exceptional severity of the Great Depression may have been partly due to the coincidence of the depression phase of the 'Kondratieff' (long waves), 'Juglar' (ten-year cycle), and 'Kitchin' (40-months cycle) cycles, his considered view was that 'the darkest hues of cyclical depressions ... are due to adventitious circumstances'. Such adventitious circumstances were the anti-capitalist, inept policies of the New Deal. 'The subnormal recovery to 1935, the subnormal prosperity to 1937 and the slump after that are easily accounted for by the difficulties incident to the adaptation to a new fiscal policy, new labor legislation and a general change in the attitude of government to private enterprise all of which can ... be distinguished from the working of the productive apparatus as such' (p. 64).[15] Schumpeter mentions that only France among the industrial countries had a similar 'most unsatisfactory recovery' (p. 65). It will be recalled that France, under Prime Minister Léon Blum, had a New Deal patterned on the United States model.

Another adventitious circumstance that accounts for the exceptional severity of the Great Depression was massive deflation in the United States caused by the collapse of the American banking system in the early 1930s and the grossly inept policies of the Federal Reserve System, which not only failed to prevent or stop the deflation but aggravated it by deflationary measures. A collapse of the banking system and horrendous mistakes in monetary policy surely are not essential features of Schumpeter's model of the business cycle.[16]

---

[15] Keynes, too, was critical of the New Deal policies. He felt that 'undue haste in the reform program' would hold up recovery from the depression. Recovery, he argued, should have priority over reform. See Harrod (1961), p. 447.

[16] In 'The decade of the twenties' (1946; reprinted in Clemence, 1951), Schumpeter mentioned 'the weakness of the US banking system' as one of the factors that 'constitute adequate explanation of the "disaster" in the United States' ... 'the-avoidable-three bank epidemics [waves of bank failures] that occurred during the crisis [depression] ... spread paralysis ... and turned retreat into rout' (p. 214 in Clemence, 1951). In an earlier paper, 'The present world depression: a tentative diagnosis' (1931), he listed a number of special factors that contributed to the severity of the depression, monetary deflation, rigid wages and tariff policies among them. He concluded: 'It is believed that these elements of the situation account for 90 per cent of the values of the measurable symptoms [of the depression]' (p. 98 in Clemence, 1951).

Further support for my interpretation of Schumpeter's thought is provided by the fact that he did not oppose government deficit spending to stop 'this vicious spiral' ... 'whenever there is danger ... of a "downward cumulative process"' (*CSD*, p. 397). I recall that in the early 1930s in a newspaper article he actually recommended a $9 billion emergency government spending programme, a very large sum by the standard of the time.

Keynes's famous posthumously published article, 'The balance of payments of the United States' (1946), must have given Schumpeter great satisfaction. For there Keynes recommended that 'the classical medicine' (Schumpeter's 'capitalist methods') should be allowed to work. Keynes castigated the radical view of some of his followers, who in the meantime had become his critics, as 'modernist stuff, gone wrong and turned sour and silly' (p. 186).[17]

Schumpeter did not live long enough to witness the various 'economic miracles' that resulted from the application of the capitalist methods—the German, Japanese, French and Italian miracles among others.[18] What would Schumpeter's reaction have been? He would have been greatly, and pleasantly, astonished that capitalist methods were applied in so many cases, but the spectacular success of this policy would not have surprised him at all. For he had argued on several occasions that 'capitalist methods' would 'speedily' solve the problems of postwar reconstruction and recovery. 'Capitalist methods have proved equal to much more difficult tasks.'[19] He expressed serious doubts, however, that in the prevailing anti-capitalist atmosphere capitalist methods would be allowed to work. In this judgement he was too pessimistic, at least in the short or medium run.

---

[17] According to various reports Keynes's radical followers tried to stop publication of that paper as unworthy of the master. In a letter to Lord Halifax, Keynes used even stronger words to criticize his radical followers. See Moggridge (1980), p. 626.

[18] Most of these miracles were performed by members of the Mont Pélerin Society—Ludwig Erhard in Germany, Luigi Einaudi in Italy, Jacques Rueff in France and Reinhard Kamitz in Austria.

[19] Schumpeter (1943), 'Capitalism in the postwar world'. There he criticizes the views then widely held—especially by Keynesians, although as we have seen no longer by Keynes himself—that there would be 'a postwar slump, threatening from a drastic reduction of military expenditures financed by inflationary methods as well as from mere reorientation of production' and 'the all but general opinion . . . that capitalist methods will be unequal to the task of reconstruction' (p. 120). Events proved Schumpeter and Keynes right and the radical Keynesians wrong. I quote two statements by radical Keynesians about the prospects of the Erhard currency reform and policy of decontrol. In 1948, criticizing the view 'that if, somehow, the German economy could be freed of material and manpower regulations, price control and other bureaucratic paraphernalia, then recovery could be expedited', John K. Galbraith concluded: '. . . There never has been the slightest possibility of getting German recovery by this wholesale repeal [of controls and regulations]' (p. 95). Galbraith's paper abounds with predictions of the dire political and economic consequences of Erhard's dash for economic freedom. Two years later Thomas (now Lord) Balogh predicted alarming political and economic consequences of Erhard's policy and, 'in a final word of warning', pointed 'to the gains which the Soviet Zone of Germany has been able to record' (Balogh, 1950). To paraphrase Keynes: rarely has modernist stuff gone wrong and turned sour and silly so fast! For further references, see my paper *The Great Depression of the 1930s—Can It Happen Again?* (1980).

THE REAL MESSAGE

The Conceptual Framework

In the introduction to this paper, the provocative and controversial conclusions of Schumpeter's book were formulated in 'desperate brevity' (to use one of Schumpeter's favourite phrases) as he himself often formulated them. 'Socialism will inevitably emerge' from 'an equally inevitable decomposition of capitalism'. Capitalism's demise is not due to its alleged failures, but to its very success. Socialism is not only perfectly feasible, but also efficient and 'a strong case can be made for its economic superiority'. Socialism is compatible with democracy.

However, these sweeping summaries must not be taken at their face value as they have been so often taken by friends and foes alike; they require most careful interpretation and closest attention to the qualifications, reservations and elucidations that Schumpeter provides in often confusing abundance.

To begin with the basic definitions, capitalism in Schumpeter's sense is not the same as what is now usually called 'the market economy'. He distinguishes between what he calls the 'commercial society' or 'bourgeois society' or occasionally 'private enterprise' economy,[20] on the one hand, and capitalism on the other. The former is defined by 'two elements, private property in means of production and regulation of the productive process by private contract (or management or initiative)' (p. 167). Commercial or bourgeois society is thus about the same as the free market or free enterprise economy.

However, commercial society is not identical to capitalist society. 'The latter, a special case of the former, is defined by the additional phenomenon of credit creation—by the practice responsible for so many outstanding features of modern economic life, of financing [innovating] enterprises by [inflationary] bank credit' (p. 167). The words in brackets have been added here to remind the reader that Schumpeter is referring to his well-known theory of the business cycle in which, it will be recalled, inflationary credit creation in support of innovating entrepreneurs during the upswing of the cycle and automatic deflationary liquidation of credit during the downswing play an essential role. But in *CSD* this business cycle mechanism is not prominently displayed. Actually, the term capitalism seems often to be used interchangeably with private enterprise or bourgeois or commercial society, leaving it to the reader to decide which of the two is applicable in any

---

[20] These terms are on the whole used interchangeably, notwithstanding occasional slight shading of meanings, depending on the problem in hand. For brevity's sake I will ignore these finer nuances.

particular context. Unlike capitalism, socialism is defined in a straightforward and non-controversial way as 'an institutional pattern in which the
control over means of production and over production itself is vested with a
central authority' (p. 167).

Schumpeter does not use the modern phrase 'mixed economy', but he
makes it clear (1943) that 'no social system is ever pure either in its economic
or in its political aspects. As regards the former, structural principles, such
as, in the case of commercial society, private management of the process of
production and free contracting, are never fully carried to their logical consequences. People were at no time allowed to do with their own quite as they
pleased, and society at all times limited the range within which they might
freely contract. In the epoch of intact capitalism law, custom, public
opinion, and public administration enforced a certain amount of public planning' (p. 114). Similarly, under socialism there is always 'left room for a
certain amount of *laissez faire*'. Here he refers to Lenin's New Economic
Policy (Schumpeter, 1943), which was reversed by Stalin with disastrous
consequences. Today we have many more examples of partial liberalization
in socialist countries, which have gone furthest in Hungary and Poland.

There are many scattered discussions in Schumpeter's works on how
much planning, government intervention and public regulation can be tolerated by capitalism or the bourgeois society without loss of identity and efficiency. Some of them will be mentioned below. Having sketched the
conceptual framework, I take up some substantive issues.

Capitalism's Economic Achievements and the Theory of Imperialism

Like Karl Marx, Schumpeter had the highest possible opinion of the productive capabilities of 'unfettered' capitalism. Some readers may be surprised that I mention Marx. But it is a fact, duly noted by Schumpeter, that
Marx in his famous *Communist Manifesto* and elsewhere described the civilizing and growth-promoting power of capitalism, especially in backward
countries, in truly glowing language. This is, of course, the opposite of what
today is proclaimed by the many self-styled Marxist leaders in less developed countries, but most of these people have probably never read a line of
Marx and would not like it if they did.

It goes without saying that Schumpeter does not accept the Marxian
theory of increasing misery of the proletariat, progressive polarization of
society and class struggle. He subjects Marx's own theory, as well as its later
elaboration, the neo-Marxian theory of economic imperialism, to a search-
ing criticism.

Since it became increasingly absurd to say that the American or European
or Japanese, or even the Brazilian or Mexican, workers are getting poorer all

the time, absolutely or relatively to other classes, the second and third generations of Marxists—Schumpeter mentions the Austrian Marxists Otto Bauer and Rudolf Hilferding, but Rosa Luxemburg and Lenin also come to mind—shifted the exploitation theory from the domestic to the international sphere. Imperialism and colonialism are interpreted as the exploitation of backward countries by the capitalists in the developed countries.[21] It would lead too far, and it is hardly necessary any more to discuss Schumpeter's criticism in detail. I confine myself to three points. First, Schumpeter shows convincingly that the neo-Marxian theory of imperialism, like its domestic counterpart of increasing misery of the working class, 'is the joint result of wrong vision and faulty analysis' (see *CSD*, pp. 49–53).

Second, Schumpeter had developed his own theory of imperialism as early as 1919 in an article titled 'The sociology of imperialism'. There he describes the phenomenon of imperialism as '"objectless" tendencies toward forcible expansion, without definite, utilitarian limits—that is, non-rational and irrational, purely instinctual inclinations toward war and conquest' that have played 'a very large role in the history of mankind. It may sound paradoxical, but numberless wars—perhaps the majority of all wars—have been waged without adequate "reason"—not so much from a moral viewpoint as from that of reasoned and reasonable interest' (*CSD*, p. 83).[22]

---

[21] Schumpeter points out that, if there was 'exploitation of *native* labor', it was the result of the most striking example of 'class cooperation' in the developed countries. 'It [imperialism] was a movement toward higher wages as it was a movement toward higher profits, and in the long run it certainly benefited the proletariat [in the industrial countries] more . . . than the capitalist interest' (*CSD*, p. 53).

[22] A beautiful example from antiquity of 'objectless' conquest is reported in *Plutarch's Lives*: King Pyrrhus, of Epirus, had a trusted advisor, 'a certain Cineas, a man . . . of great wisdom' who tried to restrain his monarch. When Cineas noted that Pyrrhus made preparations to attack Rome, he started a conversation: 'The Romans, O Pyrrhus, are said to be good fighters, and to be rulers of many warlike nations; if, then, Heaven should permit us to conquer these men, how should we use our victory?' Pyrrhus said: 'Thy question, O Cineas, really needs no answer; the Romans once conquered, there is neither barbarian nor Greek city there which is a match for us, but we shall at once possess all Italy.' After which Cineas said: 'And after taking Italy, O King, what are we to do?' And Pyrrhus said: 'Sicily is near, and holds out her hands to us, an island abounding in wealth and men, and very easy to capture . . .'. 'What thou sayest,' replied Cineas, 'is probably true; but will our expedition stop with the taking of Sicily?' Pyrrhus replied: 'Who could keep his hands off Libya, or Carthage, when that city got within his reach . . .? And when we have become masters here, no one of the enemies who now treat us with scorn will offer further resistance; there is no need of saying that.' 'None whatever,' said Cineas, 'but when we have got everything subject to us, what are we going to do?' Pyrrhus smiled and said: 'We shall have a good time, will drink bumpers every day.' And now that Cineas had brought Pyrrhus to this point he said: 'Then what stands in our way now if we want to drink bumpers . . . ? Surely this privilege is ours already, and we have at hand, without

Third, the slogan of imperialism and exploitation of less developed countries has retained a powerful appeal to this day. In its modern, non-Marxist form, it says that the terms of trade of the less developed countries have a secular tendency to deteriorate. This proposition has been disproved many times, but nonetheless it is being put forward with great aplomb by many speakers at almost every United Nations conference.

Schumpeter was very critical of the theory that vanishing investment opportunities and a slowdown of technological progress would threaten capitalism and spell secular stagnation, a theory that was very popular at the time among Keynes's followers. Today most economists would agree with Schumpeter's position.

Schumpeter's Defence of Monopoly

Rather controversial is Schumpeter's position on the monopoly problem. He had little regard for the theories of monopolistic and imperfect competition because they got lost in such trivia as the monopoly power of corner drugstores: 'We are set to wondering what world those theorists live in' (p. 85).

This criticism may be acceptable as far as it goes, that is, if applied to what might be called microscopic analysis of monopolistic competition. However, Schumpeter goes much further. Many economists, especially most 'liberal' economists, take exception to his all-out defence of monopoly, which is one of the strongest, and many would say most surprising, convictions expressed in the book and elsewhere. Schumpeter is quite contemptuous of what he calls the 'glorified' ideal of a perfectly competitive economy, which in reality has never existed (see, for example, p. 81). According to Schumpeter, monopoly and monopoly profits are inherent in the capitalist process. What often looks like excessive profits 'provides the bait that lures capital on to untried fields' (p. 90). 'Perfectly free entry into a new field may make it impossible to enter it at all. The introduction of new methods of production and new commodities is hardly conceivable with perfect—and perfectly prompt—competition from the start. And this means that the bulk of what we call economic progress is incompatible with it. As a matter of fact, perfect competition is and always has been temporarily

---

taking any trouble, those things to which we hope to attain by bloodshed and great toils and perils, after doing much harm to others and suffering much ourselves. Why not have the good times now?' Plutarch says: 'By this reasoning of Cineas, Pyrrhus was more troubled than he was converted.' He attacked anyway, and defeated the Romans in a famous battle, his last victory—which ever since has been known as the Pyrrhic victory.

suspended whenever anything new is being introduced' (pp. 104–105).[23] Schumpeter asserts again and again the superiority of 'big business' or 'monopolistic' capitalism over small business capitalism, let alone the non-existent perfectly competitive capitalism (see, for example, pp. 107–189).

It must not be forgotten, however, that the monopolistic profits of the innovating entrepreneurs are bound to be swept away by the competition of the crowd of imitators which sooner or later catches up with the innovator. Competition is only 'temporarily suspended'. In Schumpeter's scheme of things this is part of the process of 'creative destruction', which marks the downswing of the business cycle. But even in depressions deviations from perfect competition may have a useful role to play. '"Restraint of trade" of the cartel type as well as those which merely consist of tacit understandings about price competition may be effective remedies under conditions of depression... They may in the end produce not only steadier but also greater expansion of total output than could be procured by an entirely uncontrolled onward rush [presumably under perfect competition] that cannot fail to be studded with catastrophies'.(p. 91).

This surely is strong stuff; what shall we make of it? My own reaction and that of many economists is that Schumpeter greatly overstates his case in his all-out defence of monopoly and disdain for free competition. This is especially true of his defence of cartel arrangements in depressions. Temporary monopoly positions do play an important or even indispensable role in the innovating process, but the monopoly phenomenon goes far beyond that useful function. The case for anti-trust and other anti-monopoly measures may have been overstated by fanatical anti-monopoly lawyers and economists, as Schumpeter asserts. On the whole, however, anti-trust policy is not as bad as Schumpeter makes it.

On the other hand, Schumpeter is right that the future of capitalism and free enterprise would not be endangered by monopolistic tendencies if it were not for numerous government policies that create and foster private monopoly positions. The charge by Marxists, Marxo-Keynesians, and their fellow travellers that capitalism is doomed by the growth of monopolies is unfounded. Few monopolies would survive if it were not for protective government policies. The tremendous progress in transportation and communications technology, the rapid spread of technological knowledge, the development of new industrial centres in different parts of the world, including less developed countries, and the resulting rapid growth of world trade in manufactured goods have undermined monopoly positions and whittled

---

[23] Note the word 'temporarily'. Its significance will be discussed presently.

down temporary monopoly profits. It follows that Schumpeter's overall 'vision' (to use his favourite term) of the monopoly problem, and his defence of capitalism and private enterprise against the charge that increasing monopolization has sapped its viability and strength, can be upheld.

Capitalism's Cultural Achievements

Thus from the economic point of view Schumpeter gives capitalism a completely clean bill of health with respect to both past performance and future prospects, and he rejects accusations of failure due to vanishing investment opportunities, increasing monopolization, and increasingly inequitable income distribution. In addition, Schumpeter speaks highly of the cultural achievements of the capitalist era. In chapter XI, 'The Civilization of Capitalism', he discusses some of the cultural achievements and the civilizing power of capitalism in some detail. Schumpeter speaks of 'the impressive economic and the still more impressive cultural achievements of the capitalist order and the immense promise held out by both' for the future. If allowed to continue, capitalism would 'lift poverty from the shoulders of mankind' (p. 129). Then another surprise '. . . I am not going to argue, on the strength of that performance, that the capitalist intermezzo is likely to be prolonged. In fact, I am going to draw the exactly opposite inference' (p. 130). Its very success will bring about, inevitably, capitalism's decomposition.

How Capitalism's Success Brings About Its Downfall

This proposition has shocked and puzzled many people. If all qualifications, reservations, and elucidations are given their proper attention, however, the forecast of capitalism's early doom becomes less apodictic and the demise of capitalism loses much of its inevitability.

First, why does the very success of capitalism bring about its demise? There are several reasons. Perhaps the most important one, according to Schumpeter, is that capitalism 'undermines the social institutions which protect it' (p. 61). These institutions are the remnants of the feudal system on the one hand and the existence of many small businesses and independent farmers on the other. As far as the 'feudal remnants' are concerned, Schumpeter refers to the 'English case' where 'the aristocratic element continued to rule the roost *right to the end of the period of intact and vital capitalism*' (p. 136, italics in the original). The aristocracy 'made itself the representative of bourgeois interests and fought the battles of the bourgeoisie' (p. 136). It fought much more efficiently and effectively than the bourgeoisie, the business leaders, could themselves.

There is probably much truth in this as far as 19th century Britain is concerned; Schumpeter was always a great admirer of the British political system. It may also apply, 'though nowhere so effectively as in England' (p. 136), to the European continent. But it does not fit the United States at all.

Much more convincing is the proposition that the decline in the number of small and medium-sized businesses, and especially of small and medium-sized farms, weakens the defences of the bourgeois society. 'The political structure of a nation is profoundly affected by the elimination of a host of small and medium-sized firms the owner-managers of which, together with their dependents, henchmen and connections, count quantitatively at the polls and have a hold on what we may term the foreman class that no management of a large unit can ever have; the very foundation of private property and free contracting wears away in a nation in which its most vital, most concrete, most meaningful types disappear from the moral horizon of the people' (pp. 140–141). Big business is very vulnerable to socialist criticism and attacks; small businessmen and independent farmers are in a much better position to defend themselves and have always been the most formidable bulwark against socialization. Stalin had to use brute force and create a blood bath to break the resistance of the Russian farmers, the kulaks. Schumpeter recognizes, however, the limits of the argument. 'The process [of concentration] has gone less far and is less free from setbacks and compensatory tendencies than one would gather from many popular expositions. In particular, large-scale enterprise not only annihilates but also, to some extent, creates space for the small producing, and especially trading, firms' (p. 140).

The Role of the 'Intellectuals'

There is another development that, according to Schumpeter, undermines the foundations of bourgeois society. It is the rise in number and influence of the class of 'intellectuals', a 'group' or 'type' of people 'whose interest it is to work up and organize resentment' and hostility towards capitalism, 'to nurse it [the resentment and hostility] to voice it and to lead it' (p. 145). Schumpeter concedes that 'this type', the intellectual, 'is not easy to define'. His description of Voltaire, whom he calls 'an invaluable instance' of an intellectual, perhaps comes closest to a formal definition of the ideal type of the intellectual: 'His [Voltaire's] very superficiality that made it possible for him to cover everything from religion to Newtonian optics, allied to indomitable vitality and an insatiable curiosity, a perfect absence of inhibitions, an unerring instinct for and a wholesale acceptance of the humors of his time, enabled that uncritical critic and mediocre poet and historian to fascinate—and to sell' (p. 149).[24] There have been 'intellectuals' in pre-capitalist societies, but 'it was capitalism that let him loose and provided him with the printing press' (p. 147). Capitalist civilization, capitalist ethics, rationality and tolerance, and above all capitalism's very success in creating unheard-of levels of affluence increased the number and power of the intellectuals and provided livelihood and leisure. At the same time capitalist ethics, rationality and tolerance make capitalism vulnerable to or even defenceless against subversion and demagoguery.

'One of the most important features of the later stages of capitalist civilization is the vigorous expansion of the educational apparatus and particularly of the facilities of higher education.' This leads to an oversupply 'of services in professional and quasi-professional and in the end of all "white-collar" lines', and it creates 'sectional unemployment'. In addition, 'it creates unsatisfactory employment—employment in substandard work or at wages below those of the better-paid manual workers.' The 'unemployed or unsatisfactorily employed' swell the ranks of the intellectuals and the army of government bureaucrats. 'Discontent breeds resentment.' The result is growing 'hostility ... amounting to moral disapproval of the capitalist order' (pp. 152–153).

The role of intellectuals in the labour movement is especially important and destructive of the capitalist order. True, trade unions 'obviously are not the creation of the intellectual groups... Labor never craved intellectual leadership but intellectuals invaded labor politics. They had an important contribution to make: they verbalized the movement, supplied theories and slogans for it—class war is an excellent example—made it conscious of itself and in doing so changed its meaning ... and radicalized it, eventually imparting a revolutionary bias to the most bourgeois trade-union practices, a bias which most of the non-intellectual leaders at first greatly resented' (pp. 153–154).

There surely is much truth in all this; reading the whole text makes Schumpeter's analysis more persuasive than a short summary can be. But is it enough to clinch the case for the 'inevitable' and imminent decomposition of capitalism?

Qualifications

Schumpeter points out that derogation of the performance and moral condemnation of capitalism would not be enough to undermine the capitalist

---

[24] These passages come from a section entitled 'The sociology of the intellectual' (pp. 145–155). Only a few highlights of this interesting analysis can be mentioned here.

order unless it were possible to offer 'an attractive alternative'. The attractive alternative is, of course, socialism. But before discounting Schumpeter's controversial theory that socialism is not only feasible but may also be more efficient than capitalism, some general qualifications and elucidations of his theory should be mentioned that make the approaching decomposition of the bourgeois society and of the free enterprise economy decidedly less imminent and less inevitable than most commentators on the book, both critical and friendly, have realized.

First, we have to keep in mind the time dimension. Schumpeter stresses that despite all hostility and anti-capitalist legislation and regulation, 'enterprise is still active, the leadership of the bourgeois group is still the prime mover of the economic process'. So 'for the purposes of short-run forecasting . . . all this may be more important than the tendency toward another civilization that slowly works deep down below'. 'And in these things a century is "a short run"' (p. 163). Thus capitalism may, after all, continue for a century or more, and much can happen in a span of a hundred years to change the trend of events.

Second, there is another general qualification which, in conjunction with the one just mentioned, makes the demise of capitalism somewhat less than inevitable. In the prologue to the first edition Schumpeter states 'Analysis, whether economic or other, never yields more than a statement about the tendencies present in an observable pattern. And these never tell us what *will* happen to the pattern but only what *would* happen if they continued to act as they have been acting in the time interval covered by our observation and if no other factors intruded. "Inevitability" or "necessity" can never mean more than this' (p. 61, italics in the original). Similar cautionary remarks about the possibility of a change in the trend occur several times in the book under consideration and elsewhere.

The Alleged Superior Economic Efficiency of Socialism

I now come to what is perhaps the most controversial and questionable part of Schumpeter's book, his analysis of whether socialism is an 'attractive alternative' to capitalism or, as he often says in this section, to 'the commercial society'. It will be recalled that Schumpeter asserts 'that there is a strong case for believing in its [socialism's] superior economic efficiency' (p. 188) and that, in principle, socialism is compatible with democracy.

Again, close attention must be paid to the qualifications of those sweeping statements. Thus Schumpeter emphasizes that the 'superior economic efficiency' of socialism 'refers exclusively to the logic of blueprints, hence to "objective" possibilities which socialism in practice may be quite unable to realize' (p. 196). In the light of what has happened since the book was written this qualification becomes much more important than it seems to have appeared to Schumpeter. In the early 1940s there existed only one socialist country, Soviet Russia; now we have almost a dozen fully socialized economies and many others that are close to being centrally planned. Most of them have existed long enough for the transitional difficulties stressed by Schumpeter to have been overcome. The evidence of the productive superiority of the market economies has become overwhelming. Thus the striking difference in the economic performance as measured by the standard of living or output per capita of such pairs of countries as West and East Germany, Austria and Czechoslovakia, Greece and Yugoslavia, Thailand and Burma, and China and Taiwan,[25] can be explained only in terms of their different economic regimes: for the paired countries are similar in state of development, climate and resource endowment (both human and material), and they had enjoyed roughly the same standard of living in the pre-communist period.

Another important qualification is this: when discussing the 'strong case' for socialism's superior efficiency, Schumpeter usually speaks of 'fettered' capitalism. The implication is that there can be no question about the superior efficiency of what Schumpeter calls 'the vital and intact capitalism'. By 'fettered capitalism' he means the later stage (20th century) of capitalism, hemmed in and hampered as it is by an ever tighter web of regulations, a rapidly growing public sector and an increasingly heavy tax burden. The existence of a large public sector in the 'bourgeois economy' leads to wasteful 'frictions' between the two 'spheres', to 'wars of conquest waged upon the bourgeois domain [the private sector] with ever-increasing success by men of the public sphere' (p. 197). 'A considerable part of the total work done by lawyers goes into the struggle of business with the state and its organs... Not inconsiderable is the social loss from such unproductive employment of many of the best brains ... considering how terribly rare good brains are' (p. 198). Under socialism all these wastes would be absent.

Schumpeter felt strongly that a major threat to the capitalist order is high and progressive tax rates. In his last speech, 'The march into socialism'

---

[25] An example from the Western hemisphere is the centrally-planned economy of Cuba and the 'capitalist' economy of Puerto Rico. The case of Puerto Rico is especially instructive. The island is probably the most prosperous country in Central America and the Caribbean despite the fact that it is denied the use of two policy tools that are widely regarded as essential for economic development: inflation and import restrictions. Since Puerto Rico lives in monetary and customs union with the United States, it is subjected to the free competition of United States industries and its rate of inflation cannot exceed that in the United States. It should perhaps be added that by Latin American standards the rate of price increase in the United States must be classified as a case of severe deflation.

(1949; published 1950), he speaks of 'our hyperprogressive methods of taxation' which add to 'perennial inflationary pressure', which in turn quickens the march into socialism. Since then (1949) the growth of the public sector, the enormous increase in transfer payments, and inflation, have greatly enlarged the weight of the tax burden. In another paper, 'English economists and the state-managed economy' (1949),[26] speaking of the British situation, he refers to 'the pivotal question of taxation which need only be left as it is in order to make full and genuine socialism inevitable before long'. Thus, the current concern with high taxes, 'the tax revolt' of the 1970s, was anticipated by Schumpeter 40 years ago. Socialist economies are presumably not subject to the handicap of stifling taxation.

Schumpeter is surely right that the enormous growth of the public sector, ever higher tax rates and rapidly increasing regulation of the economy have greatly impaired the productive efficiency of capitalism. However, leaning over backwards to do justice to the cause of socialism, he paid insufficient attention, it seems to me, to the basic inefficiencies and weaknesses of central planning. Fettered, overtaxed and over-regulated though they are in varying degrees, the capitalist market economies still out-produce and out-perform the socialist economies.

Democracy under Capitalism and Socialism

Schumpeter rejects the Marxist theory, which at the time was widely accepted also in non-Marxist circles, that 'there cannot be true democracy except in socialism' (p. 284). Actually, 'modern democracy rose along with capitalism and in causal connection with it' (p. 296). Schumpeter's position comes close to what we may call the neo-liberal, or rather neo-conservative, view, namely that socialism and democracy are incompatible. This view is mentioned (p. 284) but not explicitly accepted. On the contrary, Schumpeter states that 'there is no incompatibility. In appropriate states of the social environment the socialist engine can be run on democratic principles' (p. 284).

But again, what counts is not sweeping general summaries but qualifications and fine print. There is a lengthy discussion on the 'conditions for the success of the democratic methods' of conducting the affairs of a capitalist or socialist country (pp. 289–296). These conditions are very exacting indeed. One limiting factor is 'the human material of politics' (p. 290), the quality of the political leaders. 'Electorates and parliaments must be on an intellectual and moral level high enough to be proof against the offerings of the crook and the crank' (p. 294). In this connection Schumpeter again refers to

---

[26] Reprinted in Clemence (1951), p. 299.

England, 'which is the only country to fulfill our condition [of high quality of political leadership] completely'. If he had a chance to revise his book today, he probably would expunge the reference to England as too optimistic.

From the point of view of the feasibility of democratic socialism, the most important 'condition for the success of democracy is that the effective range of political decision should not be extended too far' (p. 291), that certain matters be excluded from 'becoming part of the competitive struggle for political leadership' (p. 293). These 'conditions may be summed up in the phrase democratic self-control' (p. 294). The requirement of self-control is 'in principle at least' fulfilled under capitalism; for 'the importance of the role of political decisions in the bourgeois state can . . . be scaled down to almost any degree that the disabilities of the political sector may require' (p. 297). In other words, the degree of involvement of the state in economic affairs can be kept sufficiently low to be handled by democratic methods. 'In the socialist society [on the other hand] these limitations will raise a much more serious problem, for socialist society lacks the automatic restrictions imposed upon the political sphere by the bourgeois scheme of things' (p. 299). But Schumpeter points out that 'capitalism is rapidly losing the advantages it used to possess' (p. 298). This is the consequence of the increasingly serious handicap discussed above: fetters imposed on the capitalist, private profit economy by the growth of the public sector, increasingly stifling taxation and increasingly oppressive regulations.

Stopping short of declaring categorically that socialism is incompatible with democracy, Schumpeter reaches the conclusion that there 'is little reason to believe that . . . socialism will mean the advent of the civilization of which orthodox socialists dream. It is much more likely to present fascist features. That would be a strange answer to Marx's prayer. But history sometimes indulges in jokes of questionable taste' (p. 375).[27]

CONCLUDING REMARKS

Capitalism, Socialism and Democracy is a great book. It is not an easy book although, as Professor Fellner points out in his contribution to the present volume (Chapter 3), the author regarded it as a popular version of his work. Full understanding and appreciation require very careful study, and only readers with a good background in economics and history will get the full

---

[27] Already in the early 1920s Schumpeter had expressed scepticism about the possibility of democratic socialism. See his long article, 'Sozialistische Möglichkeiten von heute' ('Socialist possibilities of today') (1920/21; reprinted in Schumpeter, 1952—see especially pp. 477–478).

benefit of all the finer points and of all allusions and hints thrown out throughout the book in great profusion.[28] This evaluation of Schumpeter's book should be acceptable irrespective of the acceptance or rejection of the book's bold prognoses, which permit, as we have seen, somewhat different interpretations despite Schumpeter's own seemingly unequivocal summary statements.

I have given my own interpretation. In this interpretation Schumpeter's diagnoses and prognoses have been confirmed to a large extent by events of the last 40 years. He correctly foresaw increasing difficulties for the capitalist order resulting from the rapid growth of the public sector, the growing propensity to regulate, an increase in the tax burden and the high progressivity of the tax system, and rising inflation. These developments have reduced the flexibility, adaptability[29] and productivity of the capitalist economy and have promoted the rise of the socialist order. Schumpeter also predicted correctly that 'capitalist methods', the methods of the free market economy, what Keynes called 'the classical medicine', would, if allowed to work after the Second World War, speedily solve the problems of the transition from a war to a peace economy. He was, however, too pessimistic when he doubted that 'capitalist methods' would in fact be allowed to show their mettle in the postwar period.

Actually, the Western—or better, the non-communist—countries had a much better recovery after the war than Schumpeter and most other economists had foreseen. The war economy, an exercise in improvised central planning, was quickly dismantled and 'capitalist methods' were sufficiently restored to give the West a quarter of a century of almost unprecedented prosperity and growth.[30]

What would Schumpeter's reaction have been? He would have pointed out that he had not excluded the possibility of a short-run revival of capitalism and that 'in these things a century is a "short run"' (p. 163). But how about the longer run? It can be argued, not implausibly in my opinion, that the 'march into socialism', though it may have been slowed temporarily, has

---

[28] This does not mean, however, that the non-expert reader will not also enjoy the book and read it with profit. This is especially true of Part I, 'The Marxian doctrine', and Part V, 'Historical sketch of socialist parties'.

[29] The loss of flexibility and adaptability of the capitalist system was the theme of a recent paper by Tibor Scitovsky (1980). Scitovsky pays high tribute to Schumpeter. He speaks of 'the most celebrated performance of America's most brilliant economist' and seems to accept, without qualification, Schumpeter's pessimistic conclusion on the survival of capitalism.

[30] Since it has bothered some people, it should perhaps be stated that in this context the terms 'East' and 'West', as well as 'North' and 'South', must not be interpreted literally. The 'West' includes Japan, Australia and New Zealand; the 'East' embraces the Russian garrison state of Cuba; and the 'North' includes Australia and South Africa.

not been stopped, let alone reversed. The growth of the public sector continues in most countries, the tax burden goes up and government interventions in the economy have hardly been reduced anywhere.

I shall refrain from engaging in a detailed and unavoidably highly speculative debate on the validity of these conjectures and on whether the tax revolt in the United States or the attempt of the Thatcher government in Britain to reverse the trend is likely to be successful, but I shall give a general reason that makes me more optimistic about the chances for capitalism's survival than is Schumpeter (or Scitovsky), and shall suggest a somewhat different way of formulating the basic problem.

I argued above that Schumpeter underestimated the inefficiency and economic weaknesses of the centrally-planned economies. When he wrote, there existed only one well-established socialist country, Soviet Russia. I argued that the new experience that has become available since the war with the emergence of a dozen centrally-planned economies in Europe and Asia and of Cuba in the Western hemisphere has made an overwhelming case for the economic superiority of capitalism—fettered, overregulated and overtaxed though it is—over socialism. Is it unreasonable to assume that this will become generally recognized, perhaps not only in the West, and that it will stop the march into socialism?

It will be recalled that Schumpeter was fully aware of the fact that in real life 'no social system is ever pure'. Even in the 19th century, 'in the epoch of intact capitalism', there was a certain admixture of 'public planning'. And in no socialist economy is the principle of central planning carried out 100 per cent; there is always 'a certain amount of laissez faire', some areas reserved for the market and price mechanism.

If that is accepted, the question should be not, Can capitalism survive? but How far will the admixture of public planning go? and How far can it go in a democratic environment?, keeping in mind Schumpeter's warning that socialism 'is likely to present fascist features'. If the capitalist economies show signs of 'decomposition' (a rapid growth of the public sector and public planning), so too do the socialist economies (in both their economic and their political aspects). Perhaps there is a tendency for convergence of the two systems.

I have to stop, but a final warning is in order: in speaking of 'convergence' I do not mean to suggest (as a large part of the literature on convergence does) that there is really not much to choose between the capitalist and socialist order; far from it. As we find them in the present world, the two systems are miles apart, in both their 'economic and political aspects', and there can be no question which one is preferable. But we should follow Schumpeter's example and keep value judgements and our personal preferences separate from the analysis.

REFERENCES

Balogh, T. (1950) Germany: an experiment in planning by the 'Free Price Mechanism'. *Banca Nazionale del Lavoro Quarterly Review 3* (Rome), 71–102.

Blum, J.M. (1970) *Roosevelt and Morgenthau. A Revision and Condensation of 'From the Morgenthau Diaries'*. Boston: Houghton Mifflin.

Clemence, R.V. (Ed.) (1951) *Essays of J.A. Schumpeter*. Cambridge, MA: Addison-Wesley.

Galbraith, J.K. (1948) The German economy. In *Foreign Economic Policy for the United States* (Ed.) Harris, S.E. Cambridge, MA: Harvard University Press.

Haberler, G. (1950) Joseph Alois Schumpeter, 1883–1950. *Quarterly Journal of Economics*, August. Reprinted in Harris, S.E. (Ed.) (1951) *Schumpeter. Social Scientist*. Cambridge, MA: Harvard University Press.

Haberler, G. (1980) The Great Depression of the 1930s—Can It Happen Again? Washington, DC: Government Printing Office. (Available as an American Enterprise Institute reprint.)

Harrod, R.F. (1961) *The Life of John Maynard Keynes*. London: Oxford University Press.

Keynes, J.M. (1946) The balance of payments of the United States. *Economic Journal*, **56** (June).

Moggridge, D. (Ed.) (1980) *The Collected Writings of John Maynard Keynes, Volume 24, Activities 1944–1946: The Transition to Peace*. Cambridge: Cambridge University Press.

Plutarch's Lives (1920) Volume IX, pp. 387–389. London and New York: Loeb Classical Library.

Schumpeter, J.A. (1908) *Das Wesen und der Hauptinhalt der theoretischen Nationalökonomie*. Leipzig: Verlag von Duncker und Humblot.

Schumpeter, J.A. (1912) *The Theory of Economic Development. An Inquiry into Profits, Capital, Credit, Interest and the Business Cycle*. English translation by Opie, R. (1934) Cambridge, MA: Harvard University Press.

Schumpeter, J.A. (1919) The sociology of imperialism. English translation by Norden, H., in Sweezy, P.M. (1951) *Imperialism and Social Classes by J.A. Schumpeter*. New York: Augustus M. Kelly.

Schumpeter, J.A. (1920/21) Sozialistische Möglichkeiten von heute (Socialist possibilities of today). *Archiv für Sozialwissenschaft und Sozialpolitik*, **48,** 305–360. Reprinted in Schumpeter, J.A. (1952) *Aufsätze zur ökonomischen Theorie*. pp. 465–510. Tübingen.

Schumpeter, J.A. (1931) The present world depression: a tentative diagnosis. *American Economic Review*, March, 179–182. Reprinted in Clemence, R.V. (Ed.) (1951) *Essays of J.A. Schumpeter*. pp. 96–99. Cambridge, MA: Addison-Wesley.

Schumpeter, J.A. (1939) *Business Cycles. A Theoretical, Historical and Statistical Analysis of the Capitalist Process*. Two volumes, 1095 pp. New York: McGraw-Hill. Abridged paperback edition by Fels, R. (1964) New York: McGraw-Hill.

Schumpeter, J.A. (1943) Capitalism in the postwar world. In *Postwar Economic Problems* (Ed.) Harris, S.E. pp. 120–121. New York: McGraw Hill. Reprinted in Clemence, R.V. (Ed.) (1951) *Essays of J.A. Schumpeter*. Cambridge, MA: Addison-Wesley.

Schumpeter, J.A. (1944) A review of *Reflections on the Revolution of our Time* by Laski, H.J. (New York: Viking Press), *American Economic Review*, March.

Schumpeter, J.A. (1946) The decade of the twenties. *American Economic Review* (Supplement), May, 1–10. Reprinted in Clemence, R.V. (Ed.) (1951) *Essays of J.A. Schumpeter*. Cambridge, MA: Addison-Wesley.

Schumpeter, J.A. (1949) English economists and the state-managed economy. *Journal of Political Economy*, **57** (October). Reprinted in Clemence, R.V. (Ed.) (1951) *Essays of J.A. Schumpeter*. Cambridge, MA: Addison-Wesley.

Schumpeter, J.A. (1950) The march into socialism. *American Economic Review*, **40** (May). Reprinted in *CSD*, 3rd and following editions.

Scitovsky, T. (1980) Can capitalism survive? An old question in a new setting. Richard Ely
    Lecture. *American Economic Review*, **70** (May), 1–9.
Skidelsky, R. (1980) Myths of the 1930s. *Encounter*, June, 23–28.
Sweezy, P.M. (1951) Introduction to *Imperialism and Social Classes by J.A. Schumpeter*. New
    York: Augustus M. Kelly.
Ulam, A. (1980) In *Europäische Rundschau*. Volume 8, No. 2/80, pp. 171–173. Vienna: Eurpoa
    Verlag.

Chapter Five

Was Schumpeter Right?

ROBERT L. HEILBRONER

No. I do not think he was.

I model my answer, of course, on the apodictic style so characteristic of *Capitalism, Socialism and Democracy*: 'Can capitalism survive? No. I do not think it can.' In point of fact, Schumpeter's prognosis for capitalism was a good deal more hedged than that uncompromising verdict would indicate. At least during the short run ('and in these things, a century is a "short run"') (p. 163),[1] there was reason to expect that capitalism would adapt and survive, despite the workings of an ultimately fatal process deep within it. And so my summary judgement of Schumpeter's work must also be taken in a Schumpeterian vein. At the innermost core, I think his analysis is flawed, incomplete and inadequate. On the surface of things, however, and certainly compared with the vast majority of the writers of his time, it is a bravura performance, closer to the subsequent trends of history than the heady expectations of the contemporary Left, the naïve hopes and fears of the liberal middle, and the black forebodings of the believers in the Road to Serfdom.

There is an initial problem in taking the measure of *Capitalism, Socialism and Democracy*. It is to come to terms with the irritation aroused by its style, an irritation I sometimes think Schumpeter deliberately sought to provoke. There is a great deal of attitudinizing in Schumpeter, an open delight in *épater le bourgeois* and tweaking the noses of radicals. There is also pomposity and pedantry, mixed with an arrogance that teeters at the edge of a

---

[1] All numbered citations refer to the fifth edition, Allen & Unwin (1976).

dangerous elitism: arguing the advantages of monopoly, for example, Schumpeter declares that 'monopolization may increase the sphere of influence of the better, and decrease the sphere of influence of the inferior, brains...' (p. 101), a statement that he footnotes with the even more infuriating comment:

> The reader should observe that while, as a broad rule, that particular type of superiority is simply indisputable, the inferior brains, especially if their owners are entirely eliminated, are not likely to admit it and that the public's and the recording economists' hearts go out to them and not to the others.[p. 101n]

Perhaps of greater importance is Schumpeter's penchant for the delivery of prognostic statements with Jovian force and certitude, even when, alas, we now know them to have been based on nothing but the authority of his own convictions: '[I]t is one of the safest predictions that in the calculable future we shall live in an *embarras de richesse* of both foodstuffs and raw materials, giving all the rein to expansion of total output that we shall know what to do with. This applies to mineral resources as well' (p. 116).

Coming to terms with *Capitalism, Socialism and Democracy* requires, therefore, steeling oneself against its egregious surface blemishes; for example the statement, difficult to regard blandly after Vietnam, that 'the more completely capitalist the structure and attitude of a nation, the more pacifist—and the more prone to count the costs of war—we observe it to be' (pp. 128–129); or the declaration that 'very little influence on foreign policy has been exerted by big business' (p. 55), a view of things that will interest the historians of the Middle East. Statements such as these, with which the book abounds, set one's teeth on edge and shake our confidence in the speaker. But they do not constitute the central fault of the book. One learns to live with Schumpeter's idiosyncratic thought, his involuted style. And there are perceptive insights that redeem some of the extravagances from another side: 'The evolution of the capitalist style of life could be easily—and most tellingly—described in terms of the genesis of the modern lounge suit' (p. 126), a remark worthy of Thorstein Veblen.

Capitalism, Socialism and Democracy must of course ultimately be judged by the internal consistency and the historical cogency of its argument, not by its style. And so we come to the famous depiction of 'plausible' capitalism overcome by the hostility of the social milieu that it has itself created. The argument can be reduced to a set of interlocked propositions:

1. Capitalism is a process of continuous accumulation-and-change, the two

intimately and inextricably conjoined: 'Capitalism ... is by its nature a form or method of economic change and not only never is but never can be stationary' (p. 82).

2. The propulsive force for change consists of technological innovation: 'The fundamental impulse that sets and keeps the capitalist engine in motion comes from the new consumers' goods, the new methods of production or transportation, the new markets, the new forms of industrial organization that capitalist enterprise creates' (p. 83).

3. The process of change is self-renewing and self-vitalizing. It is not limited to the satiation of a given demand, but geared to the insatiable pull of ever-newly created demands. A 'perennial gale of creative destruction' (pp. 84 and 87) continuously infuses new life into capitalism.

4. Monopolistic profits and practices, which might endanger the accumulation process in a static setting, play a quite different and largely constructive function in a dynamic setting. 'What we have got to accept is that [monopoly] has come to be the most powerful engine ... of the long-run expansion of total output not only in spite of, but to a considerable extent through, this strategy which looks so restrictive when viewed in the individual case ...' (p. 106).

5. No reasons exist to believe that the period of capitalist growth from 1870 to 1914 was exceptional (pp. 108–110). More important, no cogent arguments lead us to believe that the period ahead—that is, during the last half of the 20th century—offers new or significant obstacles to the accumulation process. The closing of the geographic frontier does not imply the closing of the economic frontier: 'The conquest of the air may well be more important than the conquest of India was...' (p. 117). Technological exhaustion is unlikely—the possibilities of technology remain an 'uncharted sea' (p. 118). The threat of a Ricardian or Malthusian problem of resources is, as we have seen, waved away.

What remains is 'plausible capitalism', to make the most of Schumpeter's suggestive phrase. It is a depiction of a system that has many of the attributes that Schumpeter ascribed to Adam Smith's vision of a 'hitchless' economic process (1954, pp. 572 and 640). '[T]here are no *purely economic* reasons why capitalism should not have another successful run' (*CSD*, p. 163, n7), Schumpeter concludes.

I shall return to examine the plausibility of 'plausible capitalism', but it remains to complete Schumpeter's argument.

6. Capitalism has an economic 'base' and a 'socio-psychological *superstructure*' (p. 121) which is characteristically 'rationalist' (pp. 122–125). This

rationality is encouraged and expressed by such elements of capitalism as its dependence on calculation, its empirical, science-oriented encouragement of production, its style of life (the lounge suit), its essentially unheroic, even anti-heroic mentality. (Schumpeter himself does not mention, but no doubt knew of and enjoyed Miriam Beard's comment somewhere in her *History of the Business Man* that the suits of armour that have come down to us undented were made for bourgeois gentilhommes.) Thus the pacificism of capitalist civilization.

7. Ultimately this rationalist bent becomes incompatible with the belief system that supports a capitalist civilization:

> [C]apitalism creates a critical frame of mind which, after having destroyed the moral authority of so many other institutions, in the end turns against its own; the bourgeois finds to his amazement that the rationalist attitude does not stop at the credentials of kings and popes but goes on to attack private property and the whole scheme of bourgeois values. [p. 143]

This is, of course, the *trahison des clercs*, the revenge of the intellectuals (p. 146).

8. Quite independent of the corrosion of belief is the erosion of the central capitalist function of entrepreneurship. As innovation becomes reduced to routine (p. 132), 'personality and will power must count for less ...' (p. 132). 'Economic progress tends to become depersonalized and automatized' (p. 133). And so we have the gradual metamorphosis of the capitalist-entrepreneur into the managerial-bureaucrat. '[T]he modern corporation, although the product of the capitalist process, socializes the bourgeois mind; it relentlessly narrows the scope of capitalist motivation; not only that, it will eventually kill its roots' (p. 156).

9. And so the capitalist process loses its élan (p. 219). The bourgeois family, the great transmission belt of entrepreneurial values, becomes infected with the prevailing disease of rationalism. The bourgeois class loses faith in itself (p. 161). With very little resistance, it yields to the new order—for capitalism, in its dissolution, is in fact creating a new order: socialism. The drama proceeds at an indeterminate pace, with the death sentence given a century-long 'short run' reprieve in the final sentence of the final paragraph of the chapter on decomposition (p. 163). But then we turn the page: 'Can socialism work? Of course it can' (p. 167).

Thus it is plausible capitalism and the triumph of rationalism and bureaucracy that must ultimately command our critical attention. However, I think we should begin by considering a prior matter. This is to bring to centre-stage Schumpeter's evident purpose in writing *Capitalism, Socialism and Democracy*. This purpose, manifest in the opening section of the book, was to settle accounts finally with Marx. Much of Schumpeter's work, I believe, was guided by the desire to provide an interpretation of history that would do justice to Marx but would provide a view of society's workings more compatible with Schumpeter's temperament and social interest.

Moreover, the difference between Marx's and Schumpeter's views can be precisely defined. For Marx the underlying force of historical change, at least in modern times, was the class struggle with its main source located in the growing power and insight of the working class. For Schumpeter, the driving force of history is also located in a contest of classes, but not the lower classes. Just as the transition from feudalism to capitalism involved merchant and aristocrat as principal actors, with serfs and journeymen playing only background roles, so for Schumpeter the evolution of capitalism into socialism will take place out of the competition of entrepreneurs and bureaucrats, with the proletariat relegated to a position of powerlessness.[2] In Schumpeter's decomposition of capitalism, the working class plays no role at all. In the creation or administration of socialism it is only a spectator.

Schumpeter's historical vision therefore disputes Marx, with regard not to the outcome but to the motivation of the capitalist epic. But more than that. In settling accounts with Marx, Schumpeter reverses Marx's presumed subordination of the 'superstructure' to the 'base'. The thrust of Schumpeter's argument is therefore a second confutation of Marx. It is not crises and contradictions within the base of 'plausible capitalism' that bring its civilization to a finish, but crises and contradictions in its socio-psychological superstructure.

Finally, Schumpeter completes his argument with a characteristic flourish. From Marx, Schumpeter gained a historical and evolutionary view that made it impossible for him to remain a 'vulgar' economist incapable of seeing the historicity of capitalism, and from Marx he also gained a dialectical perspective that caused him to search for the seeds of capitalist decline in its own triumphs—in its 'plausible' operations, not in its failures. Nonetheless, in the end Marx is vanquished. Capitalism will not survive and socialism will come, but for Schumpeter's reasons, not for Marx's. Marx was right, but Marxism was not.[3] There is room for a conservative view, a view

---

[2] I should add that the passive role of the serfs was the prevailing view of Schumpeter's day, but is increasingly challenged in ours. See Rodney Hilton (1978) *The Transition from Feudalism to Capitalism*.

[3] See Schumpeter's 'The march into socialism' (1950).

that will permit a managerial, bureaucratic socialism to emerge. A truce has been reached. Marx is accorded every honour, including that of becoming a conservative sage. For this, the footnote on p. 58 must be read with care:

> [T]here is nothing specifically socialist in the labor theory of value; this of course everyone would admit who is familiar with the historical development of the doctrine ... In order to be a socialist, it is of course not necessary to be a Marxist; but neither is it sufficient to be a Marxist in order to be a socialist. Socialist or revolutionary conclusions can be impressed on any scientific theory; no scientific theory necessarily implies them. And none will keep us in what Bernard Shaw somewhere describes as sociological rage, unless its author goes out of his way in order to work us up.

An appraisal of *Capitalism, Socialism and Democracy* must therefore start with Schumpeter's interpretation of Marx. Immediately the complexity of passing judgement on Schumpeter begins to assert itself. For Schumpeter was without rival among conventional economists in his understanding of Marx. The opening chapters of his book, on Marx as Prophet, Sociologist, Economist and Teacher reveal an appreciation for and knowledge of Marx's work that none of his colleagues could have begun to match; indeed that is still remarkable today. Nonetheless, Schumpeter's view of Marx is wrong, and in its errors it sets the stage for substantiation of the negative summary judgement with which I have opened this essay.

The critique can commence in an unimpeachable fashion by pointing out that Schumpeter did not know the full range of Marx's work. When *Capitalism, Socialism and Democracy* was written, the *Grundrisse* was yet unknown in the Western world, and the present renaissance of Marxist scholarship had not begun. Schumpeter could not have written, for example, that Marx had a 'distinctly weak performance in the field of money' (p. 22) had he read the chapter on money in *Grundrisse*, or had he followed—as he would have—the recent rediscovery and reconsideration of Marx's treatment of money in *Capital*.[4] So, too, Schumpeter's statements about the labour theory of value, in particular the extraordinary assertion that there was 'nothing specifically socialist' about it, reflects a view of the labour theory of value that is also *passé*, a view that overlooks Marx's pointed critique of the theory as only a basis for explaining relative prices, rather than as a mode of penetration into social relationships.[5] Not less important, Schumpeter's conception of historical materialism as a simple 'base-superstructure' relationship, although representative of the understanding of Marx prevalent in his time, would

---

[4] See, among other works, Suzanne de Brunhoff (1976) *Marx on Money*.

[5] *Capital*, volume I, chapter 1.

today also be regarded as inadequate to portray Marx's analysis of history.[6]

The point here is not to vindicate Marx but to locate Schumpeter. His rebuttal of Marx is based on a reading that would not be given serious consideration among Marxian scholars today. It is not Schumpeter's fault, of course, that he was not in advance of the contemporary comprehension of Marx, but his attack is not only misdirected as regards its immediate targets but also with respect to its larger conceptual framework.

The crux of the latter difficulty is contained in the footnote cited above. The essential element of Marx's analysis that Schumpeter could not swallow—and that, being rejected, denatured or distorted much of the Marxian analysis that Schumpeter did ingest—was the revolutionary purpose and character of Marx's work. The statement that it is not sufficient to be a Marxist to be a socialist is clinching in this regard. Marx's famous XIth Thesis on Feuerbach about changing rather than re-interpreting the world was profoundly antipathetic to Schumpeter's temperament. Therefore in a fundamental way Schumpeter missed the point of Marx, and of the 'scientific socialism' that Marx espoused. The unity of theory and praxis that rightly or wrongly lies at the very centre of Marx's approach was never acknowledged by, and would surely have been unacceptable to, Schumpeter. Thus the Marx that he vanquishes is not the real Marx. The difficulty with his criticisms is not merely that they are ill-informed in textual matters, but that they are uncomprehending in spirit. The limitations of the Marxian scholarship of Schumpeter's time excuse the first fault, but the second exposes the limitations of Schumpeter's imagination.

Let us now move to a consideration of Schumpeter's prognosis. As with the relationship to Marx, one must begin by underscoring the remarkable achievement that it represents. A quarter of a century has dramatically confirmed the acuity of Schumpeter's foresight. The longest period of sustained growth in capitalism has testified to the plausibility of his 'plausible' capitalism. Monopoly and vanishing investment outlets, the spectres against which Schumpeter directed his main blasts, have so far proved to be, just as he claimed, mere wraiths. Meanwhile, the sociological side of capitalist development has also confirmed Schumpeter's perceptiveness. Bureaucracy has proceeded apace, within and outside the corporation. The 'generation gap', unforeseen by Schumpeter, has strikingly given evidence of the decline in economic patriotism that he foresaw. Thus an appraisal must begin by

---

[6] See, inter alia, Gerald Cohen (1979) *Karl Marx's Theory of History: A Defence*, Perry Anderson (1974) *Passages from Antiquity to Feudalism* and (1974) *Lineages of the Absolutist State* and E.P. Thompson (1978) *The Poverty of Theory*.

recognizing Schumpeter's prescience. As I said at the outset, there has been no performance to equal his in modern times.

Why, then, do I judge his effort to be flawed, incomplete and finally inadequate? I can best make my point by indulging in a conjectural reconstruction of Schumpeter's argument. Let us begin as he did with the assumption of the necessity of a continuous process of accumulation, made possible by a constant revolutionizing of the products and processes of the economy through the institution of the large corporations. However, now let us take the analysis in a different direction. There is an increasing rigidity of prices and wages in the monopolistic sector. This leads to growing political pressure to ensure the liquidity needed to finance a big-business wage bill that has become a semi-fixed cost. Let us further suppose that this politico-economic necessity alters the direction of the arrow of causation from $MV \rightarrow PT$ to $PT \rightarrow MV$. Further, imagine that this altered financial setting affects the behaviour of the major trade unions, encouraging them to exert a strong push for higher wage levels. Imagine, in a word, that monopolization leads to structural changes that lead towards chronic inflation. Is this not also 'plausible' capitalism?

Let us try another conjecture. Suppose that Jewkes, Sawers, and Stillerman (1958) are right, and that technological advance still depends primarily on the work of private researchers and inventors, not on large corporate laboratories. Monopolization, with its increasingly technocratic, risk-averse bureaucracies, would then create an ever less favourable climate for the independent inventor to work in or sell to. The pace of revolutionizing of the bill of final output would slacken. The gale of perennial destruction would blow more softly. Productivity would decline while the bureaucratic superstructure rose. Inflation would receive another, independent boost. Is not this also a 'plausible' capitalism?

One last alternative scenario. This time I conjecture that the innovating, accumulating enterprise discovers that indeed economic frontiers are vast and know no geographic boundaries. The firm bursts its national integument. The process of accumulation proceeds on a worldwide basis, with the great corporation serving as a conduit for the transmission of technology and capital funds. Side by side with stick-plough fields rise modern factories, and a stone's throw from a mud village is a Hilton hotel. The introduction of the technology and industrial mode of production of capitalism upsets traditional hierarchies and patterns. The backward 'host' country moves uncertainly into the modern world, equipped with fighter planes and illiterate soldiers, slavish imitations of Western styles and bitter resentments of Western hegemony. The position of the capitalist centre, the source of the dynamism that is directing the gale of creative destruction into the hinterlands, is powerful, dynamic and civilizational, and at the same time vulnerable, fragile and disruptive. Is not this also a vision of a 'plausible' capitalism?

I raise these alternative readings of the future from the vantage of 1942 (*CSD*, second edition) for only one reason. They are all entirely consistent with and, with a little argumentative skill, deducible from the same organizational premises as those from which Schumpeter began. To put the matter differently, *there was more than one plausible course for capitalism to have run.* Moreover, the successful pursuit of its trajectory of economic growth was in no way inimical to—indeed, was necessary for—the pursuit of these alternative paths. Thus what is wrong about Schumpeter's scenario is essentially that it is too narrow. What Schumpeter has designated as the 'purely economic' future of capitalism is only a partial delineation of its economic propensities and tendencies, contradictions and inner conflicts. Schumpeter was entirely right in recognizing the enormous, still unflagging power of the expansive drive of capitalism, but he failed to consider all the *economic* effects—not to mention the social and political ones—that could follow from the successful expression of that drive.

Moreover, plausible capitalism posits a dichotomy between the economic and the sociological spheres that blurs the capacity for analysis. The artificial nature of the dichotomy becomes quickly evident when we reflect on the meaning of the 'growth' that is presumably the province of changes taking place in the base. Only a small portion of this growth can be described by a simple coefficient of expansion, such as more outputs of an unchanged kind, like wheat. Most growth consists of the alteration of both inputs and outputs, with associated changes in the lives, experiences, motivations, perceptions and behaviours of the actors in the system. Some of these altered real-life properties of the system bring results we designate as 'economic', such as inflation or the internationalization of capital. Other changes bring political or social or cultural changes—an altered work ethic, or bouts of radicalism or conservatism, or a deterioration of the moral foundations on which even the purest market systems depend.[7]

It was this larger unity of capitalist dynamism that Schumpeter failed to see, despite, or perhaps because of, his intuition that 'sociological decline' would accompany 'economic rise', and despite his own emphasis on the qualitative aspect of growth. Had he widened his view he might still have predicted another 40 years of growth, but he would have stressed that 'plausible capitalism' would not for that reason be rid of its structural changes, its historic repetition of 'crises', its ever-continuing struggle to coordinate the pace of production and the flow of distribution. Truly plausible capitalism is a system undergoing a continuous transformation of its economic substructure, quite as much as continuous transformations in its psycho-sociological

---

[7] See Fred Hirsch (1976) *Social Limits to Growth*, chapters 10 to 13.

superstructure. For all its protestations of dynamics, the problem with 'plausible capitalism' is that it is a static conception.

As with the economics, the sociology is not wrong but incomplete. As I have done above, I could therefore construct alternative scenarios that would begin from Schumpeter's starting points of an erosion of bourgeois self-confidence and a bureaucratic displacement of the entrepreneurial function. For example, I might argue that bourgeois rationalism is itself a form of ideology, perfectly capable of embracing an uncritical view of 'libertarianism' and quite immune, at its core, to an unmasking of the pretensions of capitalist fetishisms. Or I might claim that the drift into bureaucracy, far from sealing the death warrant for capitalism, is in fact the only possible reprieve to its natural death at the hands of the egalitarian politics and unmanageable technology of the 20th century.

I shall not, however, pursue this course. For my central dissatisfaction with the sociological argument of *Capitalism, Socialism and Democracy* lies elsewhere. Here I must begin by capturing again the vision of socialism as it emerges in its pages. Socialism will, of course, be planned, and it will be bureaucratic (p. 185). It will differ from capitalism in that its morale may be higher (p. 211), its self-understanding deeper (p. 211) and its efficiency greater (p. 188), but it will retain from capitalism most of the terminology—and beneath the terminology, the existential realities—of a capitalist system of market relations (p. 181). The world of work, particularly as regards 'the laborer and the clerk', will be essentially unaltered (p. 203). The sphere of democracy, especially as regards production, will be suitably restricted (pp. 299–300). Good use will doubtless be made of the 'supernormal quality' of the displaced bourgeoisie (p. 204, and p. 204 n3).

Of course, things may go awry. Socialism has no 'obvious solution' to the problem of providing stable traditions (p. 302). Its task of maintaining democracy may be 'extremely delicate'; indeed, '[s]ocialist democracy may turn out to be more of a sham than capitalist democracy ever was' (p. 302). Nevertheless, the Schumpeterian expectation is plain. In place of plausible capitalism, we can have plausible socialism.

Can such a socialism 'work'? 'Of course it can.' But what is meant by 'working'? The criterion is that of efficient central planning whose feasibility Schumpeter strongly affirms (pp. 188 and 196). I suspect that this affirmation reflects the extraordinary contemporary influence of the work of Taylor and Lange (p. 173, n2). Had Schumpeter lived to witness the tribulations of the centrally planned systems today, I doubt that he would have assented so easily to their superiority.

But the nub of my criticism does not lie here. *It rests, rather, in Schumpeter's failure to recognize that a statist economic order—provided that it tolerated democratic institutions—would suffer the same contradictions as those of capitalism, although perhaps under a slightly different guise.* The central contradiction of capitalism, as Schumpeter describes it, is the incompatibility of the rational mind-set generated by capitalist processes with the necessary observance of the ir-rational rights of property. What he fails to see is that Schumpeterian social-ism would generate very similar tensions. In the place of the inviolable claims of property exerted by the bourgeoisie, there are the inviolable claims of efficiency exerted by the bureaucracy. Are not their rationales alike, in maximizing social output? In place of the bourgeois ethos, undermined by the rationality of capitalism, there is the bureaucratic ethos, undermined by the 'clarity' of socialism. Thus the overriding contradictions are unchanged. Plausible socialism is not a new and different social order. It is simply capi-talism at a new level of development.

Schumpeter himself clearly felt that socialism was bourgeois. 'The ideol-ogy of classical socialism', he writes, 'is the offspring of bourgeois ideology. In particular, it fully shares the latter's rationalist and utilitarian background and many of the ideas and ideals that entered into the classical doctrine of democracy' (pp. 298–299).

As a description of the intellectual genealogy of socialism this is indisput-able, but as a description of the historical thrust of socialism it is seriously lacking. To assume that the values of efficiency and material pursuit, of hierarchy and restricted democracy, of rationalism and utilitarianism will continue unchallenged is to assume that the advent of socialism means no more than the passage of the reins of authority from one ruling group to another, within an essentially unchanged mode of production and thought.

Such a conception of social change was indeed a prevision of capitalist trends within our own age. But is it adequate to describe the historical trans-formation that Schumpeter sought to understand? I do not think so, unless one dismisses a struggle of deeper consequence than that between ruling groups—a struggle between elites and masses, privileged and unprivileged, rulers and ruled; in short the class struggle. Schumpeter, as we know, paid no heed to this struggle, but I believe that it can be discerned as the inchoate force, now evidenced in the economic sphere, now in the social, now in the political, that moves restlessly and unappeasably deep within capitalist civi-lization.

In ignoring this buried process, Schumpeter was able to ignore the changes that it portended for plausible socialism. Almost surely these changes would have dismayed a cultivated bourgeois sensibility such as he possessed. Indeed, in their breadth and depth, the changes implicit in a more convulsive view of the advent of socialism might rob any contemporary critic of the capacity to make cogent judgements, as a critic living in ancient Rome would have been unable to evaluate the changes brought by feudalism, had he foreseen them, or a critic living in medieval times would have been incapable of understanding the changes linked to the rise of capitalism, even had he imagined them.

Approving or disapproving, mute or articulate, it is this inability to imagine the historical process as revolutionary, despite his fondness for the word, that finally delineates Schumpeter's *Capitalism, Socialism and Democracy*. Among the economists of his day, Joseph Alois Schumpeter saw further and more clearly than perhaps any other, but his vision remains bounded, consciously or unconsciously, by the bourgeois preconceptions he cherished. Perhaps that is why he was able to acquiesce with such grace in the coming of socialism, the child of good bourgeois stock. As to what might lie beyond that, I suspect he cared little. Socialism as millennium would probably have been as distasteful to him as socialism as barbarism. He remains par excellence the worldly philosopher of mature capitalism, but he does not see that the most distant reach of his thought is not a terminus but a horizon.

REFERENCES

Anderson, P. (1974) *Lineages of the Absolutist State*.London: New Left Books.
Anderson, P. (1974) *Passages from Antiquity to Feudalism*. London: New Left Books.
Brunhoff, S. de (1976) *Marx on Money*. New York: Urizen Books.
Cohen, G. (1979) *Karl Marx's Theory of History: A Defence*. Princeton, NJ: Princeton University Press.
Hilton, R. (1978) *The Transition from Feudalism to Capitalism*. London: Verso.
Hirsch, F. (1976) *Social Limits to Growth*. 208 pp. London: Routledge and Kegan Paul.
Jewkes, J., Sawers, D. & Stillerman, R. (1958) *The Sources of Invention*. 372 pp. London: Macmillan.
Lange, O. & Taylor, F.M. (1938) *On the Economic Theory of Socialism*. Philadelphia, PA: Lippincott.
Schumpeter, J.A. (1950) The march into socialism. *American Economic Review*, May, 446–456. Reprinted in *CSD*, in third and subsequent editions, London: Allen & Unwin.
Schumpeter, J.A. (1954) *History of Economic Analysis* (Ed.) Schumpeter, E.B. 1260 pp. New York: Oxford University Press.
Thompson, E.P. (1978) *The Poverty of Theory*. New York: Monthly Review Press.

Chapter Six

The Vision

HENDRIK WILM LAMBERS

THE POINT OF DEPARTURE

The contributor to a volume of articles can be seen as a one-man firm who enters into a heterogeneous oligopoly in which some dominant firms are already present. In the terminology of industrial organization, he has to think of structure, conduct and performance.

The structure is in me,[1] a teacher of economics who began teaching in 1945 and still teaches, with sidesteps into many organizations, profit seeking and non-profit seeking.

One more piece of information: during his graduate studies the author was completely captivated by F. von Wieser's 'Theorie der gesellschaft-lichen Wirtschaft' (1924). Professionals will know now what to expect; I am short on techniques, long on opaque words—for example, 'Sinn der Wirt-schaft'. Schumpeter says of von Wieser: 'The great thing about him was a spacious vision that went deep below the surface . . . But he implemented this vision very imperfectly'. Earlier in the same book—the *History of Economic Analysis*, of course—he had called vision 'a preanalytic cognitive act that supplies the raw material for the analytic effort' (p. 41).

Conduct will have to be directed at enlightening myself about the enigma of vision before I dare say anything about the meaning Schumpeter has for me now. Performance, then, will be to find an answer to the question: what

---

[1] With apologies to Machlup (1958), and with thanks to Professor J. A. Hartog for his willingness to be a partner in discussion.

107

does (did) Schumpeter's *Capitalism, Socialism and Democracy* mean to me?

As I think upon the answer, it comes to mind that the memoirs on Schumpeter are already like a panoply of the economic profession. Pellucid articles by experts and friends such as Stolper, Machlup and Haberler on the fundamentals of his thought have shown his outstanding position as a creative scholar.[2] Others have called him 'the theoretical rogue elephant in economics' (Freeman and Jahodi, 1978) and a 'Herrenbürger' (von Beckerath, 1951). A minor prose writer entering into this field might clumsily trample the ground previously sown.

A strategy has to be decided upon. I shall be in the fringe area of economics, this Dutchman's proper habitat.

One term of the question can at least be clearly defined; *Capitalism, Socialism and Democracy*'s fifth English edition (1976) will be used as a text, with the first German (Swiss) edition (1946) as an annexe. This use of a double edition may smell of conspicuous consumption; I hope to show that it is functional to my reporting because the sequence in which I read the editions has influenced my opinions.

One last remark on texts used; Dutch students who try to be efficient read the Dutch translation, which has 'visie' as the equivalent of 'vision' in English and German. In Dutch, 'visie' was formerly associated with a certain loftiness; nowadays, as every teacher uses the word many times a day, it has deteriorated to mean 'point of view'. When Dutch students meet the word 'visie' some hesitate; Schumpeter is clearly a deep man, and must have taken the high road—'visie' with metaphysical leanings. Others simply read on; they take the low road—'visie' means only 'point of view'. Those waverings have been a secondary lead towards the theme of vision.

The core of this essay will be to show how a Dutch humanitarian has wrestled with Vision (he will be lucky to get off with only a smitten hip).

To come to grips with the task, there will first be some incidental background information on Schumpeter's Dutch connections; a short excursion into the parochial history of economic thought. Following this will be the reception and appraisal of the first edition, which in The Netherlands was received shortly after the ending of war, in the aftermath of liberation.

After 35 years a new appraisal is called for. As Schumpeter remained the same, a difference in appraisal can be explained only by a different reflex in me, which makes it unavoidable to locate my position in relation to the personality of Schumpeter as an author.

Innovation in transition will be the next theme. Some thoughts, or perhaps musings, on the civilization of capitalism will lead to the comparison

---

[2] See the chapters by Haberler, Machlup, and Stolper in Harris (Ed.) (1951) *Schumpeter, Social Scientist*, and also Stolper (1979), p. 64.

of the visions of von Wieser and Schumpeter, the question which started me off.

To conclude, a point of view will be taken on Schumpeter's vision as I see it, which also means that the point of departure has been retrieved.

THE DUTCH CONNECTIONS

During the 19th century, Netherlands academic economics was part of the Faculties of Law. Mrs Irene Hasenberg-Butter, an American economist, who has done research in this field, concluded (1969) that the economists of The Netherlands in that period leaned heavily on the British classical school, analytically and politically; they were strongly policy-oriented. After 1870 The Netherlands had an original analytical economist in N.G. Pierson, with most of the leading men turning towards the Austrian School.

In 1913 the first separate school of economics was founded; it was The Netherlands School of Commerce in Rotterdam. The name upheld the Dutch tradition, but the first and, for a long time, only professor in the chair of theoretical economics, F. de Vries, was an outspoken theoretician. In his inaugural address he made this quite clear, giving much attention to the works of Schumpeter.

In 1925 Schumpeter was invited to give three lectures on monetary problems. They were published in 1925, in the weekly *Economisch-Statistische Berichten*, which was mainly oriented to current affairs. An amusing incident followed. J.G. Koopmans, a young economist, later to become well known from his contribution 'Zum Problem des "neutralen" Geldes' in Hayek's *Beiträge zur Geldtheorie* (1933), sent a—long—letter to the editor. He highly appreciated Schumpeter's original contribution on Keynes but reckoned that it underestimated Keynes.

The editor, another young economist, S. Posthuma, a future architect of the European Payments Union, reacted in the way Thomas Mun, a few centuries before, had found typically Dutch: 'leven en laten leven', live and let live; he answered that it would not be good manners to burden Schumpeter, who had graciously given the manuscript of his lecture, with the obligation to reply. Koopmans demurred; having known him rather well, I can declare that he liked good manners very much but a lively discussion even more. Posthuma found a way out: the letter was more of an article and too analytical for *E-SB* readers. The solution was found; Koopmans' notes appeared as an article (1925) in the Netherlands professional monthly *De Economist* (Posthuma, 1926). A 'fair compromise' had been reached.

There was an indirect follow-up. Another Rotterdam economist, J.E. Vleeschhouwer, a scholar of Talmudian erudition, was considering a dissertation on fundamental issues of value and price theory. He consulted Schumpeter and was invited to Bonn for a longish stay. He, like so many others, testifies thankfully to Schumpeter's unlimited willingness to give time and thought: 'during five weeks Schumpeter almost daily gave at least three hours of his time to the discussion of my embryonic propositions' (1949, p. XXI). Schumpeter advised a composition in two parts, analytical and historical. In 1949 Vleeschhouwer obtained a PhD on a thesis in two volumes; the second volume (250 pp.) contained historical references only.

Other groups in The Netherlands were interested in Schumpeter. In 1927 the Catholic School of Economics was founded at Tilburg. The first professor of economics, H.A. Kaag, had a splendid idea. Upon meeting Schumpeter he had gained the impression that there would be a reasonable chance of his cooperation in the founding of an 'economic barometer' as a joint venture with Harvard, the London School of Economics and the Wirtschaftskurve at Frankfort. Nothing came of it (Bornewasser, 1978). The same has to be said of the long-lived legend of consultations in the early 1930s about a chair for Schumpeter at the Rotterdam school. F. de Vries by then had become the dominant economist of The Netherlands. The curriculum for graduate students, as he favoured it, contained roughly equal parts of theoretical economics, monetary economics, business economics and economic history. As compulsory reading, Schumpeter's *Epochen* was brought in as well as Marshall and Cassel. Sombart had to be read as well as J.M. Clark, with Schmalenbach thrown in for good (cost) measure. It has to be said that some of us took refuge in synopses. Schumpeter, with his convictions about the width of the field and his appreciation of cost procedures (Schneider, 1951), would have fitted in beautifully.

It may all have been wishful thinking, but the origin of the wish can be well understood. So far, so Dutch.

Schumpeter left for the United States. He was still held in high esteem, but when *Business Cycles* was published (1939) there was no clamour. Attention in the field of business cycles was fixed on the work of Haberler—compulsory reading again—and of course, in The Netherlands, especially on the work of Tinbergen. I have always compared the reception of *Business Cycles* to that of Marshall's *Industry and Trade*. Both books were not what the profession expected of theoretical toolmakers; they were too broad and too heavy to fit any special chair, so practically no one was ready to receive them fittingly.

Then came war and five years of isolation. Such unspeakable things happened during those years that a slight intellectual starvation is only a feather in the balance. Nevertheless, for those who were physically free, the yearning for the world of free thought was at times to be as painful as hunger. One example may suffice. One morning I found on my desk a copy of the

Beveridge book (1944); from simply nowhere. For weeks on end we discussed it as a possible base for the reconstruction of the postwar Netherlands. I will not go deeper into this; it is no more than an indication of the eager mood in which we were awaiting new constructive material.

THE FIRST GERMAN EDITION

In 1945 came the end of the war and the liberation of The Netherlands. In the aftermath of joy, I was lucky to receive immediately upon publication a copy of the Swiss edition, *Kapitalismus, Sozialismus und Demokratie*. I was so entranced as I read it that only after quite a while did I discover that I was reading German; at that moment there could have been no higher praise.

As a group of young men we were overjoyed to hear a voice from the free world again, as erudite and ironic as we had hoped for and at the same time bringing insight to a process central to our life. Our first amazement was at its wholeness; we were proud to belong to a profession in which such a book could appear. But there was a deeper layer than that of purely intellectual joy. Schumpeter had written about the subjects nearest to our hearts and duties; many of us, in different functions, had already been drawn into the reconstruction of The Netherlands. On reading with that in mind, many were amazed again. We were aglow and aghast at the same time. Aglow I have tried to explain; why aghast? Partly through the sadness lingering in the 'Schlussfolgerung' (the inference), but directly because the Swiss edition contained a short Nachwort, written by Schumpeter, in which he said: 'Namentlich ist wenig Grund zu glauben, dass dieser Sozialismus die Heraufkunft jener Zivilization bedeuten wird von der orthodoxe Sozialisten träumen. Es ist sehr viel wahrscheinlicher, dass sie faschistische Züge zeigen wird'.[3]

After 35 years, the mildest thing I can say is that to us it seemed an untimely moment for this piece of intellectual prognostic analysis. Those of us who were socialists had the feeling that it leaned towards the sadistic. The conclusion was that we had three Schumpeters: the inspirational, the overwhelming, and the maddening.

For me there was one part where the inspirational and the overwhelming went together, with the maddening absent. As a youth I had been present at many lively discussions of socialists of divers types. Judging from perhaps too small a sample I thought of Marxism as a creed. This, during my student

---

[3] 'In particular, there is little reason to believe that this socialism will mean the civilization of which orthodox socialists dream. It is much more likely to present fascist features' (p. 375).

days, spoilt Marxist economics for me. Schumpeter, with his sublime treatment of the subject, convinced me both of the importance of Marxism and of its inaccessibility to me. Since then I have read from Lenin to Blaug, so to speak, but I still always return to part I of *CSD* as a book in itself and as a classic in itself. There is no reappraisal in this respect: I had better be careful lest 'Schumpeter on Marx' become a creed to me.

THE SORTING OUT

We were very happy at the time, very busy, and very young. My friends and I took refuge with Horace's famous line: 'I am indignant whenever good Homer slumbers'. A man of genius certainly had a right to a dark and dreary day; perhaps we had read too much in a single remark.

The qualms remained, however. They returned in full force when I tried to sort out my reactions on reassessing *Capitalism, Socialism and Democracy*. It proved to be a painful process. In essence, of course, it was the inner fight between a young man's ideals and the experience of a man going into retirement; Schumpeter was only the catalyst. (Before this turns into a true confession I had better hurry on.)

An image of the personality of Schumpeter as an author was needed. Not as a straw man to grapple with; I will certainly not do a Mark Antony twice reversed—'I have come to praise Schumpeter, not to bury him'—and then turn about again. I need a person to reason with.

In a recent wise memoir on Schumpeter, Stolper (1979) remarks that it is dangerous to try to describe a complicated man in a short compass: 'The biographer is more likely to talk about himself than about his subject, however much revered' (p. 64). That is true. A warned man had better think twice; beware of projections again and again.

I think that from his early youth Schumpeter's qualities will have been indicated with words made with the Latin e(x) root: elegant, eloquent, excellent, all of which set a man apart, make him a member of an elite.

In his introduction to Ludwig von Mises's *Erinnerungen*, Hayek (1978) refers to Mises's 'brillianten Seminarkollegen Joseph Schumpeter'. Having been in many seminars, one can see him at work and play.

Not only highly intelligent or brilliant but also, and foremost, of an original mind, Schumpeter looked for originality in all aspects of life. As an old teacher I think that I recognize his outspoken wish for quantitative methods after having first been impressed by von Wieser. Most of all he looked for analytical originality. He found it far afield, in the United States of America and in Great Britain; in the latter country he also found a cultural identity. In many memoirs there are allusions to his predilection for the Edwardian period. The hero of Edwardian fiction was a man of outstanding qualities and a man of independent means. With his strong will to work and his originality Schumpeter took up the image and turned it into an independent man of means (*CSD*, p. 322). Independence, however, also means a certain aloofness, a distance from the others. It is the characteristic also of the Bloomsbury group. Since I have actually read some of their work and even some of the books of those who now feed on their fame, I venture that a second characteristic may be mentioned of these gifted people: self-centredness, meaning complete concentration on the self-chosen task, something akin to the Carlylean concept of duty, a task one is born to fulfil and which cannot be laid down.

To prevent any misunderstandings, by self-centredness I do not mean self-seeking or any related attribute, nor by duty the normal daily round as immortalized in the Dutch educational poem: 'I have a friend with iron hand . . . and duty is his name'.

Aloofness and a self-imposed task may be necessary to a highly gifted independent man; they are not sufficient, however, if he thinks himself fit for leadership. He has to choose a field. As I see it, Schumpeter has chosen the field where Ratio is the ultimate value, which also means he has chosen to stand out on his own.

Thinking that way, one can understand the many slight and heavy ironies Schumpeter directs at those reformers who project themselves only into the masses, 'the majority of people—all in fact for whom the typical socialist cares' (*CSD*, p. 190). Sometimes I thought, 'methinks the gentleman does protest too much'. Then I thought of his friendship with Taussig. Out of nowhere, after 45 years, a sentence returned to me: 'The great mass of men are of a humdrum sort'. It is taken from Taussig's *Principles*, which in the early 1930s were still part of required undergraduate reading.[4] I also remembered how it had hurt me to read this in the midst of the Depression in a dockworkers' quarter of Rotterdam. After 45 years I know that it had nothing to do with benevolence or malevolence, with caring or not caring for people. For their analysis Taussig and Schumpeter had simply chosen a point of departure on the potential of common men to react in the short run: 'no amount of retrospective common sense will alter the fact that in reality they neither raise nor decide issues' (*CSD*, p. 264). Schumpeter then says, 'the lover of democracy has every reason to accept this fact and to clear his creed from the aspersion that it rests upon make-believe'. I am not roseate and past the Enlightenment, but I cannot free myself from this make-believe. There may have been times and systems where the common man was no more than

---

[4] Taussig (1933), p. 11. The sentence continues: 'not born with any marked bent or any loftiness of character'.

a member of a murmuring chorus(line). In a parliamentary democracy of 1980 political leaders are those who give voice to the aspirations of large groups of the population. They stay only as long as they succeed in doing so. The common man co-decides and is co-responsible. He should be told so and not that he does not mean a thing politically. I know very well that, next to observation, there is emotion in this point of view. I am unhappy when a man of Schumpeter's stature speaks of collective psyche (*CSD*, p. 264). Leaning heavily upon Dutch tradition—which Schumpeter appreciated—I'll go on thinking in terms of individual persons.

In *Capitalism, Socialism and Democracy* Schumpeter accomplished the feat of moving five layers of thought—the firm, the markets, the institutions, the cultural values, the leaders of society—as one interwoven dynamic process. With incomparable skill he made history go through time as one stream. None the less, as Haberler noted, he himself called the book a parergon, a work of the left hand.[5] Psychologists have great interest in obiter dicta—passing remarks—as they often reveal the intermingling of the rational with other elements of the inner personality. Schumpeter called his work one long passing remark in comparison with all his other accomplishments. C. Jung, the Swiss psychologist, would probably have called it the second voice where vision speaks.

It is a pity that Schumpeter did not find reason to weave one more layer explicitly into his dynamic process.

Enough may have been said to ascertain, at least for myself, what it was that in youth made me angry and, with retirement approaching, leaves me still unresigned.

INNOVATION IN TRANSITION

How may one approach such concepts as innovation and creative destruction? In a way it would be like carrying water to the sea. Let us turn to the measured analytical reasoning of Heertje (1973) or, for empirical studies, to a sound review article such as that of Kamien and Schwartz (1975): 'Market structure and innovation'.

On both counts, analytical and empirical, the evidence is inconclusive; it does not fit any generalized hypothesis. However, the outcome, as Schumpeter saw it, is there, the continuing process of concentration, certainly in the Western European countries (Jacquemin and de Jong, 1976, 1977). We shall have to find answers to that. One is apt to fall in with Mason's remark: 'it is difficult to the point of impossibility to derive from Schumpeter's

---

[5] Haberler (1951), p. 39: 'The author regarded it as nothing more than a parergon'.

"process of creative destruction" an analytical framework, on which applicable and effective antitrust standards might be built' (1957, p. 101). That, however, was not at all Schumpeter's aim; thus, though from experience I agree with the remark, it cannot be accepted as an objection. In this field a recent remark by J.J. Klant (1978), a leading Dutch methodologist, has my complete agreement: 'where economics as a science should fail, there is always, especially in applied research, the extra possibility of economics as an art ... done by a researcher who dares to choose his way because he trusts to his common sense and practical instincts' (p. 411).

This is a long quotation; we shall put it to double use as an introduction to an example of a perfect case of innovation in transition.

In 1959 large sources of natural gas were discovered in The Netherlands, which made the country one of the 'haves' in the energy field. A clearer possibility of innovation out of the blue could not have been found. There are historical examples of this kind of bonanza happening to a country. The silver fleets of Spain come to mind, and how they were squandered in war and corruption. I always like the example of 18th-century Rome where the Counter Reformation brought a rich stream of tithes to the Holy See: they were used for a quietly consumptive life for many and also invested in an outcropping of baroque architecture and sculpture.

What happened to The Netherlands? The country was in full upswing after reconstruction. Technical capabilities and organization were present (Royal Dutch Shell). In a few years natural gas had gained an important share in industrial use and household consumption, with the government holding a considerable share in the income from domestic sales and export.

Here was a genuine gift from the sweetest of fairies; or was she? Analytically a number of decision trees could be built. What really happened from a mix of economic and political causes has been carefully analysed by Maria Brouwer (1978), in an article entitled 'Natural gas and our economy: blessing or curse?' On the one hand the export of natural gas, even at prices that are too low for equivalent substitution with other sources of energy, maintains the Dutch guilder at a level which impedes the export of other Dutch goods. And domestically, on the other hand, the flow of income to the state coincided with a massive expansion of the social security system. From 1974 to 1977 government income from natural gas rose from 2777 million guilders to 8684 million guilders; in that period, government transfers to social security soared from 1800 million guilders to 5900 million guilders.

Now the economy stagnates and unemployment rises: the budget deficit surpasses even the limits set by progressive economists. We are back to the routinely pessimistic views of the preceding century.

Social security has become a fortress, every stone of which is defended by some vested interest. Trade-union leaders discover that their members prefer material consolidation to solidarity. Business firms hesitate to invest because their margin of profit is small in view of the uncertainties they meet in the market and institutionally. The government has published a Blue Book on Innovation, which in essence says we need it to survive as a highly developed society.

The Netherlands have their share of well-trained economists; they even have those who are able to blend science and art. These have not been silent over the years, to use an understatement. Be it science or art, however, they have not been directors: at best they came under the subtitle 'also playing'; the performance has left the stage a shambles.

This story has also been told to show that Schumpeter's analysis in *Decomposition* and in the Preface to the third edition (reprinted in the fifth edition, *CSD*, p. 415) is now being vindicated in The Netherlands. His insights, gained from the analysis and knowledge of facts and formulated 30 years ago, seem to describe the momentary situation, just as his prediction, that under certain assumptions real income per head could well be doubled again over the period 1928–78, has come true for The Netherlands; in fact it was multiplied over that period by a factor of 2.5. He added: 'this would do away with anything that according to present standards could be called poverty' (*CSD*, pp. 65, 66). The restriction to be pondered is: according to present standards.

In fact, the increase in real income per head came in a spurt, doubling income between 1950 and 1970. The rapidity and continuity of the rise surpassed all published long-run expectations. A feeling arose that these professional people habitually underestimated possibilities. A new level of income just became a station on the route to the next stage. What once had been proudly labelled 'discretionary purchasing power' was tied to a level of expenditure which did not leave any discretion. Dr Admiraal (1976) has shown that a reversal of the relation income/expenditure took place. The level of expenditure, reached or aspired to, became the base for the demand for income.

There were at least two sustaining factors: first, a vulgarization of Schumpeter's thesis, which he had meant contrariwise, 'that innovation had become a routine'. Progress in technological potential was taken for granted; there was confidence in science. In an extensive inquiry into the status of professions, university professors came out first (it is over now). Second, the commercial world, wishing to have its share of that purchasing power, found ways to encourage spending by means of short- and long-term debts.

Parallel with, and partially made possible by, the income increase, went a widening of the concept of infrastructure, seen as the obligation imputed to the state to create acceptable working conditions of the social economic system (see Lambers, 1977). Many of us can still recall in our sleep that the classic system knew three of them: defence, law, and the monetary system. Today even one very much awake will miss out something on cataloguing the field of infrastructure: education, national health, social security, social welfare, the cultural sector, income policy, and subsidies to declining industries.

Due to high employment and social security measures for groups in restricted circumstances, the poverty line as a minimum standard of the 1930s was left behind. Poverty, however, is also a social phenomenon; in that sense the rise in income has sharpened differences. Government income had to be found to deal with it. Tax levels increased; it is one of the amusements of historical work to see how, through the decades, the unacceptable level of taxes and governments' share in national income is pushed upwards.

Taxes met a frozen level of expenditure; inflation was a way out; Schumpeter's 'March into Socialism' fits completely.

Why, however, has it to be the march into socialism? We have had it drummed into us, and we taught the computers, that it is an either/or situation; a third possibility is excluded. Why should an economist, trained in the substitution of factors, not try to combine elements of both systems by eclective method? Is it because the two terms have been used in antithesis for so long that one can only think that if the one is absent the other has to be present?[6]

Schumpeter, careful as ever in economic analysis, builds in a caution: under certain historical and cultural conditions socialism does not even have to come (CSD, p. 163). Seven years later, however, the march to socialism takes place in England; the small Western democracies are much akin; what about them?

At the moment we are in a phase of transition. A market economy and a budget economy of equal importance coexist within the same economic system, with two different sets of aims and motives. Popular attention has first been switched from technical innovation to social innovation; the next switch will be to political innovation. The number of people who, weighing realities, ask for reasonable solutions instead of pragmatic rigidity increases. Taught by Schumpeter, and life, I know that the taste of power is seductive and that the first reaction to a turning tide is often to stay put.

Schumpeter ironically says that the bourgeois and his professional entourage are weak in defence. I would say that they have been taught that action rests upon a subtle mind and solid knowledge; they have been taught away from force. Behind every measure of government policy are executive officials, who, however intelligent and valiant, cannot ward off inventiveness incited by self-interest. In a period of decline of old values, such as

---

[6] Cf. Koestler (1974), p. 21; 'wars are fought for words'.

respect for the law of the land, some of those who see a way and an advantage in circumventing it will do so to the distress of law-abiding others and possibly by jeopardizing law-abiders' very standards. This applies to the field of tax practices as well as to the field of social security.

These are moves and counter-moves in a stage of transition. The law of heterogony is the one law that always works.[7] If one has been taught, as in my case, by Chinese friends that in historical perspective a generation is the time-span for the short period, one could perhaps turn towards neoclassical economics.

Some friends, if they ever read this, might wonder that in old age one may turn that way. Well, I have never denied that, within wide margins, there are at work economic laws or tendencies which one can see as the reactions of the modal man to economic reality, but the tendencies are only lines drawn ex-post, obscured by short-run uncertainties. Governments, seeking the popular vote, search for the upper limit and get stuck when they hit the limit, because retreat is a difficult task in politics. Here we live, and at the moment uncomfortably, so we had better take measures within a time-span more fitted to Western minds than the Chinese precept.

In The Netherlands now much thought is directed at the joining of the micro- and macro-level of the economic system; in economics, some workers seek the instruments in information theory and some in institutional economics. The field is mostly indicated as meso-economics. Again, Schumpeter has a pointer: 'Democracy does not require that every function of the State be subject to its political method' (CSD, p. 292).

I shall not turn to this field; I prefer to speculate a little on the Vision needed if any good is to come out of this. Friedrich von Wieser at last will make his entrance.

CIVILIZATION OF CAPITALISM AND 'FREIHEITSMACHT'

As I stated in the beginning of this essay, I shall try to compare Schumpeter's vision with what he called the spacious vision of von Wieser. In doing this I have turned to CSD, Part II, Chapter XI, 'The civilization of capitalism'. First because, as he says, the superstructure has been added; so, without being spelled out, his social vision becomes clear. A minor reason is that I cannot think of von Wieser without coupling him with the image of civilization; and a very minor reason might be to follow Schumpeter since, having laid a solid foundation, he does not leave a stone unturned in his quest for the pervasive influence of rationalist attitudes.

---

[7] The law of heterogony as formulated by Wundt reads: the effect of certain psychic causes always exceeds the aims anticipated by the motives and out of this effect new motives arise.

The task he sets himself is to show the widening influence of rationalism, which found its root in the economic sphere. He first agrees to the existence of non-rational attitudes, quickly making them similar to the behaviour of neurotics, then takes up his argument for the rationalist attitude in life, founding it in economic necessity. Then he takes it forward into the super-structure; with deft strokes he comes to a new arrangement of the system: the aristocracy as a distant overlord and protector, and the bourgeoisie as the *classe passive*. It is an impressive performance.

In economic history I have been taught how to tackle a monument of learning: by chipping away at facts or statements or by nibbling at hypotheses. It is alluring to do so because spontaneous answers keep arising. It is not to be; patience and courage to approach all the sources fail me now that a once-strong memory pays the price of missing files.

One could try satire. At the height of vital capitalism in Great Britain—the epitome of rational society—there were an aristocracy which was, or which thought itself to be, above sordid commerce and financial calculations; a group of entrepreneurs and bourgeois followers who, due to the un-certainties of the gale of competition, could not follow 'the lore of nicely-calculated less or more'—they just got rich; and the modal man, who was the only one who had to calculate very accurately to make ends meet. It is not fair to Schumpeter[8] but it is a satisfying picture of the British distri-bution of personal income at the end of the 19th century.

To make a somewhat more serious remark on a subject I at least know something of: Schumpeter comments on the group of regents of the Repub-lic of The Netherlands in the 17th and 18th centuries 'that in practically every emergency it had to hand over the reins to a warlord of feudal com-plexion... Which amounts to saying that it needs a master' (*CSD*, p. 138).

The Amsterdam burgomasters would first have replied that, formally speaking, they were the group literally born to lead. Through the system of letters of contract among leading families they had, illegally, tied the seats of authority, even on behalf of children yet to be born. Then there would be a haughty silence; because they did not hand over to a feudal warlord as an active decision. When it happened they were pressed into this by the mass, sometimes by its vanguard, the mob. The rabble, as they called it, sensed when the situation was so desperate that a symbol was needed for the common aim; a master suppressing—not protecting—the regents' eternal conflicts of commercial self-interest. (Shades of William III, of Holland and Great Britain, a calculating diplomatist if ever there was one; the real warlord was the Admiral de Ruyter, who had risen from the ranks, coming

---

[8] *CSD*, p. 201: 'I submit to socialist friends that there is a better way of encountering them [home truths] than sneering'.

from before the mast as the old saying has it.)

And the thought that an etching of Rembrandt in the final outcome is just another product of capitalism is just as satisfactory an explanation as to say . . .

I had better stop and meditate for a long time. 'I've come to praise Schumpeter, not to bury him.' Well, I am fully serious when I say that these chapters are wonderful, but that this is so too because at the same time they are great fun. They make one think of the conversations of highly intelligent men like Tolkien and C.S. Lewis at their meetings of Inklings (Carpenter, 1978). There was deep feeling and high thinking and quick repartee; yet not every word could stand up in the cold light of morning.

To resume the main argument: having shown how rationalist behaviour, springing from capitalism's centre—the economic system—permeates all manifestations of culture, Schumpeter typifies the whole as Individualist Democracy (*CSD*, p. 126). He then concludes to what has to be quoted in full: 'Things economic and social move by their own momentum and the ensuing situations compel individuals and groups to behave in certain ways whatever they may wish to do' (p. 129). He then adds: 'by shaping the choosing mentalities and by narrowing the list of possibilities from which to choose' (p. 130).

There is no place left for Voluntarism. Or does he, ever cautious as an analyst, leave a little opening in 'the list of possibilities from which to choose'?

At this point I will introduce two notions out of von Wieser's profound vision. First 'anonyme Führung', nameless leadership, exercised by various leaders through the example of inventiveness. Von Wieser places their influence in small groups, working on a base of continuity or at best slow change. In counter-position he places the personal leader who has power over large groups and is indispensable to the working of society: 'The great progress to new turning points requires great leaders, who come to the fore personally'—it might be Schumpeter—but then the passage continues: 'though they only fulfill what has been historically prepared for a long time') 1924, p. 114).

Not for nothing has he been called the man of the method of historical genesis. Not for him innovation like a bolt from the blue.

Anonymous leadership forms part of the second, broader, concept, 'Freiheitsmacht'; the literal translation, 'freedom power', conveys little. Von Wieser describes it as follows: 'these powers are experienced as aids by the individual, which alleviate for him the identifying and development of his being; one feels them as an enlargement of one's own force' (p. 113). To paraphrase: Freiheitsmacht is a freely acknowledged power which has a liberating influence on the individual. Although difficult to formulate, the notion has a recognizable meaning to me. Perhaps it is best to bring the notions together in an example from real life.

Since student days, 'anonyme Führung' and 'Freiheitsmacht' have intrigued me; I have always been on the look-out for them. During the winter of 1953 large parts of Western Holland were inundated. A group of authorities stood talking together at one of the threatened dykes, seeking ways to find sand to fill sandbags. A roadworker standing with them quietly remarked: 'there is plenty of sand here: three months ago we put a foot of sand under the bicycle path over a distance of four kilometres'. The anonymous leadership is clear but also his wish to help authority, because he was part of them, having the same aim. He could just as well have let them drive away and then with his colleagues filled the bags to shame authority.

These two notions are then embedded in von Wieser's vision of the individual person, which he thinks is strongly influenced by social environment, and 'consciousness has countless points of entrance, which makes it accessible for social influences, which conduct it, deep down, in socially determined ways' (p. 117).

This is written in desperate briefness. Then why write it at all? Because I would think it dishonest towards Schumpeter not to give some of von Wieser's—sometimes misty and practically untranslatable—passages on the social individual; and because in 1938 (and in German, where leader is Führer with a capital F) reading it gave me great difficulties. I am completely convinced that for von Wieser there was a clear-cut boundary between individual moral responsibility and the wish to belong. In less noble hands, however, it may become a wafer-thin line. I greatly prefer Schumpeter's at times harsh individual independence to the possible consequences of this kind of social belonging. If ever I think of mythical values it is in the direction of the wisdom of a fully developed individual, not in the direction of mental collectivism.

Man is an individual person and social creature simultaneously. Taking this as a starting point, we will have to see how von Wieser applies it to the field of economics. He agrees to methodological individualism as a basis of pure theoretical economics but continues 'one has to leave this, following the method of decreasing abstraction, for the (solidaristic) group approach which is common in life, if one wishes to understand the concrete phenomenon of life' (p. 116). Here we are on the edge of economic sociology but, as I see it, within the field which Schumpeter at the beginning of his chapter on the civilization of capitalism has staked out for rational thought, by trying to make the best of it by the rules which we call logic, and by doing so on assumptions which satisfy two conditions: that their number be a minimum and that everyone of them be amenable to expression in terms of potential experience (CSD, p. 122).

From introspection and experience I am satisfied that the concepts of anonymous leadership and liberating power may be expressed as potential experience. I am further convinced that in trying to make the best of the dynamic process of social–economic institutions, we might come to fruitful assumptions if we added these concepts to our analytical apparatus.

To give some examples: using the existence of anonymous leadership as an assumption in analysing the decision-making of top management in large business firms, or the overall success/failure of innovation in small business, has given me a clearer insight. The same goes for the mechanisms of Workers' Councils and University Councils. These modest applications alone would not justify much attention to these concepts in this text. I am out for a wider hunting ground: the potential they may have in lessening the impact of the opportunity cost of change.

CHANGE AND THE LAW OF HETEROGONY

If I take as a starting point Schumpeter's dictum that capitalism is a form or method of economic change (*CSD*, p. 82), the postwar years were certainly capitalistic. It has been a period of swift and comprehensive change; I do not need to catalogue it. The rapid succession of changes made continuous adjustment necessary. Comprehensiveness results in the intermingling of changes from different spheres of life. It follows that adjustment in the patterns of living, patterns of thought, and patterns of ethics will proceed in ruptured sequences. The consequence might be seen as the reversal of Gossen's first law of satisfaction: with every repeated dose of change, the ability to adjust decreases until total indifference has been reached. If that tendency has been correctly diagnosed, it may become a rationalist economic question of how the opportunity cost of an innovation, a species of change, compares with its expected revenues. And after a period of comprehensive change, the majority answer might be that it is too high.

Even if, like Schumpeter, one saw innovation as the motor that drives the increase in real income, one might ask: what price innovation? The whole of Book II of *CSD* contains the answer to that question for the system as a whole. The implied price of continuous innovation in a capitalist environment is the system's unavoidable end, not with a bang but with a whimper.

Having again passed in review his arguments as to the situation under transition, he concludes: 'considering this state of things, we need not project the tendencies inherent in it very far ahead in order to visualise situations in which *socialism might be the only means of restoring social discipline*' (*CSD*, p. 215) (Schumpeter italicizes this sentence). If one thinks of the cultural indeterminateness of socialism (*CSD*, p. 170), many questions remain to be answered on the welfare consequences of this statement. Schumpeter goes into them systematically, giving great stress to the cultural traditions and the phase of development of an economy in deciding the shape of the system to come. As a certain kind of Dutchman I react to Schumpeter's answers in a way that, though hopefully rational, will be bounded by strong cultural and historical convictions on individual freedom. Leaving exogenous forces aside, I do not expect a clear-cut choice between the two systems. Historically The Netherlands have tended to look for countervailing power against processes they did not like rather than to produce dogmatic answers. It may be a deep sense of smallness in international affairs, or it may be economic necessity not to diverge too much from dominant trade partners; whatever the causes, the observation, I think, can be defended. In reality there will be a period of further tension while the sorting out of conflicting institutions continues.[9]

Majority opinion in The Netherlands since 1945 has shifted towards more direct intervention of government in the economic process. Numerous people believe that government-initiated institutions in the economic process hold out a more certain promise of the satisfactions they want: a steady income and job security, the feeling that one need not be ashamed of the conditions others have to live in, and an equitable distribution of income. Having gone a certain distance in that direction, we have come to a standstill. If government measures in one direction (e.g., social security) threaten their wishes in another direction (e.g., steady income levels), they react. Their reaction is clear and simple: do not take it away from me. To socialists of the early 20th century such a reaction would have been impossible, perhaps morally, but certainly materially; they had not much to be taken away. We are removed one phase from classic capitalism. Many more people now have an income and acquired rights to defend. They give the classic answer: that they wish to be left free in their negotiations. Schumpeter gave a brilliant exposition of why one economic system came to an end. In the end, after the unmeasurable period of transition, something permanent should be left. So, on his horizon, there rose not a Marxian dawn but Protean Socialism (CSD, p. 171). I wonder whether the law of heterogony, which is virtually part of my creed and which he loves to refer to, has not by now got the better of him. Being a micro-observer, I sometimes fear that the deepest problem awaiting The Netherlands will be the tension between those active in economic life—be it in private business or government-sponsored organizations—and those outside it; between economically active and formally inactive persons (who may be very active on the sidelines,

---

[9] Institutions as formulated by Commons (1934): 'collective action in control of individual action'.

which is one of the causes for tension).

After a long detour I at last come to the point I wish to make. When Schumpeter compares the efficiency of economic systems, he chooses as a yardstick the expected stream of consumer goods in equal units of time. Then he himself concludes that his definition does not identify economic efficiency with economic welfare. After some explanation he says: 'I do not think that we lose much by adopting a criterion that neglects those [welfare] aspects'. Then, with complete openness: 'This, however, is a very debatable matter' (CSD, p. 190).

I think so too. Now that I come to the point of welfare, however, I have discovered that it merits a book, a book that I cannot write. If I had a rational mind I would turn tail and fly. Instead I will take flight forwards.

An observer who had used the Schumpeterian measure to judge the performance of The Netherlands economic system from 1954 to 1974 would surely have awarded it an honourable mention among comparable systems. A different situation exists in the second half of this decade. The Scientific Council on Government Policy states in a recent report (1980) that the aims of industrialization policy in the early 1950s—prevention of unemployment and safeguarding of the balance of payment—at this moment are prominent again. 'It is a paradox', the Council says, 'that as late as 1976 a Blue Book on the structure of the economy should have been published that pleaded "selective growth", i.e. growth strongly bounded by welfare restrictions' (p. 8).

The solution of that seeming contradiction lies in the emergence of noneconomic aims and the securing of certain welfare elements as part of an acceptable economic system. Having given earlier in this essay some indication of the forces behind this phenomenon, I will now keep to the main points.

During the 1950s and 1960s, economic policy and social policy were not only administered by separate government departments but they were also compartmentalized in the minds of very many people. On one level there was the desirability of growth, and on a different level there were our obligations to the aged, the invalids and the unemployed. The separation was due to two factual developments: long periods of overfull employment and the revenues of natural gas made it easy to overlook interdependence.

Now we are in the position of having to state our priorities, assuming at best a zero level of growth. People have become aware of the rudiments of economics—opportunity cost—again. They see the price of welfare policies but have also become thoroughly aware of the price to be paid for innovation, privately in job security and lifetime income, socially in external effects.

The difference from the 1950s is that we have lost our innocence. We know now that the means for innovation and the means for welfare obligations both have to come from the same national product; we also know that in government policies the two are competitors for the consumers' guilder. Innovation, economic and social, the two of them combined, is necessary to maintain our style of life, socially and economically. There will have to be a trade-off between the short-run cost of economic growth and the social cost, the short-run price in welfare. It can be achieved only by co-alition and compromise. I do not condemn it.[10]

To that end we shall need above all von Wieser's spacious vision. We shall need the inventiveness of the thousands of nameless leaders, in business, in the social world and in the cultural world. We shall have to adjust or reno-vate some of our institutions so that they will get the remuneration and rec-ognition they deserve by their example and activities, whether they are gainfully employed or engaged in socially valuable work. As these people work for continuity, their recognition will also have to be expressed in clear information and participation in the aims of the organization to which their contribution is given. People ask for clear decisive personal leadership: a programme has to be developed which reasonably combines economic ef-ficiency with respect for the dignity of man. But above all we need to imple-ment von Wieser's 'Freiheitsmacht'. There will not be unity of aims, but there has to be unity of purpose, to get us on the move again. That can only come true if we find the liberating power, which for the individual joins private and common ends.

Once a Dutch socialist poetess wrote the still famous line: 'the mild forces will overcome in the end'.

I do not know what the end will be; I am as shy of prediction as Schum-peter. I do not even know precisely any more what the mild forces are. But I feel there is truth in her poetry: in a democracy, group interests must be willing at times to give way to the larger long-run interest; otherwise a mixed economy might not be able to stave off the outcome that Schumpeter so gravely holds up to us at the end of *Capitalism, Socialism and Democracy*: 'As a matter of practical necessity, socialist democracy may eventually turn out to be more of a sham than capitalist democracy ever was' (p. 302).

VISION AND vision

Schumpeter has given to *Capitalism, Socialism and Democracy* the full force of his personality, trying to keep it within the bounds of rational analysis.

---

[10] See also Jöhr (1958), p. 52: 'Auf Grund des antinomischen Verhältnisses, das zwischen verschiedenen Werten besteht, erweist sich der Kompromisz häufig als die—auch vom eth-ischen Gesichtspunkte—beste Lösung'.

Within these bounds a vision can be clearly discerned: innovation is the moving force in material progress. Still, kept within bounds, the vision expands: pervasive rationalist attitudes condition (favourably) institutions for the development of innovations. A third pre-analytic cognitive act has been present from the beginning: historic movements tend to have an end; how will the end come in this case?

An exceptional array of gifts allowed him to create out of this pre-analytic material a synthetic image of history, which, for once, may rightly be called unique. I have heard no other opinion from anyone who thought it part of his profession to read the book. More important perhaps, after 40 years he still inspires young people. While talking things over after many an oral graduate examination, I have often heard remarks like: 'to be honest, the one stimulating book was Schumpeter'. The commonest young judgement is 'mooi werk', a compound of beautiful work, beautifully done, an aesthetic valuation with a connotation of work perfectly completed. That is the opinion of radical and conservative students alike. Yet both groups say, each in their own way, 'he keeps me puzzled: is it my fault or did he intend to?'

Looking for more mature—not ex definitione more valuable—judgements I took a test. I went through ten or so articles and monographs—not handbooks—in the field of micro-economics and industrial organization just as they came to hand, looking for their notions on Schumpeter. He is mentioned often but in many cases his work has been reduced to one-sentence capsules: 'the Schumpeter innovation', 'Schumpeterian creative destruction', and so on.

In a way this may be the hallmark of fame: 'Schumpeter's innovation', like Solomon's wisdom and Job's patience. Is it enough?[11]

The *History of Economic Analysis* will ensure that Schumpeter remains a legendary name in economics for as long as it will be a subject of scholarship. Will *Capitalism, Socialism and Democracy* be put next to it? I wonder; not because he himself thought of it as a parergon. On the contrary, I think its survival will rest on its being a hologram, created by the light of Schumpeter's personality instead of his scholarship alone. As I see history, themes—not solutions—will recur again and again, not the least among them those of rise and fall. Once, in writing a memorial article, I had to read through a century, 1852 to 1952, of the Netherlands professional monthly, *De Economist*. National feeling should make me say that it was a glorious experience. Let me say instead that I have practically forgotten many an article but have kept one vivid impression. With nearly monotonous regularity, the doom of the economy was pronounced; either we were stagnating in

---

[11] Dr Admiraal of the Erasmus University Rotterdam, after having himself written an article on Schumpeter, said to me: 'he has been reduced to the footnotes'.

dormant pools or we had now certainly reached the state of maturity. As long as people are free to think so long will they, looking for explanations, turn to Schumpeter, even if for a while it were quiet around him.

Will they also find a Vision, a star to lead their way? Schumpeter, I think, would have denied that this was possible. One could only give light, not a leading light. Still I think he did. Many have remarked upon his images and his preference for military ones. His mythical images are still more impressive, I think, and, at least to me, of the highest interest. I wish to connect two small sentences of genius which I think only Schumpeter fully understood as he wrote them down: 'For mankind is not free to choose' (*CSD*, p. 129) and 'The Stock Exchange is a poor substitute for the Holy Grail' (*CSD*, p. 137). He stresses that his bourgeois capitalist or his entrepreneur is a non-hero, an anti-hero even. That is true if one defines hero in the romantic sense as one who sacrifices himself to the Absolute. To an economist that is unthinkable. It is, however, a definition which is bound to a special period in history. There is another hero image that has come to us through ages of cultural history.

Schumpeter loved the Greek tragedies, especially Euripides.[12] So he must have been fully aware that there the hero is the actor who sets in motion the chain of reactions which will fulfil his moira, his pre-ordained fate, 'for mankind is not free to choose'.

He goes a step beyond the Greeks with: 'The Stock Exchange is a poor substitute for the Holy Grail'. One might cavil a little at this, though it would be like a squire sitting in judgement upon Merlin. The Holy Grail can never be an object of exchange, nor can it ever change, its quest being the timeless symbol for the completing of personality.

This does not matter much, however. What matters is that Schumpeter here introduces one of the deepest symbols of myth. I refuse to think that it was done to *épater le bourgeois*, as witness the line preceding the image: 'There is surely no trace of any mystic glamour about him [the industrialist and merchant] which counts in the ruling of man' (*CSD*, p. 137).

Even if these are remarks in passing, they could not be more telling. Myth, metaphysics, stood before his eyes. Greek tragedy is intended to bring Katharsis, a feeling of purification. Myth will bring insight into truth, needed to continue amidst the slings and arrows of outrageous fortune: it points a way; it gives a base for hope.

Marx knew this; his message pointed to a coming dawn. Schumpeter will have known all this. He refused. He wished to enlighten, not to lead towards stars he did not see. He stayed with the Greeks: moira itself—above the

---

[12] Stolper (1974), p. 65. My thanks are due to Drs M.H.J. Dullaart of the Erasmus University Rotterdam for alert help in tracing sources.

Gods—decides the outcome, and rational man can only decipher what has led up to it.

Schumpeter wrote a book of scholarship; at the same time he wrote a myth, the saga of ascendency and decline as one organic process. But he would not have the young hero come winning through in the end, having struck down the ancient monsters on the road, to begin a new life (and, without knowing it, a new cycle). Schumpeter deeply felt the human potential for failure; he may have seen life that way. That is the sadness that pervades Part IV of *CSD*.

We have come to the parting of ways: 'Je tire ma révérence et quitte par hasard', venturing into a future, needing a Vision, a grain of hope.

Making my bow to the unfathomable master, this almost mysterious mind (Tinbergen, 1951), I shall borrow the words Odysseus spoke to a King's child: 'sebas m'echei eisoraonta', a timid respect takes hold of me as I look at you.

REFERENCES

Admiraal, P.H. (1976) *Besluitvorming in het Konsumptieproces*. Leiden: H.E. Stenfert Kroese B.V.

Beveridge, Sir William (1944) *Full Employment in a Free Society*. London: Allen and Unwin.

Bornewasser, H. (1978) *Katholieke Hogeschool Tilburg*. Deel I, *1927–1954*, p. 45. Baarn: Ambo B.V.

Brouwer, M. (1978) Het aardgas en onze economie, zegen of vlook? In *Samenleving en Onderzoek* (Ed.) Klant, J.J., Driehuis, W., Bierens, J.J. & Butter, A.J. p. 293. Leiden: H.E. Stenfert Kroese B.V.

Carpenter, H. (1978) *The Inklings*. London: George Allen and Unwin.

Commons, J.R. (1934) *Institutional Economics*. 2 Volumes. Madison, WI: University of Wisconsin Press.

Freeman, C. & Jahodi, M. (Ed.) (1978) *World Futures, the Great Debate*. p. 207. London: Martin Robertson and Co.

Haberler, G. (1951) Joseph Alois Schumpeter 1883–1950. In *Schumpeter, Social Scientist* (Ed.) Harris, S.E. p. 24. Cambridge, MA: Harvard University Press.

Hasenberg-Butter, I. (1969) *Academic Economics in Holland 1800–1870*. The Hague: Nijhoff.

Heertje, A. (1973) *Economie en Technische Ontwikkeling*. Leiden: H.E. Stenfert Kroese B.V. English edition (1977) *Economics and Technical Change*, London: Weidenfeld and Nicholson.

Heertje, A. (1979) Economie, technische ontwikkeling en economie. In *Preadvies voor de Vereniging voor de Staathuishoudkunde*. Leiden: H.E. Stenfert Kroese B.V.

Jacquemin, A.P. & de Jong, H.W. (Ed.) (1976) *Markets, Corporate Behaviour and the State*. Nyenrode Studies in Economics, Volume I. The Hague: Martinus Nijhoff.

Jacquemin, A.P. & de Jong, H.W. (Ed.) (1977) *Welfare Aspects of Industrial Markets*. Nyenrode Studies in Economics, Volume II. Leiden: Martinus Nijhoff, Social Sciences Division.

Jöhr, W.A. (1958) *Der Kompromisz als Problem der Gesellschafts-, Wirtschafts- und Staatsethik*. p. 52. Tübingen: J.C.B. Mohr.

Kamien, M.I. & Schwartz, L. (1975) Market structure and innovation, a survey. *Journal of Economic Literature*, **XIII**, 1.

Klant, J.J. (1978) De methodologie van Keynes. In *Samenleving en Onderzoek* (Ed.) Klant, J.J.,

Driehuis, W., Bierens, H.J. & Butter, A.J. p. 411. Leiden: H.E. Stenfert Kroese B.V.

Koestler, A. (1974) *The Heel of Achilles, Essays 1968–1973.* p. 21. London: Hutchinson.

Koopmans, J.G. (1925) De zin der bankpolitiek (Schumpeter contra Keynes). *De Economist,* pp. 798–918.

Koopmans, J.G. (1933) Zum Problem des 'neutralen' Geldes. In *Beiträge zur Geldtheorie* (Ed.) Hayek, F.A. p. 211. Vienna: Verlag von Julius Springer.

Lambers, H.W. (1977) Een historische schets. In *Haagse Vingers, de Veranderende Relatie Overheid-Onderneming.* Scheveningen: SMO Boek Extra.

Machlup, F. (1951) Schumpeter's economic methodology. In *Schumpeter, Social Scientist* (Ed.) Harris, S.E. p. 95. Cambridge, MA: Harvard University Press.

Machlup, F. (1958) Structure and structural change: weaselwords and jargon. *Zeitschrift für Nationalökonomie,* **18,** 280–298.

Mason, E.S. (1957) *Economic Concentration and the Monopoly Problem.* p. 101. Cambridge, MA: Harvard University Press.

Posthuma, S. (1926) De zin der bankpolitiek. *De Economist,* pp. 798–818, 423–458.

Schneider, E. (1951) Schumpeter's early German work 1906–1917. In *Schumpeter, Social Scientist* (Ed.) Harris, S.E. p. 55. Cambridge, MA: Harvard University Press.

Schumpeter, J.A. (1925) Oude en nieuwe bankpolitiek. *Economisch–Statistische Berichten,* pp. 552–554, 574–577, 600–601.

Schumpeter, J.A. (1939) *Business Cycles: A Theoretical, Historical and Statistical Analysis of the Capitalist Process* (2 Volumes). New York: McGraw-Hill.

Schumpeter, J.A. (1946) *Kapitalismus, Sozialismus und Demokratie.* Bern: Einleitung von Edgar Salin, Verlag A. Francke A.G.

Schumpeter, J.A. (1954) *History of Economic Analysis.* New York: Oxford University Press.

Schumpeter, J.A. (1976) *Capitalism, Socialism and Democracy.* 5th Edition. London: George Allen and Unwin.

Scientific Council on Government Policy (Wetenschappelijke Raad voor het Regeringsbeleid) (1980) *Plaats en Toekomst van de Nederlandse Industrie.* p. 8. 's-Gravenhage: Staatsuitgeverij.

Stolper, W.F. (1951) Reflections on Schumpeter's writings. In *Schumpeter, Social Scientist* (Ed.) Harris, S.E. p. 102. Cambridge, MA: Harvard University Press.

Stolper, W.F. (1979) Joseph Alois Schumpeter—a personal memoir. *Challenge,* January/ February, p. 64.

Taussig, F.W. (1933) *Principles of Economics.* Volume I, 5th Edition (revised), p. 11. New York: The Macmillan Company.

Tinbergen, J. (1951) Schumpeter and quantitative research in economics. In *Schumpeter, Social Scientist* (Ed.) Harris, S.E. p. 53. Cambridge, MA: Harvard University Press.

Vleeschhouwer, J.E. (1949) *Economische Rekenvormen.* Deel I, *Waarde en prijs-theorieën als leer van menschelijke motieven*; Deel II, *Geschiedenis van de leerstellingen.* 's-Gravenhage: Martinus Nijhoff.

von Beckerath, H. (1951) Joseph A. Schumpeter as a sociologist. In *Schumpeter, Social Scientist* (Ed.) Harris, S.E. p. 110. Cambridge, MA: Harvard University Press.

von Mises, L. (1978) *Erinnerungen, mit einem Vorwort von Margrit von Mises und einer Einleitung von Friedrich August von Hayek.* p. XIV. Stuttgart: Fischer.

von Wieser, F. (1924) Theorie der gesellschaftlichen Wirtschaft. *Grundrisz der Sozialökonomie.* Abteilung I, II, Teil, 2nd Edition. Tübingen: J.C.B. Mohr (Paul Siebeck).

Wundt, W. as cited (1950) *Handboek van het Moderne Denken.* 3rd Edition, p. 308. Arnhem: Van Loghum Slaterus N.V.

Chapter Seven

Schumpeter's Predictions

ARTHUR SMITHIES

Schumpeter entitled his last (brief) paper 'The march into socialism'. It was written at the end of 1949, just before he died. As he had done in *Capitalism, Socialism and Democracy*, he still defined socialism as 'that organization of society in which the means of production are controlled, and the decisions on how or what to produce and who is to get what are made by public authority.'

He states that he doesn't predict or 'prophesy' socialism. His task is 'to diagnose observable tendencies and to state what the results would be if those tendencies should work themselves out according to their logic.' But he recognizes that events, external to those inherent in the capitalist process, can accelerate or retard the advent of socialism. However, the argument in all of his writings attaches overwhelming importance to accelerating factors, particularly great wars. He holds out little prospect that the march to socialism can be arrested or diverted into other channels.

Schumpeter's central thesis in *Capitalism, Socialism and Democracy* is that 'the actual and prospective performance of the capitalist system is such as to negative the idea of its breakdown under the weight of economic failure, but that its very success undermines the institutions that protect it, and inevitably creates conditions in which it will not be able to live and which strongly point to socialism as the heir apparent.'

In his *Encyclopedia Britannica* article (1946), he characterizes the 19th century (in England) as the period of 'intact capitalism', which involved individual freedom at home, free trade, sound money and limitations on the powers of government to interfere with economic processes. If those conditions had been permitted to continue, capitalist success could have continued indefinitely. But that was not to be because, from 1898 on, the system itself generated political conditions that brought about its failure.

In this paper I shall first outline, with some critical comments, Schumpeter's central thesis that capitalism is undermined by its 'success'. Second, I shall argue that failures inherent in capitalist evolution as well as its successes must be taken into account. Third, factors external to the capitalist process will be considered. The final question is whether the trends in capitalist development inevitably lead to socialism as Schumpeter defines it. Or is there a possible 'half-way house'? Or can the 'march to socialism' be wholly or partly reversed? Or are there successors to capitalism other than socialism?

CAPITALIST TRANSFORMATION AND DECAY

To make way for his theory, Schumpeter is first concerned to discard the breakdown theories that assert that in the structure of capitalism are basic contradictions that inevitably lead to its breakdown. In that connection he pays particular attention to the theories of Marx and Keynes.

With respect to Marx, he easily disposes of Marxian economic causes of breakdown, such as a falling rate of profits, immiserization and crises of increasing violence; but by now there are few supporters of these propositions, apart from the unregenerate faithful. The importance of Marx for Schumpeter lies in other directions, as we shall see.

Keynes was a different matter. As soon as the 'stagnation thesis' was propounded in the *General Theory* (and subsequently in the works of Alvin Hansen), Schumpeter took vigorous exception to it. The 'stagnation thesis' maintained that, as a country grew richer, most investment opportunities would diminish absolutely, but at the same time the propensity to save would increase absolutely as income increased. Consequently, saving and investment could be balanced only at a chronically high level of unemployment. Full employment could be maintained only by *permanent* government action to increase investment or increase consumption. And, as Keynes states, nationalization of investment was clearly called for.

If valid, the long-run Keynesian argument provided an impregnable case for socialism. But at best the case was not proved. Schumpeter argues persuasively that, despite slowing population growth and limited frontiers, the stagnationists underestimate the investment that can result in a favourable climate for innovation. There may be room for argument on that score. Schumpeter's decisive point is that in Keynes's view the propensity to save increases according to a 'psychological law' regardless of investment opportunities. Keynes himself is explicit in the *General Theory* that the independence of savings and investment decisions is an assumption of his short-term model (pp. 96, 97 and 110). Yet without argument or evidence he makes it the basis of his prediction of the long-run failure of capitalism. Schumpeter, on the other hand, maintained his sanity. He saw that the saving–investment problems of the 1930s were cyclical and not secular. But the danger to capitalism lay in the belief of economists and politicians that breakdown was at hand.

We hear little of the stagnation thesis nowadays. 'Stagnation' is not even indexed in the modern textbooks. Perhaps Schumpeter does not deserve as much credit for rejecting the thesis from the outset as the rest of us, including Keynes, deserve censure for an uncritical acceptance of it.

The potential excess of saving is, of course, crucial to Keynesian breakdown. Without it, declining investment opportunity, if it occurred, would be accompanied by a declining propensity to save. The rate of growth would slow down as the economy approached its 'full complement of riches', in the manner of Adam Smith. That agreeable state would not be capitalist breakdown, and would not necessarily lead to any form of socialism.

There is no breakdown in Schumpeter's theory. For him, the worst that can happen is a stationary state. Capitalistic development in his view depends on the ability, imagination and ambition of profit-seeking entrepreneurs who can shake the economy out of its equilibrium lethargy by introducing new consumer goods, enlisting new technology, opening up new markets, discovering new sources of supply or winning new strategic positions in industry; in short, by achieving 'new combinations' or innovations. In the age of individualistic capitalism, at any rate, all this is a matter not of marginal adjustments or appraisals of risk, but of explorations of the oceans of uncertainty. To evoke the talent required, suitable and even grandiose rewards are necessary.

His main emphasis is on profits as an incentive to entrepreneurship. He gives less attention to profits as the main source of accumulation. Presumably this is because his original model begins with an economy in general equilibrium and virtually zero saving. Innovators obtain their resources with newly-created credit which enables them to raid the circular flow, in a process that is essentially inflationary. Even in the early model, the feasibility of the process depends on the willingness of the rest of the economy to tolerate an inflationary transfer of resources from consumption to investment.

The initial model becomes substantially modified as the analysis goes forward, or as capitalism evolves, and Schumpeter does, implicitly, at any rate, recognize that for the system to work, incomes generated by innovation must be largely saved, and the rate of saving depends on the distribution of incomes. In other words, a structure of the economy that yields a high rate of saving as well as innovation is necessary for capitalistic success.

With respect to the distribution of income he is more concerned to make the point that capitalistic success produces increased equality. Relatively speaking, Queen Elizabeth I had a far higher standard of living than does Queen Elizabeth II. 'The capitalistic achievement does not typically consist in providing more silk stockings for queens, but in bringing them within the reach of factory girls in return for steadily decreasing amounts of effort' (*CSD*, p. 67). This is a signal aspect of capitalistic achievement, but statisticians obscure the fact by focusing attention on the distribution of money incomes.

The other main element of success is the rate of increase of total output. In the eloquent words of the *Communist Manifesto*, 'The bourgeoisie during its rule of scarce one hundred years has created more massive and more colossal productive forces than have all preceding generations together . . .' And, as Schumpeter maintains, the process has not been associated with the Marxian horrors of exploitation and immiserization. That is his picture of capitalistic success.

We can now ask whether the internal logic of the capitalist system will bring about its demise or transformation. Schumpeter's view can be briefly summarized (see *CSD*, Chapters XII and XIII).

1. The age of the individual innovating entrepreneur did give way, and in Schumpeter's view must give way, to the large-scale enterprise. The entrepreneurial function becomes bureaucratized. Organized research and development are a main source of innovation, and the innovating process is carried out by executive committees and finance committees. While ownership is still legally vested in the stockholders, they have been stripped of their decision-making functions, and have virtually become rentiers. Thus high executive incomes as well as dividends are functionally unnecessary. They are already exposed to heavy taxation; Schumpeter's clear implication is that the corporation might as well be transferred to public ownership.

I feel his argument is incomplete. He does not undertake to show that capitalistic performance in terms of innovation is impaired by the advent of the corporation. Nor does he show that it would be improved with public ownership. Most economic arguments suggest that effective corporate performance requires some shelter from the gales of politics. Nevertheless, there is strong political hostility to corporations, especially those concerned with oil, and to corporate profits, even if they are saved and invested. Schumpeter may, in the end, or within 25 years, turn out to be right.

2. His next point is that capitalism is bent on destroying its 'protective strata'. Capitalism and bourgeois ideology ousted feudalism, but not completely. In England during the period of intact capitalism, the bourgeoisie

ran the business of the country, while the government was supported by the aristocratic tradition. Even today, Labour governments are well represented by the Old School Tie. The aristocratic tradition, in Schumpeter's view, provided the element of irrationality that is necessary for the working of a 'rational' system. In more general terms he states: 'No social system can work which is based upon a network of free contracts between (legally) equal contracting parties and in which everyone is supposed to be guided by nothing except his own (short-run) utilitarian ends.'

Not every antecedent stratum meets Schumpeter's requirements. The British aristocracy may have had the necessary flexibility and adaptability, but in the case of France, it is generally held that the remnants of the French aristocracy that survived the Revolution played no constructive role.

Of course, the United States immediately comes to mind. Schumpeter is merely prepared to say that it was exceptionally favoured, but he expects it to suffer from the absence of a protective stratum (*CSD*, p. 138). One might ask whether the higher levels of American business do not attempt to fill the gap by the formation of organizations such as the Council on Foreign Relations and the Committee for Economic Development, which attempt to take a long-run national point of view rather than a strictly business point of view such as that of the American Chamber of Commerce.

To return to England; capitalism has suffered and the protective stratum clearly has declined in strength and influence since the time of Lord Salisbury, largely under the impact of egalitarian policies sponsored by Lloyd George, Winston Churchill when younger, and their successors. But whether this decline and these policies can be attributed to the internal logic of capitalism is another matter.

3. Schumpeter's third point—possibly I should have put it first—is that capitalistic success has raised the *absolute* economic position of all classes, particularly labour, agriculture, the aged and the unemployed. This improvement in absolute standards has strengthened the *relative* political power of those classes *vis à vis* the bourgeoisie, on whom capitalistic success depends; and the consequence is anti-capitalistic policies, with business profits as a principal target and with 'welfarism' as a major objective. This conclusion is very Schumpeterian and paradoxical. It implies that the political achievement of welfare measures such as health insurance and abatement of pollution derives from the economic success of the recipients rather than from their misery. Compare, for instance, the ability of the labour movement to finance a political campaign today with what it was 100 years ago. Compare the concepts of poverty in the West and in South Asia.

4. As an all-embracing point, bourgeois civilization is essentially 'ration-

alistic'.[1] Its spreading influence tends increasingly to destroy the protective strata, but it eventually turns on capitalism itself, particularly under the influence of the intellectuals that it breeds. Capitalism itself is perceived as an 'irrational' system. We have already noted that incomes from large corporations are attacked on the grounds that they cannot be justified in terms of the way in which a bureaucratized organization performs its functions. But what of the Schumpeterian entrepreneur in Intact Capitalism? He is a romantic and heroic figure motivated by the drive to win prizes that can be described not in terms of hedonistic enjoyment but in terms of the 'dream and the will to found a private kingdom', 'The will to conquer; the impulse to fight, to prove oneself superior to others, to succeed for the sake, not of the fruits of success but of success itself' and, finally, 'the joy of creating, of getting things done, or simply of exercising one's energy and ingenuity.'

This may have been a picture, or was it a caricature, of some of the capitalistic giants at the end of the 19th century. He may have been thinking of Andrew Carnegie and Friedrich Krupp, among others. But were those imperial characteristics necessary conditions for entrepreneurship? To go back to the beginning, both James Watt and George Stephenson were far more interested in the progress of their inventions than in the accumulation of fortunes. In fact, Stephenson protested against the 'railroad mania' of 1844 and Watt tried to get legislation enacted to prohibit the use of high-pressure steam for engines, because he believed it was dangerous to the public; not typical Schumpeterian behaviour. I suspect that the wealth of the early industrial revolution in England came as much from the ownership of coal mines as from successful entrepreneurship. And at the end of the century how much of the vast fortunes came from financial manipulation and monopolistic privilege? Those factors do not fit easily into Schumpeter's model.

In his zestful pursuit of his own major thesis, Schumpeter tends to neglect the savings side of the picture. As I pointed out earlier, he never really establishes the necessary link between innovation and the willingness to save. Other theorists of development, notably Simon Kuznets, take the opposite point of view, that opportunities for innovation are abundant, but the willingness of the economy to save is the limiting factor that determines the rate of development.

Schumpeter, however, is right in the emphasis he gives to the effect of 'rationalistic' attitudes on the capitalist process. But the criticisms, it seems,

---

[1] I follow Schumpeter in putting 'rationalistic' in quotes. He cannot give precise definition to the term and, a fortiori, neither can I. It seems to relate both to ends and to means and to be both analytical and normative. Ends must seem reasonable to those brought up in the tradition of the

are directed at the inequalities of income and wealth, however they arise, that are inherent in capitalistic development. Whether functionally justified or not, that distribution is anathema to the 'rationalistic' intellectual. How far does one get if one argues that increasing profits of oil companies are an important part of a solution of the energy crisis?

The supreme achievement of rationalism in economics is the proof that a regime of perfect competition yields an efficient allocation of given economic resources, and thereby lends support to *laissez-faire*. But that system does not provide rational justification for the distribution of income. It may seem fair that wage earners get the marginal products of their labour, but the system does not justify the rent of land accruing to private owners. From the point of view of efficiency, the system would work equally well if land were nationalized, or rent were confiscated by taxation, an idea that occurred both to John Stuart Mill and to Henry George.

The distribution of income cannot be justified by a hedonic calculus. It must be justified as a determinant of the rate of economic development, of the rate of saving and investment or of incentives for entrepreneurship. Within wide limits, the rate and character of development is not a matter for 'rational' argument. Schumpeter makes no such claims for Intact Capitalism. On emotional and aesthetic grounds he clearly prefers it to any successor that he can envisage. He does not argue that on rational grounds a system of modified capitalism or socialism would be inferior, however, even though he would probably argue that the rate of increase of total output would be lower under those systems. Other eminent authorities differ widely. Adam Smith said: 'The progressive state is the hearty state, the stationary state dull, the declining state melancholy.' John Stuart Mill (under the influence of his wife) applauded the idea of a stationary state of plenty as the happiest outcome of economic development.

Consequently the state of development is open to attack from all sides. The attacks can be concerned with monopolies, pollution, safety, discrimination, and so forth, all reflected in the increasing trend towards government regulation and single-issue politics. All these attacks may be 'rational' in their own contexts and may be the outcome of the rationalistic tendencies

---

philosophical and social thought of the Eighteenth-century Enlightenment. These could include freedom and justice. Means should follow logically from ends. These could include application of the principles of *laissez-faire* and utilitarianism. Alternatively, those principles could be accepted as reasonable and their consequences could be regarded as rational. But the trouble arises when the application of the principles can yield conflicting results; as it does with *laissez-faire* and utilitarianism. Then a reasonable system of 'weighting' the conflicting consequences must be contrived. Rather than get further enmired in this subject, I follow Schumpeter's example and use the quotation marks (when I remember them). And everybody uses the term and, presumably, knows what it means.

of Schumpeter's thesis, but in the aggregate they can lead to consequences that can accelerate capitalist decline.

I have tried to summarize in a very brief space Schumpeter's thesis embodied in the aphorism that capitalism succumbs to its successes. Incidentally, the aphorism, while it appeals to Schumpeter's sense of irony, seems to be misleading. Success is defined by him, as we have seen, in terms of the rate of increase of total output and increasing equality in the distribution of *real* incomes. It might have been equally valid for him to say that capitalism deteriorates because of the failures that accompany success. In fact he himself says: 'There is not so much difference as one might think between saying that the decay of capitalism is due to its success and saying that it is due to its failure.'

CAPITALIST FAILURE

Are there any other items that should be added to Schumpeter's list, whether on the side of success or failure? It seems to me that there have been ideological movements that have profoundly influenced capitalist development, but do not fit neatly into Schumpeter's pattern.

One of these is Marxism itself. That doctrine cannot be said to depend on bourgeois rationality. Its analytical conclusions, such as exploitation and immiserization leading inevitably to class warfare, have been shown by Schumpeter and others to be wrong. Yet Marxism survives and even flourishes, and 'Marx the Teacher' (*CSD*, Chapter IV) is the rallying cry of the slogans, even though they are false, but he is by no means fully dependent on them. I do not think that Schumpeter has fully explained the hostility to capitalism that the continued success of Marxism implies. He ascribes that hostility mainly to the intellectuals, but there may be something more.

John Stuart Mill (1848), in his famous chapter on the stationary state, says: 'I confess I am not charmed by those who think that the normal state of human beings is that of struggling to get on; that the trampling, crushing, elbowing and treading on each other's heels which form the existing type of social life are anything but the disagreeable symptoms of one of the phases of industrial progress.' In the next chapter, on 'The probable [sic] futurity of the labouring classes', he advances proposals, to which I refer later, designed to ameliorate that condition.

Marshall (1920) draws special attention to those who virtually drop out of the economic race. On the second page of the *Principles* he says: 'Those who have been called the residuum of our large towns have little opportunity for friendship; they know nothing of the decencies and the quiet, and very little of the unity of family life; and religion often fails to reach them. No doubt their physical, mental and moral ill health is due to other causes than poverty, but this is the chief cause.' One has only to pick up the morning newspaper to be reminded of the fact that the problem is still with us and still unsolved.

O.H. Taylor (1955) writes in similar vein. He states: 'I cannot believe that the main causes of extreme opposition threatening liberal capitalism lie at all in its economic imperfections, even with respect to distribution or instability of its great and growing output of economic benefits reaching the greater part of all the people . . . The fundamental causes lie, I suspect, in excessive frustrations of people's inevitable natural, human and legitimate emotional needs; for sufficient tolerable degrees of relative stability, continuity and security, not of their incomes alone but of their local, personal, family, group and community ways of life.'

These quotations relate to objective features of capitalistic development, and not to ideologies. Yet they provide a fertile field in which hostile ideologies can take root and flourish. Without them Marx, by now, could have been a historical episode, rather than a living force. In Schumpeterian terms those features of capitalism must be recorded as failures, not successes.

The revolution in Iran illustrates my argument. The 20 years of the Shah's reign witnessed an extraordinary capitalistic expansion. Not only did total (non-oil) output grow dramatically, but sectoral incomes, including agriculture, increased as well. No segment of the economy was condemned to building pyramids, but traditional values were attacked and the population exposed to tension and uncertainty. All this could not have been achieved under a political democracy and the Shah and the ruling élite almost inevitably became very rich.

The revolution reverted to traditional values and established a religious dictatorship, with considerable intellectual support, and inflicted severe economic losses on the country. I venture to say that neither Marx nor Schumpeter would have predicted this outcome. However, we can borrow the aphorism and say that the Shah was destroyed by his successes.

Another instance of capitalist failure, or an attribute of success (depending on how you look at it), is the tendency of the capitalist system to generate booms and depressions. Of course, under intact capitalism the economy fluctuates, according to Schumpeter's system, during successive periods of innovation and adaptation. And until 1929 the system, at any rate in the United States, accepted periods of unemployment without great social strain, partly because the unemployed in industry had a refuge in agriculture. The 1929 depression was of unequalled severity. Previous depressions in the United States had involved a slowdown of economic growth, but never in recorded history an absolute decline of gross national product. Between

1929 and 1933 GNP declined by 25 per cent and non-agricultural employment declined correspondingly.

Marxian economists rejoiced in the belief that this was the beginning of the period of crises of increasing violence. Had they been able to sustain that thesis, Schumpeter's thesis would have been overwhelmed. Most non-Marxists were simply bewildered at the time. Schumpeter, as early as 1931 (*Essays*, p. 96), undertook to argue that a severe depression at that time fitted in with his model. It was an accidental coincidence of troughs in his three cyclical pattern, and did not represent any inherent weakness in the system. He subsequently argued that the depression was deepened by special factors inherited from the 1920s, particularly the banking situation, heavy mortgage indebtedness in agriculture and the speculative mania of 1927 to 1929, all of which were accidental factors.

He also argued that a normal process of recovery was under way by 1934 and that, if the 'capitalist engine' had been allowed to do its work, full recovery would have ensued at a reasonable pace. As it was, full recovery was delayed until President Roosevelt substituted Dr Win-the-War for Dr New Deal. The delay in Schumpeter's view was due to the anti-capitalist attitudes and policies of the government (*Business Cycles*, Ch. IX), and those represented the cumulative antagonisms that had built up in accordance with his theory and had been suppressed during prior periods of capitalistic success. It is consistent with Schumpeter's general thesis to argue that anti-capitalistic measures themselves follow a cyclical pattern. The political climate is more favourable to their adoption when the economy is depressed than when it is booming. More economic measures confirming his thesis were crowded into the 1930s than occurred before or after that decade. Whether those measures can be attributed to capitalistic success or failure is a matter of taste.

One aspect of the 1930s that deserves attention is the 'Keynesian revolution' and in particular the long-run stagnation thesis.[2] As Schumpeter has shown, the thesis is without foundation. Yet the anti-saving ideology it induced has had profound effects on political life and may be an important factor in producing our present inflationary woes. Nor can the thesis be attributed to the growth of anti-capitalist attitudes. Keynes himself only became a 'Keynesian' with the onset of the Great Depression. Until then he was a good Marshallian with faith in the ability of capitalism to benefit all mankind in the future through accumulation and technology (see his 'Economic possibilities for our grandchildren', 1930). The *General Theory* grew out of Keynes's efforts to comprehend the Great Depression. Underconsumption had a long history going back to Malthus, and the declining

---

[2] *CSD*, p. 392, and *History of Economic Analysis*, Part V, Chapter 5.

investment opportunity idea goes back to Adam Smith. Consequently the anti-saving ideology may be regarded as a powerful force that impinged on capitalism, but not as one that followed from the logic in the Schumpeterian sense of capitalistic development.

On the other hand, the Great Depression could have occurred only under capitalism. The system must be judged not only by it successes but by its vulnerability to inflation. In that sense, the susceptibility of the system to the ideologies of Keynes can be regarded as a failure of the system. For purposes of organization, I have included the depression as a failure. The reader can take his choice.

I am tempted to go back and think of Adam Smith in Schumpeterian terms; when Adam Smith wrote, capitalism had little to do with individualism and the liberal ideology. It was more accurately portrayed by his famous diatribes against merchants and manufacturers. For instance, 'people of the same trade seldom gather together, even for merriment or diversion, but the conversation ends in a conspiracy against the public, or in some contrivance to raise prices.' And, with respect to mercantilist restrictions on trade, 'The niggling arts of the underling tradesmen have become the principles that govern a great empire.' *The Wealth of Nations* can be regarded as a rational protest against an irrational system, but, in contrast to Schumpeter, the protest emerged from the failure rather than the successes of 18th-century capitalism. It became the dominant orthodoxy of the 19th century.

THE INFLUENCE OF EXTERNAL FACTORS

In Schumpeter's words 'this epoch [since 1898] witnessed a complete reversal of the attitude toward capitalism and of almost all the tendencies of the liberal epoch ... We find revival of protectionism, growing antagonism between nations, rising public expenditure and taxes, increasing regulation of economic activity... Again, all this may be linked with corresponding changes in social structures, philosophies of life, schemes of values' (1931, p. 190). All this sounds like a reversion towards the system against which Adam Smith rebelled; and much more besides the internal logic of capitalism is needed as an explanation.

Of course, the most spectacular and catastrophic external factor is war. While there is a wealth of discussion, largely Marxist, on the economic causes of war, no one appears to have attempted a systematic treatise on the economic consequences of war, possibly because the subject does not lend itself to easy generalization.

Schumpeter (in 1945) summarizes his general position as follows: 'Whether or not economically conditioned it [the First World War] visibly accelerated, in Europe at least, existing tendencies unfavourable to the survival of capitalist institutions. On the one hand, it produced situations of stress, though due to a chance combination of factors, that caused permanent breakdown of social patterns, which without such stresses might have persisted indefinitely; this is strikingly exemplified by the case of the USSR. On the other hand, it produced a permanent change in the distribution of political weights that produced policies which prevented the capitalist engine from working: this is exemplified by the case of England. A similar argument applies of course to the war that broke out in 1939' (pp. 203–204). We can grant him the Russian case. The United States situation is an exception. But what of England and Germany? We can agree that the conditions for intact capitalism were impaired by the First World War, but what of the march towards socialism?

In England, the advent of the first Labour government in 1924 and the general strike of 1926 made the march seem plausible. But by 1931 the Labour government had given way to the national government and that gave way to the governments of Baldwin and Chamberlain. Those governments did not represent capitalistic success, but it is hard to contend that the march to socialism accelerated between 1924 and 1939. Schumpeter would accept these facts, but would attribute them to the incompetence and pusillanimity of the Labour movement. But should not the human element be recognized as a factor in the process?

English history repeated itself after the Second World War. In 1945, Churchill's government was overthrown, and a Labour government with strong socialist inclinations took its place. Churchill was restored in 1952. The march to socialism did not accelerate under succeeding Labour governments, and now there is an effort to decelerate it.

England is without question more socialist today than it was in 1914, but how much of the change can be attributed to the decay of capitalism according to its internal logic?

The history of Germany under the impact of the two world wars is more interesting. As Schumpeter would have expected, the Social Democrats came to power after the First World War. They and the democratic system they represented proved unequal to their task. The beginning of the 1930s saw the rise of Hitler. I find it totally incomprehensible that Schumpeter hardly says a word about Nazism; surely that sinister episode has a bearing on both his analysis and his predictions.

He did not live long enough after the Second World War to see the capitalist phoenix arise from the German ashes. He would have seen a period of virtually intact capitalism lasting for more than 25 years. Is this to be ignored in the long sweep of history in which socialism is the ultimate outcome?

At the other side of the world, in Japan, the consequences of the war combined with the benign American occupation ushered in a period of capitalistic success at least comparable with that of Germany.

Also in the Orient, Hong Kong, Taiwan and Korea have achieved successes under capitalism that have not been paralleled elsewhere in the Third World.

That concludes my brief survey of Schumpeter's theory. One can applaud his point of view that capitalism must be analysed as an organic process that is continually being transformed. One can also agree that the process of transformation impairs the 'capitalist engine', compared with 'intact capitalism', but we lack empirical evidence on how the system would work out if left to itself.

As Schumpeter is at pains to assert, capitalism is influenced by factors external to his model. I have pointed to the ideologies stemming from Marx and Keynes as examples. They were not inherent in the Schumpeter model, but they did work in the same direction, and seemed to strengthen his argument. But other ideologies such as those of Friedman and Hayek may work in the opposite direction. Evidence from the past is lacking, and I would not venture to make predictions.

Of course, the most significant external events have bedevilled the 20th century. The history of the 30 years since Schumpeter died does not confirm or, in the long run, necessarily refute his generalization quoted above, that the dislocations of war will strengthen his predictions concerning the march to socialism.

IS SOCIALISM THE FINAL OUTCOME?

My final topic in this discussion is Schumpeter's prediction of socialism as the outcome of capitalistic development. I shall not touch on his trenchant and foreboding comments on 'Russian Imperialism and Communism'. The establishment of communist states by military force in Vietnam, Cambodia and North Korea is excluded from this discussion. On the other hand, the performance of Russia since the revolution is clearly disconcerting to socialist ideologies in the West. And the history of the Eastern European countries, particularly Yugoslavia, since the Second World War does not suggest that their association with Russia represents the triumph of socialist ideology.

Schumpeter adheres to his prediction through thick and thin: 'It is only socialism in the sense defined in his book that is so predictable;[3] nothing else

---

[3] He became a little less dogmatic about 'prediction' in his last paper. See the quotation in my first paragraph.

is. In particular, there is little reason to believe that this socialism will mean the civilization of which orthodox socialists dream. It is much more likely to present fascist features. That would be a strange answer to Marx's prayer. But history sometimes indulges in jokes of questionable taste' (*CSD*, p. 375).

He distinguishes between 'socialization in a state of maturity' and 'socialization in a state of immaturity'.

Mature socialism is supposed to occur after the process of capitalist development has worked itself out. In particular, the entrepreneurial function has become bureaucratized and no longer requires special incentives. A major task of socialism would be to eradicate capitalist inequalities that have now become functionless, and to establish the values of the socialist commonwealth.

Socialism would be established through democratic elections, but its administration would necessarily be entrusted to the Central Planning Board. 'No responsible person can view with equanimity the consequences of extending the democratic method, that is to say the sphere of "politics" to all economic affairs.'

As socialist economists, particularly Barone, Lange and Lerner, have shown, a socialist system can allocate given economic resources so as to achieve 'economic efficiency'. But fundamental matters, particularly the desired distribution of income and the rate of economic growth, lie outside the field of technical competence. (Lange would agree.) Those objectives must be established by the democratic legislature, if democracy is to survive. On this point Schumpeter is sceptical. He states: 'The prime minister of a democracy might be likened to a horseman who is so fully engrossed in trying to keep in the saddle, that he cannot plan his ride, or to a general so fully occupied with making sure that his army will obey his orders that he must leave strategy to take care of itself' (*CSD*, p. 287). In that realistic situation the values held by the planning board are likely to prevail over those of the legislature.

On the other side of the coin, however, the rationalistic thinking of capitalist civilization has demolished the idea that capitalism yields a 'maximum of satisfaction'. And there are modern planners and programmers who prefer the arbitrary coherence of planning to our present untidy solutions.

The discussion of mature socialism is really a (useful) academic exercise. No Western socialist party now includes it in its platform, and Schumpeter does not predict that mature socialism will come about. A more likely outcome, in his view, will be 'premature socialism'.

There are two major interconnected questions I want to discuss. First, given the socialist tendencies in our society, is there 'a habitable half-way house'? In other words, is the present mixed economy (of the United States or the United Kingdom) a viable and enduring arrangement? Second, if the mixed economy becomes unworkable, will the outcome be socialism in Schumpeter's sense of public ownership or control of the means of production?

Schumpeter virtually answered the first question in the negative (in 1950), even though the British Labour Party had abandoned socialism as a formal goal and American 'liberals' never had it. He felt that the process of capitalist decay, in accordance with his theory, was the overriding influence. Moreover, the politics of the mixed economy would accelerate the process and would do nothing to arrest it. He gave the mixed economy a life of 50 years or so. Whether the experience of the last 30 years would make him alter his opinion in any way is a matter for speculation.

Schumpeter seems to me to give insufficient emphasis to an important aspect of the matter that follows from his own argument. Surely the march towards socialism is achieved at increasing cost in terms of material output, compared with what is possible under (modified) capitalism. If the march continues under democratic auspices, it is likely to result in decreasing rates of accumulation, and public interference with the allocation of resources is likely to satisfy the public less than the operation of an (imperfect) market system. Continued efforts to redistribute income and wealth may involve costs that are generally regarded as not worth paying.

Moreover, organized economic groups within a capitalist economy acquire a strong vested interest in the system. It is no accident that American labour is anti-socialist, to say nothing of anti-communist. It realizes that capitalist profits are essential to its own success. Radical demonstrations in New York are broken up not by the tame capitalists of Wall Street, but by hard-hatted construction workers. Of course, that is much less true of British trade unions, with consequent impairment of the British economy.

Again, American agriculture is itself becoming increasingly capitalistic. One cannot expect an Iowa farmer with an investment of half a million dollars or more in his farm to be in the vanguard of the march. He not only reaps capitalist profits but is protected against losses.

I could go on and refer to veterans, welfare mothers, school teachers and even universities.

My contention is that all these groups, in the United States at any rate, prefer to trust their fate to the competitive struggle within the present system. But they realize that they will not succeed if they kill the capitalist goose that lays the golden eggs ('golden' may be an anachronism in a modern context). I therefore believe that there are forces that will tend to stabilize the mixed economy, and its outlook is not as bleak as Schumpeter expects.

However, voluntary association or competition among individuals or groups cannot work without some overall restraint. While those groups and individuals may recognize their interest in capitalism there is no assurance that their unrestrained collective or competitive action will ensure its survival. In a democracy, the traditional restraint is the monetary system, and to serve its function the monetary authority must have shelter from democratic processes. A weak monetary authority is the prime cause of inflation. Inflation, Schumpeter contends, is the most important factor that will accelerate capitalist decline. That brings me to the second question posed above.

Schumpeter, like other continental economists of his generation, saw at first hand the inflations in Germany and Austria that followed the First World War, and preoccupation with the dangers of inflation is reflected in all his writings since that time. Anglo-American economists tended to think his concern was obsessive, but since the Second World War they have come to share it. Even in that period, nevertheless, the concern was slow in growing.

Schumpeter argues (1950) that the modern mixed economy is bound to create demands for public expenditures which will increase aggregate demand and raise employment above its 'natural' rate. That in turn will set in motion the all-too-familiar wage–price spiral, with the consequence of general inflation. For all this to happen, however, the central bank must be willing to 'accommodate' the inflation by creation of money. But this is likely to happen since the bank itself will be under continual political attack. It may be nationalized, as in England, or it may be harassed by a democratic legislature, as in the United States, or it may remain strong, as it has until now in Western Germany. Apart from such exceptional cases, Schumpeter believes that inflation will become endemic. He then (in his 1950 paper) considers whether anything can be done to reverse or mitigate the process.

First, he considers the 'orthodox' remedy of monetary or credit restriction. He points out that this remedy was designed to work under conditions of price and wage flexibility. Under modern conditions of rigidity, the main impact would fall on employment and would immediately provoke government action to neutralize it.

Second, there is the possibility of increasing taxes. But Schumpeter argues that in modern political conditions, such taxes would concentrate on profits and hence investment and the rate of economic growth. They might decrease inflation for the moment, but would increase it in the longer run. He might have added that the alternative, taxes on consumption, would be reflected in money wages and, consequently, prices. He could also have added that any taxes that decreased aggregate demand would mean the political liability of increasing unemployment.

Third, reduction of public expenditures is perhaps the most orthodox of remedies. Schumpeter considered this possibility in 1948 in *Essays* (p. 244), but rejected it in his 1950 article, presumably because, as he argued in 1948, the vested interest in all forms of expenditures was too great for general reduction to be a practical possibility.

His conclusion is that the most likely outcome of 'serious' endemic inflation is direct control of prices. (He does not specify wage control, but in practice wage controls have proved less effective than price controls.) Price control, in his view, would appeal to bureaucracies, whose authority over the economy would be increased. It would also appeal to the anti-capitalist interests, since profits would be squeezed. For the moment it would halt inflation and would not increase unemployment. But as a consequence of the weakening of capitalism that would be involved, the control system could not endure, and the final outcome would be socialism as Schumpeter defines it.

Schumpeter's analysis may not seem strikingly original in 1981, but remember that he was writing in 1949, and how many economists, in the United States at any rate, saw the inflation problem as clearly as he did? The USA is now struggling to escape his conclusion concerning direct controls. A promising possibility is to emphasize 'the supply side', but Schumpeter would contend that measures to increase productivity would run into the formidable political barrier of anti-capitalist ideology. His prediction concerning direct controls may eventually turn out to be right.

Let us now turn to his prediction that a central system will give way to centralized public ownership and control of the means of production. How does he arrive at that conclusion and are there alternative outcomes?

Schumpeter did not live to explain this prediction, so one is forced to conjecture. He cannot believe that a modern democracy, under inflationary pressure, will vote to establish a fully-fledged system of central planning and control, including not only quantities, but wages and prices. That would require a revolution and the extinction of democracy.

He must have had in mind more gradual processes. One of these is that under controls, according to his argument, the government must supply an increasing proportion of investible funds; and the bureaucrats who supplied the funds would have an irresistible urge to allocate. Of course, if the bureaucracy was intent on full socialization, it would have a powerful weapon in its hands. Even without such ambitions the bureaucracy, with some justice, may feel that it can allocate capital resources as well as can private financial markets.

Thus, if the control system remains intact and profits are increasingly squeezed, we can agree with Schumpeter that the final outcome will be full socialization of investment. This, in conjunction with the price controls, would amount to socialism as he defines it. Although the administrative mechanism would differ from his physical planning operation, the results would be essentially the same.

However, will the control system endure? It is a fact that enforcement problems increase the longer the controls are attempted, for two main reasons. First, in the state of suppressed inflation, there is an accumulation of liquid balances that cannot be legally spent. Consequently more controls are needed to prevent illegal spending at home or the export of capital. Second, a control system requires constant revision to permit necessary changes in relative prices. The process of revision exposes the system to political pressures that make enforcement increasingly difficult. Finally, current output is likely to suffer. Revisions of the controls will not fully exempt producers from the cost pressures the controls imply. They will inevitably produce less than they would under a free market, with consequent dissatisfaction on the part of both themselves and the public.

All this is not mere speculation. What I have said is confirmed by experience after the Second World War. When the war was over the United States abandoned controls and preferred to take its chances with open inflation, partly, however, because it had strong ideological objections to controls. Other countries, for example the United Kingdom and Norway, saw continued controls as the way to socialism, but after a few years they too realized that the control system was not viable. I know of no Western country today that, in its calmer moments, would opt for controls as a permanent way of life but, if inflationary pressure continues and other methods of controlling it prove unavailing, controls may be adopted as a course of last resort. If they are, I predict they will have a short unhappy life.

To return to Schumpeter, he may in 1950 have been unduly pessimistic concerning the inflationary tendencies inherent in the mixed economy. Inflation for the 20 years after the Second World War was moderate and manageable. The acceleration of inflation since 1965 has been mainly due to the direct and indirect effects of factors that are external to Schumpeter's model. The main external factors are the inflationary finance of the Vietnam war, the agricultural crises of the 1970s and particularly the oil crises. The legacy of those factors, which may last for years in terms of inflationary expectations and increasing real costs, combined with new external factors that are bound to occur, may strain political patience to the limit. A controlled economy may again be perceived as the solution, combined with an increased political determination to make the control system work, despite its manifest difficulties.

Schumpeter's prediction of a socialism involving central control of the means of production may be right, but 'external factors' may play a more decisive role than the internal logic of capitalism in bringing it about. It should also be borne in mind that the socialism he envisages as a practical possibility is 'unlikely to mean the civilization of which orthodox socialists dream. It is much more likely to present fascist features.'

Another possibility is suggested by the recent history of Brazil, Uruguay and Chile. In all three countries, the policies of left-wing governments had produced astronomical rates of inflation. These rates, if allowed to continue, might well have resulted in Schumpeter's scenario. But to avert that outcome, military governments took power.

The objective of those governments was not socialism or fascism but the creation of conditions necessary for capitalistic success. The methods employed were the suppression of political dissidence and the curbing of the spending propensities of democratic legislatures, but not the extinction of bureaucratic institutions. In economic terms, the policies of the military governments consisted of fiscal and monetary reforms designed to reduce inflation, and to establish conditions necessary for the successful working of the market system, both nationally and internationally.

These policies have succeeded in Brazil during the past 15 years, even though the rate of inflation remains very high by 'Northern' standards. Uruguay and Chile are still suffering from the traumas inherent in the restoration of market systems after periods of hyperinflation.

I do not venture to predict the long-run outcome in any of these countries, but for the time being, whether we like it or not, the alliance between military government and private capitalism seems to have arrested the march into socialism as Schumpeter defines it.

A possibility more congenial to the United States and Western Europe is some form of participatory economy. Countries such as Sweden, with nation-wide organizations of business and labour, are closer to cooperation of those groups with the government than is the USA with its decentralized system.

Progress towards a participatory economy should reduce the competitive struggle among organized groups and its inflationary consequences, but participation will not remove the need for the fiscal and monetary restraints that are needed to make any mixed economy work.

Finally, the mixed economy of the United States may work. This essay would have had a very different tone had it been written in the early 1960s. For reassurance, I invite the reader to glance at the Economic Reports of the President of those years. The presidential advisers of those years had not read Schumpeter, nor had they experienced the 1970s, which are but one decade in the span of history. In the final chapter of *Capitalism, Socialism and Democracy*, Schumpeter seems prepared to concede that the mixed economy in the United States might have a chance, 'But only for the next half-century or so. The long run diagnosis elaborated in this book will not be affected' (p. 398). We have until the year 2000.

I have to conclude that Schumpeter's prediction of socialism as the long-run outcome of capitalistic development is not supported by experience.

Other outcomes may be possible and half-way measures may be more durable than he expects. But neither can his thesis be refuted. He believes that whatever happens in the meantime, the internal logic of the system will validate his prediction in the long run. But that prediction must be regarded as an apocalyptic vision.

Schumpeter's greatness, in the present context, lies in his vision and analysis of capitalism as an evolutionary process of transformation and decline. In that sense, his theory can be appraised in the light of historical experience. And in view of the importance he attaches to 'vision' in scientific endeavour, he would be disappointed if his theory did not provoke disagreement.

His greatness, however, did not depend on a single book. With undue modesty, he used to refer to *Capitalism, Socialism and Democracy* as a potboiler. He would regard the *Theory of Economic Development* and the *History of Economic Analysis* as the true monuments to his fame. For those who knew him, the qualities of his personality deserve equal rank. Unhappily, those qualities cannot be adequately recorded for the benefit of later generations.

REFERENCES

Clemence, R.V. (Ed.) (1951) *Essays of J.A. Schumpeter.* p. 244. Cambridge. MA: Addison-Wesley.

Keynes, J.M. (1933) Economic possibilities for our grandchildren. In *Essays in Persuasion.* New York: Macmillan.

Keynes, J.M. (1936) *The General Theory of Employment, Interest and Money.* London: Macmillan.

Marshall, A. (1920) *Principles of Economics.* 8th Edition, Chapter I. London: Macmillan.

Marx, K. & Engels, F. *The Communist Manifesto.* English edition (1964) with a Foreword by Huberman, L. & Sweezy, P.M. p. 10. New York: Monthly Review Press.

Mill, J.S. (1848) *Principles of Political Economy.* Ashley edition (1926) published by Longmans Green.

Schumpeter, J.A. (1911) *Theory of Economic Development.* Chapter 24. English translation by Opie, R. (1934) Cambridge, MA: Harvard University Press.

Schumpeter, J.A. (1945) *Economic Essays.* pp. 203–204.

Schumpeter, J.A. (1946) Article in *Encyclopedia Britannica.* Reprinted in *Essays of J.A. Schumpeter* (1951). Cambridge, MA: Addison-Wesley.

Schumpeter, J.A. (1950) The march into socialism. *American Economic Review, Papers and Proceedings,* May.

Schumpeter, J.A. (1954) *History of Economic Analysis.* Part V, Chapter 5. New York: Oxford University Press.

Schumpeter, J.A. (1964) *Business Cycles.* Abridged Edition, Chapter IX. McGraw Hill.

Schumpeter, J.A. (1976) *Capitalism, Socialism and Democracy.* London: George Allen and Unwin.

Smith, A. (1776) *The Wealth of Nations.* 1950 Edition, London: Methuen.

Taylor, O.H. (1955) *Economics and Liberalism.* pp. 309–311. Cambridge, MA: Harvard University Press.

Chapter Eight

A Sovietological View

PETER WILES

SCHUMPETER'S PREDICTION PSYCHOANALYSED

Capitalism, Socialism and Democracy is a great book.[1] Without hindsight, this writer could not have written one a quarter as good. There are brilliant passages that at present do not concern us. The four chapters (VII–X) that establish the importance of technical progress, and so destroy much of the then fashionable argument for competition, were a revolution in economic theory, too long in reaching the textbooks; they should figure for ever as a standard part of the history of economic doctrine. The long footnote on the distribution of Soviet incomes (pp. 381–382) is in its own way equally brilliant. It shows that Schumpeter was not easily fooled, even when far outside his own specialities.

There are, it is true, *des longueurs*: mainly all those passages on political parties. But it is with another brilliant four chapters (XI–XIV) that I wish to take issue. Is capitalism the architect of its own decline? I do not think so now, and I believe that this, the second main message of the book, is quite misleading. But no one should be blamed for having thought so in 1942.

It follows that since the first main message has entered our blood-stream and the second is wrong, *CSD* is a great book but not an urgent one any more.

Schumpeter was a German-speaker from Central Europe. Coming from where he did, he knew much more about Marx than a gentleman of that time

---

[1] I have used the fifth edition (1976) of *Capitalism, Socialism and Democracy*. The book is referred to as *CSD*.

needed to know. He must also have been familiar with Thomas Mann's *Buddenbrooks*. The famous, eloquent and convincing chapters referred to define an *Idealtypus* of the capitalist economic order, and present it as being in inevitable decline. This order can only be described as Hanseatic (like *Buddenbrooks*, which is set in Lübeck). The upper middle class found capitalist family dynasties; they have permanent seats of residence in both town and country (p. 158). They also effectually rule the *polis*, having displaced the aristocracy:[2] 'The capitalist order entrusts the long-run interests of society to *the upper strata* of the bourgeoisie. They are really entrusted to the family motive operative in those strata' (p. 160, my italics).

This stress on the family motive is extremely interesting and has been, to my knowledge, little noticed or praised. Textbooks of economics, for instance, say nothing of it. A famous article on income distribution sets inheritance at zero (Modigliani and Brumberg, 1954). The new economics of family size determination (e.g., in the *Journal of Political Economy*, March, 1973, Part II) omits this aspect. Even when we admit the influence of age on human behaviour, and engage in 'longitudinal studies', we assume lifetime *consumption* maximization, which directly does away with inheritance. These absurdities had not come to Schumpeter's attention for he was a pre-Chicago man. But his insistence on the bourgeois family through many generations not only runs counter to a lot of nonsense: it tells us a great deal about capitalism. The system in its classical form depended indeed on inheritance or, better, on the will to bequeath. The corporation does not itself bequeath: it is either immortal, merged or bankrupt. Individuals continue, of course, to bequeath blocks of shares, but it is not the same thing. However, the corporation's officers pro tempore do strive for its immortality, and that *is* nearly the same thing.

The decline of a society based on such dynasties is utterly Hegelian: it is due to their own success and their liberal principles. They create, by private patronage and public expenditure, a hostile radical intelligentsia (pp. 145–153). They enrich the proletariat by the dynamic technical efficiency that is immanent in their system; and these, though less radical than the intelligentsia, allow themselves to be led. They invent limited liability, and so let in small shareholders who do not care (p. 156). Their businesses are thus much enlarged and bureaucratized, and the new managers do not care either (pp. 153–156). They themselves cease to believe in their fathers' ideology, so fail to defend their system with violence or conviction (p. 410). The whole

---

[2] Or at least adapted them to purposes fundamentally bourgeois: a good example, we might say, is Britain, where an *aristocratie embourgeoisée* governed on behalf of a *haute-bourgeoisie aristocratisée*. Indeed, on p. 298 Schumpeter tells us the haute-bourgeoisie seldom forms its own political class.

picture is suffused with an elegiac regret: the author bravely faces the future like a doomed scholar and gentleman. It charms, nay it hypnotizes, the Anglo-American world. It is very good compulsory reading for students brought up in the Benthamite tradition. The vulgar certainties of homo economicus are left far behind: motives are clouded, but before darkness the twilight is subtly beautiful.

But is this really Anglo-Saxon, is it even German, capitalism? The 'Hanseatic' merchants[3] of his imagination are so gentlemanly and exclusive that they even keep shopkeepers and bank clerks out of government. *They are a ruling class*, but a very lukewarm one. However, I was born sufficiently far West not to believe in Marx at all, and so to be extremely doubtful that any economically defined class was ever a ruling one in any society. What is plainly untrue of the USSR may well be untrue elsewhere. It does not seem to me true that in any country the 'upper strata of the bourgeoisie' are the sole efficient guardians of capitalism. On the contrary the mass vote for it, and the readiness to use violence in its favour, come from smaller capitalists, especially small farmers and shopkeepers. This is a matter of much notoriety, already perfectly evident in 1942. And always a substantial proportion of other social classes—the aristocracy, the intelligentsia, the proletariat—also support the system permanently, for this or that reason. Members of these classes are most certainly not kept out of political power in capitalist countries: they rather tend to monopolize it. Capitalists, as Schumpeter correctly observes on p. 298, tend to stick to their counting houses.

To this extent, then, Schumpeter must be faulted as being too Marxist. It might further be objected—it surely has been, from the far right—that large corporations do after all maximize their profits (the mere existence of the managerial revolution is of course fully recognized in *CSD*, though not by that name).[4] Such opponents can point to the compulsory minimum of shares that a director must have; to the habit of giving him cash bonuses and stock options for good performance; to the ever-present threat of the take-over bid for those whose management depresses share-values or dividend pay-outs. I think Schumpeter would have answered that the short-term policy of the corporation was none of his concern; and that this kind of petty micro-efficiency formed no part of his view of capitalism at any stage; it was the passion and the ideological commitment that concerned him. A small bureaucracy can indeed be trained to maximize profit, but not to defend its employer against nationalization, or indeed to stand up for him/it in a culturally hostile environment, or to save and invest at inhuman rates.

---

[3] And, presumably, self-employed professionals.

[4] It seems that Schumpeter had not read Burnham's book (1942) with that title.

And in all this he would have been right. There is no capitalist ideology any more, or only amongst marginal groups. I think here of all those brash young executives from the less well-known business schools; the ethnic minorities coming up, and the immigrant bourgeois of the second and indeed the first generation. I think of certain fashionable new fields: pornography, television, advertising, pop music, Chicago economics. It is evident that driving, unscrupulous self-dedicated people have not disappeared (as is suggested on p. 156), but it is true that they have no ideological stability. In addition, they are not gentlemen, they are not upper middle class (Schumpeter's phrase) or Hanseatic (mine). Though surely that is less important, it still matters. You cannot lead people if you have no style, and are wholly wrapped up in yourself.

It is of the essence of capitalism that one man works for another's profit. The worker makes the effort now, and it is a tiring and boring effort: always in the marginal hour, and nearly always in the intra-marginal hours too. He receives a reward rather strictly commensurate with his effort. The capitalist merely saved some money in the past—abstinence has disutility, but not very much; and took a decision to invest his money, also in the past. What disutilities does he currently bear? Merely those of risk. All this is very trivial compared with the pain of labour, especially the pain of the last hour. The monetary rewards are not commensurate, certainly not where inheritance makes a man a capitalist, and very probably not in any case at all.

Marx grasped this simple point, and so do Western proletariats down to the present day. The Soviet proletariat also grasps it. Indeed how could it not?—since it is about the only valid point in the whole of Soviet propaganda. The 'exploitation of man by man' under capitalism is reiterated in the USSR, and essentially by every Western trade union too, ad nauseam.[5] In fact, it is only one consideration among many. It may be expedient—it *is* expedient—for workers to forget it. They should—many of them have—accumulate enough to become 'exploiters' in their turn. Political freedom and some aspects of economic efficiency (but not all) are better served this way. Workers as such under capitalism enjoy many other advantages.

Nevertheless there the great fact is. Does Schumpeter face it? Yes and no:

> 'a sensible workman, in weighing the pros and cons of his contract with, say, one of the big steel or automobile concerns, might well come to the conclusion that, everything considered, he is not doing so badly and that the advantages of this bargain are not all on one side'. [p. 144].

But this is a little indirect, and then he goes on to spoil it all by an instant switch to what intellectuals think. Clearly he was more at home with the

---

[5] Service workers, especially those in the public sector, are not exploited in Marxist theory. The lacuna is a gross one, but seems to worry very few Marxists.

latter group. He thinks they are quite wrong but bound to win, as we saw above. He seems to say nothing more about the workers and their attitude. Yet it is of course 'exploitation' and nothing whatsoever about the intelligentsia that makes capitalism so unlovable, and undermines it.

Note that 'exploitation' is not the same as income inequality. Each family, if not each individual, may receive about the same net of tax from all sources combined, but still there will be the fact of working for another's profit. Yet there is almost nothing in CSD about inequality either: only, it seems, the postwar afterthoughts on pp. 381–382.

Nevertheless capitalism, despite increasing malfunction since the late sixties, survives well enough for a reason Schumpeter did not at all foresee. The cultural environment has turned out rather less hostile than he foresaw, and this is because of the autonomous failure of socialism in all its forms, whether as a practice or as an ideology.

SCHUMPETER'S IGNORANCE OF SOCIALISM

He is really quite incurious about socialism. He eschews all detail, referring in a rather grand manner to 'socialism'. Britain after 1945 figures, of course, only in Chapter XVIII and the appendices. In the body of the work there is only the USSR, and the chapters on the Socialist Blueprint (XVI–XVIII) are astonishingly jejune. They exhibit no serious attempt to come to grips with fact or to empathize. He has observed the USSR briefly and through the wrong end of an economist's telescope. Only the two pages on trade unions (pp. 216–217) come alive. Yet already by 1942 there were plenty of good books in English and German.

It is not that he was not a Sovietologist! But he is careless and distant about what should have been a prime concern in a book with such a title. The collectivization of agriculture, the artificial famine, the Great Purge, the expansion of forced labour all indicated that if Capitalism turns inevitably into Socialism, there is a poor look-out for Democracy, and indeed for our daily bread. It is absolutely not enough to dish up a little welfare economics (Chapter XVI) and assure us that the 'planner's problem' is soluble. If we are really rolling into Soviet socialism through a sort of Buddenbrooks collapse, we should be warned of what is in store. Today, of course, the USSR looks better than that, but it still presents an exceedingly grim prospect—if it is a prospect.

I am unable, then, to take Chapters XVI–XVIII seriously, and consider them well below the standard of the others. And this leads me straight to my main complaint: he failed, in the body of the book, to spot the military messianism of Russian Marxism–Leninism, and he forgot that the world consists of independent sovereign states.

THE FORGOTTEN PRIMAT DER AUSSENPOLITIK

Writing in 1941 and revising up to 1949, Schumpeter describes (except for the implicit assumption of an Allied victory) a foreign-policyless world, in which each country is, as in Marx, the master of its own fate. How could an Austrian, of all people, have forgotten the 'Primat der Aussenpolitik'? But perhaps he did so only because economists always do! For in fact socialism has spread by force of Soviet arms: and not, therefore, in developed countries or in underdeveloped countries, nor in countries politically prepared for it (like Czechoslovakia?) or unprepared for it (like Poland), but in contiguous countries. There are very few exceptions to this simple military rule,[6] which is much more important than all talk of convergence (a concept Schumpeter did not use), or of automatic peaceful socialization (which he did—it is not quite the same thing, since it presupposes no change on the Soviet side). We need conquest theories, not convergence theories.

At the end of Chapter XXVIII (written in 1946) Schumpeter makes handsome amends for this omission, in a section entitled 'Russian Imperialism and Communism'. He reveals himself here a cold warrior before the Cold War, and the reader may wonder what my real complaint is. It is that this little passage destroys his whole thesis: if that is what socialism is like, capitalism will not peacefully grow into it.

As long as foreign policy dominates the conduct of governments, quasi-automatic internal social processes will be brought under control if they threaten 'freedom' as locally understood, territorial integrity, military strength, state sovereignty, etc. Only fully automatic processes will, by definition, be permitted to run their course; but there are few such processes, and they do not directly threaten any half-rational social order. Thus every political system except those of Pol Pot and Mao Tse-tung can live with technical progress, which is indeed automatic and hard to stop. But the nationalization of the means of production is not automatic. Any government, any people, can stop nationalizing things, and even reverse the process. Many have.

---

[6] Let us list them. Yugoslavia (1944) became communist under the shadow of Soviet arms, but before the Red Army set foot on the territory. Cuba turned communist in about 1960 after Castro, long in power, had quarrelled irredeemably with the USA; there was no Soviet military force present at all. North Vietnam (the takeover lasted from 1945 to Dien Bien Phu in 1953) had of course Soviet and Chinese help, but used no foreign troops. The same is true of Mozambique (1975) and South Yemen (1978). In every single other case there have been Soviet or Cuban or Vietnamese or indeed Yugoslavian (Albania 1944) troops. Even China is a suspect case, since Soviet troops occupied Manchuria in the crucial years 1943–6; whatever else they did there, they did not help Chiang Kai-shek. In Czechoslovakia the troops were on the border, and the threat of invasion sufficed in 1948 (but not in 1968!) to tip the balance. The rule of geographical continuity has been relaxed by the growth of a Soviet fleet and an air transport command.

Today nationalization in its commonest form is associated in the minds of people who live under advanced capitalism with military aggression, the GULAG and the KGB. Today it remains the case, as it always has since 1917, that political émigrés flow in their vast majority from countries that have nationalized a lot (*whatever* their detailed economic policies) to countries that have not. Economic émigrés flow, of course, from poor to rich, which is another matter, but even they feel a severe political constraint: there are no Portuguese in Latvia, but there are in France.

Such, then, is the fate of thorough-going socialism in the view of the Western world, for and about which Schumpeter was writing. The backlash upon Social Democracy (to which he gave the fullest consideration along with communism) has been terrific. Only the British Labour Party and the Chilean Socialist Party[7] remain formally committed to thorough-going socialism. A majority in the British party's apparat believes no such thing. The Chilean party is smaller and has slipped to the left of the communists. Here, of course, it is equally important that the widespread experiments with nationalization and other socialist policies (workers' self-management, high public expenditure, price control)[8] have had unimpressive results. They have by no means led us down the Road to Serfdom, but rather back up it.[9]

WHY SHOULD NOT THE THIRD WORLD GO COMMUNIST?

Schumpeter at no point mentions the Third World, or takes it into implicit account; and this again is typical of his foreign-policy-free suppositions. It is the poorest countries that have gone for socialism. Having experienced only capitalist imperialism or some native tyranny, the Third World produces *volunteers* for communism: North Vietnam, Cuba, Mozambique and South Yemen up to now. The Russians themselves put up a stronger resistance to communism in 1917.

CSD was not intended to cover such a phenomenon. We cannot rightly blame its author for deliberately excluding the Third World—which was not then liberated. Besides, the book is long enough as it is. Yet I cannot pass by this sentence without exclaiming over its absurdity:

---

[7] Among major social-democratic parties known to the writer.

[8] I confess to a certain obliquity at this point. The text does not list price—and wage—control, which I consider to have been successful when strongly pursued (by non-social-democrats), or the moderate equalization of incomes, a subject on which I remain obstinately left-wing.

[9] Wiles (1972, pp. 463–471). Schumpeter had read Jewkes before he died (p. 411) but evidently not Hayek. In this connection the pedantic reader should be warned that the index to my edition is imperfect throughout, and does not cover pp. 409–425 at all.

'Can socialism work? Of course it can. No doubt is possible about that once we assume, first, that the requisite stage of industrial development has been reached and, second, that traditional problems have been successfully resolved'. [p. 167. Cf. also p. 178]

There is of course no such requisite stage, however primitive, and this proves Schumpeter's unconscious Marxism. For an Austrian he was very German. *CSD* is a late-19th-century *Stufenlehre*, and its author must be denominated a *Kathederkapitalist*.

The real history of humanity knows no *Stufen*. Mozambique had every reason to go communist; Sweden has none. Mozambique had to overthrow the Portuguese yoke—and only the USSR and China helped her. She has never known personal liberty or the orderly succession of elected governments, and could not provide them if she tried. So she looks around to see what system mobilizes people for development best. Command, the suppression of the market, the nationalization of large enterprises, are all important. It may turn out disastrous as in Cuba, or not at all bad as in Albania and North Korea; but it is inevitable, and something Schumpeter did not, and could not possibly have, foreseen.

Meanwhile Marxism–Leninism has not spread to advanced capitalist countries except for the GDR and Czechoslovakia, and it is likely to spread to others only as a result of similar military occupations. Simultaneously any internal capitalist evolution towards even British-type socialism is blocked by the evident bankruptcy of its ideology and techniques, the perpetual threat in central Europe and the alarm about the Third World.

Therefore Chapters XI to XIV of *CSD* have ceased to be a tract for the times. Much of their argument remains correct, however, and it is of absorbing interest to see just what, in detail, is going wrong, and what is happening.

THE LIKELY FUTURE OF WESTERN POST-CAPITALISM

There is no capitalist ideology any more, and Schumpeter's 'elegy' is correct at least on that. Few capitalist state machines were ever seriously in the grip of such an ideology: for instance, British and French imperialism had quite other sources. The last state to be gripped in this way was the United States of America until about 1960. It was not strictly Hanseatic: based on stable family fortunes held by influential city fathers;[10] but rather what one might

---

[10] Boston, with its unostentatious old families living off trusts and grumbling about the Irish takeover of city politics, was profoundly Hanseatic; but it stood alone.

call proto-Chicagoan: political and intellectual freedom (not strong Hanseatic values) depend on economic freedom, and the latter is defined as being capitalist. The acceptance of Keynesian economics and the welfare state, followed by the Vietnamese defeat, put an end to this too. Capitalism must now survive without spiritual support, and even without state support. My prophecy is, to repeat, that it will, because (a) we don't want to go communist and (b) non-communist but still socialist alternatives have been tried and failed.

This survival is thus negatively motivated. We

> 'keep a-hold of Nurse
> For fear of finding something worse'.

Can an economic system last on such a loveless basis? Obviously, in periods when people do not think about economics, it easily can. Thus the nascent capitalism of northern Italy or Catholic Flanders, or even of Anglican England in the 16th to the 18th centuries, rubbed along very well in the face of official neutrality.[11] In more economically minded periods like the present the thing is more difficult. But a particular economic system can still seem to be the pragmatically best available and indeed *our* system, the one *we* have chosen. Thus Hungary has chosen market socialism, and defends it, without love, as the best available—without being invaded by the same enemy as ourselves.

Advanced capitalism will, then, remain unless or until it is swept away by Soviet invasion. What exactly will it look like, however, and how will it differ from what Schumpeter knew? He was no expert on institutions, and thought fit to leave vague almost all detail about socialism, as we have seen. None the less, the present writer considers vagueness (as opposed to direct confessions of uncertainty) shameful, and prefers to chance his arm. If he thus renders himself more certain to be wrong, it will at least in the event be clear whether he was wrong!

1. There will be state capitalism (the Marxist phrase) or corporatism (the fascist phrase). Both have somewhat false connotations. State capitalism implies that the bourgeoisie still owns the whole of the means of production, and uses the state machine to forward its own interests by protecting the yield on its property. But the proletariat now owns indirectly great chunks

---

[11] I choose areas where Max Weber's Puritanism thesis (1905) does not apply. English capitalism was not strongly marked by Puritanism in these centuries. Puritanism and Judaism (Sombart, 1911) were the ideologies of nascent capitalism—which, however, it hardly needed.

of the means of production through pension funds,[12] and still more of less political assets such as their own houses, large savings bank deposits, and durables. And the state machine protects very inefficiently the yield on private property, partly because it is under the control of trade unions. Corporatism, then, is a slightly less loaded name, and I shall use it here. It implies, however, in its fascist use, that the state founded the corporations and herded people into them; while what we mean about postwar capitalism is that the corporations (cartels, trade unions, etc.) have become stronger and stronger and penetrated or terrorized the state.

2. There will be a great deal of very serious co-determination[13] by labour. At no point did Schumpeter's sureness of judgement fail him more than in this unqualified contempt for all such ideas (p. 300). Yet how could he have anticipated Tito's chance decision of 1950, or have taken seriously the decisions of the occupying powers as to the administration of iron and steel enterprises in Germany (1946)? Blame him or not, he did not hear the music of our times.

The exact forms of co-determination will vary between Yugoslavia and the capitalist countries. In the Federal Republic of Germany they have fallen into the hands of trade unions. These conduct the elections and provide most of the candidates. They even have the right to get outsiders, permanent experts from the union bureaucracy, elected. Yugoslavia's unions, on the other hand, remain wholly Stalinist and ineffective. It seems certain that other capitalist countries will follow Germany.

3. It is, however, no longer certain (to one writing in May 1981) how much stronger trade unions will be allowed to become in the exercise of their original function, collective bargaining. For in about 1968 there was a real turning point in advanced capitalism: *cost inflation*, due to irresponsible union wage-claims that leap-frog each other. The date is different for different countries, but most marked in Britain and France;[14] there at least it is definitely prior to Yom Kippur, 1973, when cost inflation through imports was added. There were indeed elements of cost inflation in the system since

---

[12] A Marxist will—should!—object that such funds are administered by the bourgeoisie. But then he has admitted that managers are separated from owners.

[13] In German, Mitbestimmung. I use the same weak word of Yugoslavia, rather than the official 'self-management', because the councils seldom meet; are chaired by the enterprise directors; are still trammelled by the Party; and in large enterprises (which means most of the labour force) form an indirectly elected hierarchy of councils.

[14] *Les évènements* in France ended predictably in a large wage claim that bought off the Communist trade unions and divided them from the students. British unions were much impressed by this event, or by the new radicalism of British students—which had in fact preceded the French student radicalism, but on a much smaller scale.

1939–40, and Schumpeter recognizes the whole syndrome on p. 422. This was written in December 1949, at a time when many other economists were warning about the role of trade unions, and discussion was quite uninhibited by monetarist blinkers.

4. A Latin American might be surprised by these dates. For in fact the idea of cost inflation as a policy began to be practised by Uruguay about 1920, and this little-known fact deserves a short excursus. Even before this date the public sector had grown like a cancer, mainly because of the public-sector trade unions on whom no market pressure was exercised.

This phenomenon can be analysed as an attack on:

(a) restraint in public expenditures;
(b) the level of costs in general (because if public salaries and wages rise, others must follow suit);
(c) budgetary balance, this last leading to a permanent inflation as much through demand as through costs.

Uruguay is the father of us all. It is above all false that Uruguay had to await economic stagnation for the beginning of this inflation, for the stagnation of its economy, with all its tragic political results, began in 1955; but prices, stable enough during the Second World War, rose at about 6 per cent per annum in 1944–55, that is to say during a period of reasonably rapid real growth. It is only true that stagnation worsened a situation already grave.

To be sure, Uruguay is only a small country while Argentina, a larger country that Europeans think they know, suffered the same evils but under a non-democratic form of government, Peronism, of which the ideology, the so called Justicialismo, is precisely an ideology of cost inflation. The unionized proletariat was supposed to agitate against urban capitalism, while the government took care of rural capitalism (an export industry) by overvaluing the peso. This peculiar deviant left-wing fascist ideology has concealed from us the effects of cost inflation, which were identical in the two neighbouring countries.

Indeed Uruguay also had in its way an ideology, in this case a very democratic one, the generous 'state populism', called Batllismo, which was behind the expansion of the public sector and the support for trade-union excesses. It is, of course, Batllismo and not Justicialismo which has spread or been spontaneously re-created everywhere in the capitalist world. Batlle was in fact a great man, a veritable 'giant in a mezzanine', and he already had this to say in 1920 about cost inflation. He replied to the 'empresistas' (i.e., those who supported the entrepreneurs against cost inflation) as follows:

'They say that the rise in wages is at the origin of the rise of product prices; and that is true ... the rise in wages with the inevitable consequences of the rise in product prices will again improve the situation of the workers: one part of the rise, not all. Suppose that the total value of the rise of wages of a trade union is one million pesos and that, in consequence, the value of all the products of the union rises by one million, who pays this million to the workers? The consumers. But these consumers, are they all workers? No. Suppose that half of them are not. The million which must finance the rise in wages is accounted for as follows: one half of these same workers which have benefited and the other half by the consumers which have not benefited. The union comes out gaining half a million!'[15]

5. Indeed the *inflación estructural* about which Latin American economists argue is little more than cost inflation plus budgetary laxity, dressed up as somehow being part of development economics. The usefulness of a special name and a special development theory is to present the phenomenon as inevitable and to acquit Latin American governments and peoples from responsibility for what is in fact a disease of society as a whole.

Latin American trade unions are peculiarly grasping and restrictive, when not engaged in revolution. They are also occasionally brought under control, by peculiarly vicious right-wing tyrannies. The Brazilian indexation scheme, for instance, rests on tight and quite effective wage control. Chile, on the other hand, uses monetarism with effect on prices, though at a predictably disastrous cost in unemployment and output. It is highly significant that these extremely different but quite successful policies rest on military dictatorships that set the police above the law and persecute trade unions. It seems unlikely that we shall come to this in Europe. It is even just possible that our stronger and more tolerant state machines will master cost inflation by more civilized means. But the writer would prefer an intermediate prophecy: we shall neither abandon democracy nor control cost inflation, trade unions will continue to be too powerful and too greedy, and we shall find the situation hopeless but not serious. Meanwhile communist trade unions will continue in thrall to their governments, especially the central organs, and at all levels in respect of wage rates. There will be, as before, no collective bargaining—a huge advantage to any economy.

6. Suspended between the First and the Third Worlds, neither imperialist nor underdeveloped, Latin America is above all forgotten. Yet it is a large part of capitalism, and no work with 'Convergence' or 'The Future' in its title should forget it. The Latin American scene is a very grim one, and the survival of capitalism in this part of the world should make all professional prophets think very hard. If capitalism, associated as it is, rightly or wrongly, with the manifold evils of Latin American society, can survive in

---

[15] *El Día*, 6 Feb. 1920. Cf. Rama (1974, p. 128). Part of this section has been taken by me from Wiles (1976).

all countries but one, it has 'something going for it'. We know of course that external forces operate: the CIA does back right-wing governments; Cuban refugees stream out to convey an awful warning, etc., etc. But the writer is convinced, albeit inexpertly, that these matters have been secondary. Whatever its intellectuals allege, Latin America decides its own destiny, and has *chosen* capitalism, much as it has chosen coups d'état, highjackings and, of course, cost inflation. The choice may very well be wrong, but it would not have remained the valid choice for so long in so many countries without some rather genuine advantage to at least a third of the people.

7. Until about 1975 it was held, in flat defiance of Latin American experience, that perpetual cantering inflation at rates between, say, 8 and 50 per cent per annum was intolerable. Pensioners would die, the canter would become a gallop, no one would invest, everyone would delay his/her tax payments, the real rate of interest would turn negative ... Schumpeter shared this vision of gloom, saying in his addendum of December 1949:

> 'A state of perennial inflationary pressure will have, qualitatively, all the effects of weakening the social framework of society and of strengthening subversive tendencies (however carefully wrapped up in "liberal" phrases) that every competent economist is in the habit of attributing to more spectacular inflations.'

He was pretty well altogether wrong. Inflation at our level is a shame and not a catastrophe. As this is written 12 years after 1968, the real rate of interest is indeed negative, but we save a great deal and private investment is reduced only by monetarist governments' trying to stop inflation altogether. Since most things are covertly indexated, pensioners die only when striking coal-miners give them hypothermia (which is indeed more often than in the 1960s). The canter has not become a gallop.

The art of prophecy, in which Schumpeter so bravely engaged, is hardly anywhere more dangerous than here. Perpetual cantering cost-inflation, a danger dimly foreseen by many in 1949, dropped out of 'the literature' until about 1973, and out of reality until about 1968. It has been with us since that latter date. Most economists have remained within their methodological blinkers and have not even admitted its existence. This is probably because it is a political and sociological phenomenon, the remedies for which must be prescribed by others other than economists (Wiles, 1980). The present writer, for all his vehement discontent (Wiles, 1973), cannot presume to bear the burden of correcting a whole profession—he has specialized in studying the USSR and such things do not happen there!

Can the canter indefinitely not become a gallop? That is, can trade unions be kept adequately in check for ever? Can unemployment eventually stabilize at a high level? Will this appalling new defect in capitalism be accepted by those who live under it? Schumpeter implied No (previous quotation). I state, from the vast heights of 12 years' experience, that the answer is yes.

He also drew attention to the horrors of trying to stop inflation. Thus the next two sentences after the previous quotation read:

> 'But this is not all. In addition some of the standard remedies for such situations will not mitigate, and may even aggravate, the present one.'

The cures, then, are worse than the disease. I agree, and so predict that they will nowhere be seriously applied. The disease will persist, and capitalism will survive, since it is not fatal.

Inflation, then, is and will continue to be tolerated, since:

(a) the poor are indexated;
(b) the powerful (MPs, top civil servants and—effectively—top management) are indexated;
(c) capitalism is not directly, perhaps not even indirectly, to blame. Trade unions and governments are to blame, and this is not merely the truth but also how people see it;
(d) we must, as always, see our own defects within the world context. Compared with Yugoslav self-management we do not have very much inflation. Compared with the USSR we have an unquestionably superior social order, warts and all. Inflation is just one of these warts.

CONVERGENCE

How will the major competing system fare?

1. Take first the decision-making process. *Some techniques* have been imitated by Soviet-type planners: futurity discounts, rational shadow prices, etc. This imitation was indeed a form of convergence, and a big one, but it was a single step, not a trend. The planners' *purpose* has never changed: to find a *cost-effective* answer to the Politburo's orders as to the final output vector, and not a *cost-beneficial* one to the effective monetary demands of the people. The Politburo directs the planners as it always did, and nothing has changed in that. They are meant to be in charge, and they are. There is nothing remotely like this set-up or these intentions under capitalism. It is safe to predict that all this will continue, and that imitations at technical level will have no more effect in future than they did in the past.

2. Hungary will continue to be an exception, with the planners primarily deflecting market initiatives rather than imposing their own. Her fiscal and

banking controls are so tight, however, that it is permissible to say of Hungarian industry, only one thing is ever profitable, so you might as well have been commanded to do it. As this is revised (May, 1981), even Kania's Poland shows little tendency to imitate Hungary.

3. Since the Soviet-type system will not greatly change, there will continue to be suppressed inflation or at least non-market-clearing prices—it hardly matters which from the citizen's point of view, and the controversy on this may be neglected here. Capitalist prices used to clear the markets and be stable too: now they can only do the former. There really are advantages in the 'choice' that capitalism has made, since queues are very irritating indeed and waste a great deal of time in Soviet-type economies. So yet again cost-inflation is a minor, not a major, disaster in relative terms. But Soviet-type retail prices will continue to be much more stable.

4. One could continue to make indefinitely many predictions of increasing detail and doubtfulness. I shall confine myself to the *three weak sectors* of Soviet-type communism: R and D, agriculture, construction. These have in common that their product is unpredictable and their technology is variable. So they work best when decentralized, with the greatest play given to individual initiative and so to profit and the market. Consequently it is not a question of the desirability of good shadow prices (to facilitate good central allocation), but of the necessity of good market prices.

R and D is the most important of all sectors for future growth, yet capitalism will continue to generate most of the technical progress in the world, since Soviet-type R and D is extremely inefficient, and likely to remain so. This failure is ideologically disastrous; for clearly the superior mode of production is the one that develops most inventions. For all his interest in technical progress Schumpeter did not foresee this, though he would surely not have been surprised to hear it. To begin with R, its product being new knowledge or a new machine it is by definition unpredictable or, in the phrase common among specialists, a prototype. It may not be produced at all; or it may be subtly unexpected, or there may be a surprise by-product—in both cases the producer must find another use. Its cost of production cannot be planned. The specific inputs that make up this cost cannot be predicted; so they cannot be acquired through the usual channels of the command economy but must be organized ad hoc, through the very topmost channels of command or perhaps by corruption. Over and above these problems, researchers must meet foreigners at conferences and make friends with them. For this they require a quick supply of foreign technical journals, good international telephone links, and exit visas. The KGB is very obstructive about all this.

D consists in making this prototype commercially workable. In the Soviet system this means persuading the director of an ordinary enterprise to organize the new channels of supply and risk his plan-fulfilment bonus on an untried process. He resists, and even when he has finally overcome its problems the next director is almost equally recalcitrant.

Agriculture is also a sector of communist inefficiency. Here again the output cannot be predicted, even though it is of standard type. The sowing pattern is part of the command plan, but the harvest is not. There are compulsory delivery plans, which do not and are not meant to exhaust the crop. The unpredictable rest trickles away into auto-consumption or the (this time, legal) free market. With the weather a variable, neither can cost be predicted nor can the best use be made of the labour and capital available. This has to be decided suddenly, by the man on the spot.

A further and very great difficulty is that peasants are traditionally minded people, not socialists at all. They remember the forced collectivization or nationalization, they see through the claim that efficiency has grown, they spend 'too' much time on their private plots, they are very hard to discipline on large farms when the boss's back is turned, and they keep, in a very general way, the pre-revolutionary culture, including religion and the love of private property in the means of production.

In *construction*, as in R and D, each product is unique and therefore a sort of commonplace prototype. Even a repair job is of this sort; perhaps only a house in an estate built on the modular principle is not. As before, weather changes, unexpected difficulties with the ground site, the easy substitutability of materials and the nomadic character of the labour put a heavy premium on decentralized choice of technology; and of course the cost is unpredictable so that 'cost plus' is fairly usual.

In all these respects construction has not changed under socialism but, like the two other sectors named, it has been plunged into a rigid and centralized system unsuited to it.

5. One further trend should be named, very fashionable as this is written, though surely not about to become vieux jeu: the *black* or *second economy*. It is indeed a welcome change in the methodology of economics that this informal and confidence-destroying subject, so dependent on sociology and even anthropology for data, should have attracted at last so much attention. More than the erosion of the neoclassical methodology is at work, however: the volume of illegitimate production, distribution and transfers has increased in all countries. Under capitalism this coincides with the tax burden's reaching the 40 per cent mark; under Soviet-type communism with the death of Stalin or in China with the Cultural Revolution. Moreover, it seems that everywhere there is a decline in morality. All these things may be, some of them must be, coincidences. But the end of it is that the black economy's

expansion is one of the few certain elements of convergence in the near future.

The Third World has of course long set us an example of superior dishonesty; and the word 'example' is meant seriously. Schumpeter evidently fell, along with most economists, into the White Man's Trap: 'we' have nothing to learn from 'them', or the rich never imitate the poor. There is little evidence for this proposition, either in the case of cost-inflation (above) or in that of systematic pilfering. It is indeed rather the same attitude that resulted in the implication that Mozambique would not choose to be socialist before it 'successfully resolved its traditional problems' (above).

Men are cheats, then, all over the world: and there is already plenty to cheat about in a market-place or as the employee of a large firm. An important consequence is almost inevitable: in the Soviet-type black economy errors of detailed planning rank second to old-fashioned theft and tax evasion (Wiles, 1981). To be sure, as we have seen, extreme centralization is bad for building repairs, and encourages a black market in them; but so do cash payments, which are easier under capitalism. There comes a point, then, where tax rates render dishonesty inevitable, and nearly all countries in all systems passed that level long ago. Poverty, religion, traditions, family structure, even national pride,[16] play their part.

6. The previous sections have skirted an important new point, unperceived either by Schumpeter or modern prophets of Convergence. Corporatism involves the state in the economy, but all states are different. There has been little or no convergence of political arrangements in the world of corporatism-cum-parliamentary-democracy since about 1870. Even the European Economic Community has had little effect. The French still have prefects, and their Fifth Republic is more peculiar than their Fourth; the Belgians have introduced federalism for reasons wholly inoperant in other countries; and the British House of Lords remains hereditary! Outside the EEC political convergence is still smaller, of course. Thus the Americans still elect a politician to be both prime minister and king, every four years, while their northern neighbours content themselves (except in one province) with a king over the water. This contrast is not about to change. One solid case only of convergence there has been: the restoration of such constitutions in Japan, West Germany, Austria and Italy in 1945. Exactly as in the case of communism, this was achieved by military force!

---

[16] Thus the Soviet minorities undoubtedly practise corruption more than do Russians, in part as a gesture of independence. Per contra, East Germans are proud to make an imported Russian system work better than the Russians can. Or again, it does not enter into the American self-image to be incorruptible and proud of it; but the English-speaking Canadian does so see himself.

Not only are the constitution and its modus operandi special to a given country. Its churches and religions are of course highly diverse, going back a long way into history, and quite irrationally based. Its other private associations, notably its trade unions, perhaps its banks and largest corporations, are equally special. Only petty capitalism is rational in most ways, so fairly uniform. We really can, especially as economists, generalize about polypolistic markets and small owner-managed businesses. But they grow into large businesses, and this growth is the last uniformity they exhibit.

Capitalism develops into heterogeneity, as capital concentrates, trade unions grow strong and the state intervenes. Rates of growth of real income, and of the price level, differ very greatly in face of apparently similar problems and policies. Decision-making processes, the influence of one body relative to another's, and the machinery of government intervention differ greatly from one corporate-capitalist country to another. It is in the increasing (or large and stable) institutional divergence of one country from another that I see the main cause of such divergent performance.

In just the same way there is divergence of institutions under communism. While Stalin was alive this concerned only countries outside the Soviet block, such as Yugoslavia; now it affects them all. The reason is of course that few generalizations are valid for countries. Only purely economic systems operate on a universal logic, and socialism is partly political, like corporate capitalism.

FREEDOM

I define freedom here as all the normal civil liberties plus the apparently necessary substructure of parliamentary (or indeed direct) democracy, including an opposition and genuine opportunities to elect a new government. Such things are of course totally impossible under Marxism–Leninism, by the definition of that creed. If freedom were to come in the USSR it would be through revolution or an anti-Leninist, hardly even Marxist, Revisionism. We put this question aside, just as Schumpeter put it aside in his Chapter XXIII (pp. 296–302, entitled 'Democracy in the socialist order'). He was perfectly well aware that freedom is impossible under Marxism–Leninism (Chapter XXVIII/III), and discusses only freedom under 'English' socialism, or what we now call social democracy. A mature society, he says, will be able to preserve freedom under such a socialism.

Strangely, he finds it unnecessary to mention the problem of publicly-owned means of communication. If parliament allocates newsprint and 'the people' own the printing presses, how can opposition flourish? Is not the gross political bias of French radio and TV just what a reasonable man would expect? The empirical answer is unclear. Switzerland, Belgium and above all

Luxembourg also broadcast in French; and neither is newsprint allocated nor are the printing presses nationalized. Take away these two constraints and the French example is undoubtedly but a foretaste of what would happen— to France. But would it happen elsewhere? My guess is that despite the relatively clean record of parliamentary democracy in countries where it is more deeply rooted, the French road would be trodden to the bitter end. Partial nationalization of the means of communication may even increase freedom, but their total nationalization would be a total disaster. Whatever we think of this answer, the question poses itself urgently to anyone writing under the title of *CSD*, and its omission is a serious blot.

In this same chapter on freedom there is too much about efficiency. Will parliament's calendar be clogged with the details of administering the economy? It is a good question, but not a freedom question. Indeed, it only touches democracy by reducing the government's efficiency (for it is that, not the rationality of economic choice, that is on Schumpeter's mind here); and inefficiency makes for freedom! For what it is worth, his notion that parliament could and would stick to its traditional jobs while leaving the economy to the planning board strikes me as absurdly, nay culpably optimistic. It has certainly been utterly falsified.

A PESSIMISTIC CONCLUSION

Every English-speaking person has heard of the Dutch Elm Disease. Not less important but too little known, I think, is the Dutch Economist's Disease: the belief that the neoclassical economics does not mean what it says, but that the same methodology can be redirected and the capitalist market economy itself manipulated in a decent centre-left wing manner so that all will eventually converge on an optimum society, in which there are equality, stable prices, full employment, rapid growth, no pollution, optimal resource allocation, Peace on Earth and Goodwill towards Men. *Nomina sunt odiosa*; but the Dutch reader will be able to suggest several to himself. In a book of Dutch inspiration I take leave to differ strongly. The neoclassical methodology rests on premises that are often but not always demonstrably wrong: it has to be supplemented ad hoc by boring empirical research. But it has grasped one point correctly: men are bad. It errs in supposing they are bad and rational,[17] whereas I have suggested that they are bad and irrational—which may well be a better combination.

---

[17] The absurd error of the Chicago variant is to suggest that bad plus rational equals good: i.e., that extreme selfishness and a disregard for other people which verge on the psychopathic (which is the definition of homo economicus) are morally tolerable and an adequate basis for human society.

Schumpeter did not belong to the Dutch School. His own methodological position was not neoclassical at all.[18] The whole of *CSD* is a monument to pessimism and to the importance of ideology.

I agree. There are few grounds for optimism. If human communities are founded on ideology or morals (irrational?!) they will fight each other. Indeed the *smaller* such distinctions are between them the more likely it is that they will fight: so that convergence might be very dangerous. In any case, however, convergence is, beyond what has already taken place, very unlikely; and if ideology and morals do not cause fighting, greed and stupidity will suffice. The author of *CSD* would have concurred.

REFERENCES

Burnham, J. (1942) *The Managerial Revolution*. London.

Modigliani, F. & Brumberg, R. (1954). In *Post-Keynesian Economics* (Ed.) Kurihara, K.K.

Rama, C. (1974). *Historia Social del Pueblo Uruguayo*. Montevideo.

Schumpeter, J.A. (1959) *History of Economic Analysis*. Oxford: Oxford University Press.

Sombart, W. (1911). *Die Juden und das Wirtschafitsleben*. Leipzig.

Weber, M. (1904/5). In *Archiv für Sozialwissenschaft und Sozialpolitik*. Cf. Weber, M., *The Protestant Ethic and the Spirit of Capitalism*, translated (1958) by Parsons, T. New York.

Wiles, P. (1973) In *Economic Journal*. June.

Wiles, P. (1975/6) In *Annales d'Economie Politique*. Paris.

Wiles, P. (1972) In *History and Theory*, 1.

Wiles, P. (1979/80) In *Journal of Post-Keynesian Economics*. Winter.

Wiles, P. (1981) *Die Parallelwirtschaft*. Cologne: B.I.O.S.

---

[18] Though he was most reluctant to admit this, or to admit any element of true *Methodenstreit* into his *History of Economic Analysis* (cf. Wiles, 1980).

Chapter Nine

Capitalism, Socialism and Democracy: the 'Vision' and the 'Theories'

HERBERT K. ZASSENHAUS

Reading this large book (hereinafter quoted from the fifth edition, 1976, as *CSD*) again after some 40 years—large as well by subject matter as by physical volume—shows the passage of time, or perhaps the passage of the reader through time, much the same thing. Read when it first appeared, it resisted the attempt to identify it with any familiar orthodoxy. It seemed to be on both sides of too many issues; it refused, irritatingly, neat rubrication into the pigeon-holes that often serve as the initiates' devices of intellectual self-orientation. Now, as perhaps it should have been then, this is rather one of its attractions.

A conservative admires the Marxian 'vision'. He deplores (or at least admonishes reflection on) the passing of the 'capitalist civilization', while convinced of the workability of a socialist centrally-planned economy. Poignantly describing the autocratic terror of the Soviet system, he declares socialism and democracy perfectly compatible. The pure theorist who wrote and lectured brilliantly in obvious admiration of what was then a succession of analytical and econometric discoveries condemns them all to relative irrelevance before what he describes as the real task of socio-economic analysis—explaining, out of their own dynamic, the evolution of such systems as capitalist economic development ('development' then meant something less pat, and 'dynamic' something less limited, than they do now). The fascination with the 'entrepreneur' goes side by side with undisguised contempt

170

for the 'bourgeois'. The cultural sociologist who plans a book on the 'Ideen-seele des Sozialismus' yet produces the most realist and least ideology-ridden analysis of democracy and imperialism. It was all a little hard to take in the 1930s and 40s, and though we did not mind at all participating in one of Schumpeter's favourite sports, to *épater le bourgeois*, he seemed to run the danger to épater everybody else as well.

Today, all this and much more has retained its fascination and lost much of its irritation. To be sure, the book remains a colossal *tour de force*, and much of it—Schumpeter would probably not have minded calling this its 'vision' (as against its 'theories')—remains economic sociology over-stretched and at times overdrawn. But, even though one must realize the near impossibility of mastering, with one universal theory, the enormous range of the book's objectives, one can find the realistic eclecticism in many of its details a merciful virtue. Many are the analytical essays, the theoretical mini-monographs, the historical *aperçus* that remain unsurpassed; or so is my impression now.

Perhaps this is because the passage of time has also meant the passage of what used to be the continental (European) philosophistics where every judgement had to be a matter of principle. Progress in the social sciences seems to lie, more modestly, in the reaching of limited objectives. On the other hand, it is perhaps because there has more recently been a surfeit of jejune attempts—and not only from 'those intellectual denizens of our newspaper world to whom the gods seem to have granted the gift of eternal youth' (*CSD*, p. 47)—to diagnose the 'limits of capitalism' or the 'cultural contradictions of capitalism', based on passing, however spectacular, hap-penings of the 1960s and 70s. Schumpeter's book, in all its complexity, stands head and shoulders above such efforts in the ephemeral, if only because of its basic combination of wide historical knowledge and rigorous economics.

It is worth a few lines to revert to the Schumpeterian distinction between 'vision' and 'theory'. He employs it, rather benevolently, in his evaluation of the Marxian system (*CSD*, Part I).[1] With often cutting criticism that a gen-erous general critique does not disguise, he rejects Marx's 'theories' (e.g.,

---

[1] But also in his obituary article on Keynes (1946): 'The social vision', he says of Keynes, 'first revealed in the *Economic Consequences of the Peace*, the vision of an economic process in which investment opportunity flags and savings habits nevertheless persist, is theoretically implemented in the *General Theory*' . . . and . . . 'simplicity of vision is in part a matter of genius and in part a matter of willingness to pay the price in terms of the factors that have to be left out of the picture.'

The passage shows, incidentally, that Schumpeter could not explain to himself Keynes's savings-investment doctrine other than by associating it with that of the 'Vanishing Investment Opportunity' of really other origin. See below.

the mechanics of Marxian economics of value and accumulation, of the 'immiseration' of the 'proletariat', but also his theory of social classes) and the Hegelian convolutions derived from them; but he praises the 'vision': 'Through all that is faulty or even unscientific in his analysis runs a fundamental idea that is neither—the idea of a theory, not merely of an indefinite number of disjointed individual patterns or of the logic of economic quantities in general, but of the actual sequence of these patterns of the economic process as it goes on, under its own steam, in historic time, producing at every instant that state which will of itself determine the next one' (*CSD*, p. 43). This vision of 'the economic theory of the future' (*ibid.*) is the fulcrum of Schumpeter's admiration of Marx.[2] And to this vision Schumpeter's book is to be a contribution. In his own summary: 'The capitalist process not only destroys its own institutional framework, but it also creates the conditions for another'. 'With every peg from under the capitalist structure vanishes an impossibility of the socialist plan. In both these respects, Marx was right.' 'In the end, there is not so much difference as one might think between saying that the decay of capitalism is due to its success and saying that it is due to its failure' (*CSD*, p. 162).

This is the 'vision', and I believe it is mistaken—as was Marx's. But for very different reasons. The 'theories' which are offered to support it—so utterly unacceptable with Marx that not a single one of his 'visions' came true—are far superior, or at least a good many of them are. Thus, the principal lines of the Schumpeterian analysis of the economic mechanism of capitalist economic development would seem to withstand critical review well enough, as do some of the consequences he draws from them. And the bulk of the detail, as set out in his *Business Cycles* (1939), is probably far more resistant to serious critique than its fate in professional appraisal has indicated; a full appreciation of that impressive analysis is, even after so many years, still to come. Again, many of the elements of Schumpeter's sociological analysis of capitalism, socialism and democracy remain remarkable for their insight and at the very least for the analytical stimuli they provide: Schumpeter's doctrine of 'creative destruction', of the function of monopolistic market forms, his rejection of the (largely post-Marx) Marxian doctrine of capitalist imperialism, the focus of the socialist debate not on the (theoretical) possibility of a planned economy but on the wider social requirements and consequences of a socialist order, the thesis of the 'supporting strata' of

---

[2]Schumpeter wrote practically no biographical essay—from that on Böhm-Bawerk (1914) to that on Keynes (see footnote 1) (1948)—and not excluding so surprising a subject of comparison as Gustav von Schmoller, without using Marx's structure as the example, though not always as the model, by which to illustrate his biographical encomia. See J.A. Schumpeter, *Ten Great Economists* (1951) and 'Gustav von Schmoller und die Probleme von heute' (1926).

capitalism and of democracy, and altogether the emphasis on historical explanations. The 'theories' are views and suggestions which the analyst neglects at his cost. Thus, one finds—quite the opposite to what Schumpeter found in Marx—a wealth of penetrating and successful 'theories' in Schumpeter, even though one cannot befriend the 'vision'.

And there is one more reason to prefer Schumpeter to Marx—'theories' *and* 'vision'. Visions tend dangerously towards dogma, even activist dogma, and dogmas spawn schools. Schumpeter abhorred schools and did not form one. We have therefore mercifully been spared the spectacle of the exegeses of the disciples. The horizon of his ideas is too wide to lack tolerance, and the figures and colours, though not always free from dissonance, of that intellectual carpet are far too polyglot and brilliant to be cut into the chasubles of a priesthood.

What follows is offered as ideas, very briefly indicated, on re-reading the book, both its economics and its sociology, both its 'vision' and its 'theories'.

Consider, first, Schumpeter's analysis of capitalism, its nature and its development.

The roots of Schumpeterian economics can perhaps be traced to his earliest work better than those of his socio-cultural vision. Astonishingly early in his life he had studied and made thoroughly his own the Walras–Pareto system, and then, as one of the first university teachers to do so on the continent, propagated it. His admiration for it never ceased, even after the decisive advances beyond it in the work of J.R. Hicks and Paul A. Samuelson in the 1930s and 40s. Almost as early, however—in fact after his contact with J.B. Clark during his first visit to the United States[3]—he had become aware of its static (in the old sense) limitations. Its basic assumptions did not permit (and were not designed to) the building upon it alone of a dynamic (again, in the old sense) theory of capitalist development. The *Theory of Economic Development* (1912), elaborated but not basically changed in the next 25 years, was Schumpeter's grand proposal to address these shortcomings, and his *Business Cycles* was his equally large-scale attempt to underpin his 'dynamic' analysis with statistical and historical material. It reappears, if only in summary, in *Capitalism, Socialism and Democracy*.

The core ideas are well known. Economic 'innovations' whose carrier is the 'entrepreneur' break the static Walras–Pareto ('circular flow') equilibrium. Combined with their financing from sources outside static savings (i.e., from 'created credit') they set in motion the process of capitalist economic development. Since innovations occur in waves, this process

---

[3] See the long footnote (2) pp. 91–92, in *Theories der wirtschaftlichen Entwicklung* (1926).

inevitably takes the statistical shape of cyclical movements of the principal economic aggregates of various amplitudes—'Kitchins', 'Juglars' and 'Kondratieffs'—along a secular rising trend: '2 per cent capitalism' for the last Kondratieff before the First World War, for instance. The detail is set out with great care by the marshalling of an astonishing volume of detailed historical erudition in *Business Cycles*, whose 'Historical Outline' chapters belong to the most fascinating pieces of *histoire raisonnée* written anywhere. Into this we cannot enter here; it must suffice to make only two notes to it. First, this theoretical structure would seem to be fully compatible with, and in part still much ahead of, the bulk of much work that has since been done in this field. In particular, the fitting of the Walras–Pareto 'static' system into 'dynamic' analysis of historical phenomena, problems and systems would seem to retain its value as an analytical device.

Second, all of Schumpeter's work, not only on cycle theory but down to his analyses of current economic developments—from the 'Tax State' article (1918) to his contributions to economic journals, through his contributions to periodicals such as the *Deutsche Volkswirt* in the 1920s and 30s, to the book here under discussion—has been consistently based on this analytical scheme. It is a structure which made it very difficult for him to feel comfortable with post-Marshallian post-Wicksellian analysis, and he could only with some effort find anything but fault with Keynes's *General Theory* and with much of aggregative economics that followed the 1930s. This is apparent from Chapter XXVIII of *CSD* ('The Consequences of the Second World War'), added to the third and later editions of the book, and there is no indication that Keynes and all his works (and that of the Keynesians) were meant to be exempt from the motto of that chapter, 'mundus regitur parva sapientia'; a regrettable failure of reciprocal understanding, costly to economics and much commented on.

As for the particulars, in *Business Cycles* we find the most concentrated definition of capitalism: 'Capitalism', Schumpeter says in Volume I, p. 223, 'is that form of private property economy in which innovations are carried out by means of borrowed money, which in general, though not by logical necessity, implies credit creation' (see also *CSD*, p. 167). And 'the individuals who carry out [innovations] we call entrepreneurs' (*ibid*, p. 102). This purely economic definition was much amplified in *CSD*, in a manner which had already been indicated in the third section of Chapter 2 of the *Theory of Economic Development*. But before we consider the amplification, it is worth examining two or three by-products of the business cycle analysis proper which do figure prominently in the book here at issue and remain of validity and considerable relevance.

Ever since the elaboration in the 1930s—its discovery is of course very much older—of the analysis of imperfect or monopolistic competition as market forms rather more realistic than that of perfect competition, anti-monopoly (anti-trust, etc.) policies seized on the new inventions for respectable support from modern economic theory. Monopolistic (oligopolistic) pricing as practised by large enterprises with large market shares was judged predatory of consumers, detrimental of efficiency, distorting income distribution, and thus to reduce the public welfare. Schumpeter is far from denying his praise to the modifications which these analyses made to the 'classical' or to what he calls the post-classical 'Marshall–Wicksell' economics. The theory of monopolistic competition, he says, was 'one of the major contributions to postwar [i.e., to post-First-World War] economics' (CSD, p. 79). But for him, the trade-off faced by public policy-makers who confront this phenomenon is not—as it has been from at least Adam Smith to Arthur Okun—between efficiency and equity in a given static economy but between (static) efficiency at a point (or a short run) of time and efficiency á la longue of the dynamically evolving capitalist process. 'The introduction of new methods of production and new commodities is hardly conceivable with perfect—and perfectly prompt—competition from the start. And this means that the bulk of what we call economic progress is incompatible with it' (CSD, p. 105). An innovation requires initial protection, but its powerful consequences in the course of progress will wipe out what adverse effects in the initial position there might have been; '. . . perfect competition is and has always been temporarily suspended when anything new is being introduced' (ibid.). Far from being an argument against, say, the deregulation of railroads and of airlines, this is in fact an argument in its favour. And so, in an appropriate cost–benefit analysis of 'big business' regulation, it is in other cases. 'What we have got to accept is that it [the large-scale unit of control] has come to be the most powerful engine of that progress and in particular of the long-run expansion of total output not only in spite of but to a considerable extent through, this strategy which looks so restrictive when viewed in the individual case and from the individual point of time. In this respect, perfect competition is not only impossible but inferior, and has no title to being set up as a model of ideal efficiency' (CSD, p. 106). Perhaps this is a rather dated stricture, but it does no harm at all to recall it.

The reason why Schumpeter felt it to be so important to lay so much stress on these conclusions is that 'capitalism is by nature a form or method of economic change and not only never is but never can be stationary' (CSD, p. 82). However valuable the (static) analysis of any particular part of the capitalist process, such as that of the textbook theory of the individual firm under various market forms, may be, it alone does not yield a judgement of that process. 'Every piece of business strategy acquires its true significance only against the background of that process and within the situation created by it. It must be seen in its role in the perennial gale of creative destruction' (*CSD*, pp. 83–84). The competition between firms and industries which produces this 'creative destruction' is the competition that really matters.

The thesis of creative destruction is, then, another element of Schumpeter's economic analysis of the capitalist order which it is worth recalling now. Innovations that are successful in the competition between new processes and products and old, and that means, at least for the last hundred years of capitalist development, successful monopolistic competition, must replace and destroy old processes and products, even though aged plant may subsist on (Marshallian) quasi-rent. It is this phenomenon of creative destruction that puts the evaluation of the employment and exploitation of monopolistic positions on a basis that is fundamentally different from the textbook theory which began with the work of Joan Robinson and E.S. Chamberlin. These theoretical advances, however meritorious in themselves, are misapplied in condemning the growth of large-scale enterprises in the successful capitalist development process of the last century. Delayed destruction of antiquated plant, or protection of it from the fate of retiring into quasi-rent existence, can be nearly fatal for industries and regions, as may be seen from the examples of the American steel and automobile industries or from the long semi-recession of Massachusetts textile areas before high-technology industries took over. The argument that the preservation of bankrupt enterprises (e.g., collecting them into the public sector à l'anglaise) prevents unemployment Schumpeter meets with the convincing thesis that nothing stimulates employment so much as the virulent development through the 'gales of creative destruction'.

No simple policy rules follow. In particular, propositions are not necessarily reversible: that successful capitalism implies creative destruction does not mean that the destruction of enterprises creates successful capitalism; and that this latter is accompanied by the (at least temporary) exploitation of monopolistic competition does not mean that the establishment of monopolistic positions creates successful capitalism. We cannot here follow Schumpeter's invitation (*CSD*, p. 99) to speculate on the 'psychology of political discussion' which leads to the misapplication of well-established economic theories. It may just be mentioned that the two cases here at issue are examples of political psychology of the kind that includes also the misapplication of Keynesian economics to less-developed countries or to stagflation (two situations which are surprisingly similar to each other). One is tempted to recall the celebrated passage in the *General Theory* about the 'madmen in authority, who hear voices in the air ... distilling their frenzy from some academic scribbler of a few years back', and the 'practical men, who believe themselves to be quite exempt from any intellectual influences', but 'are usually the slaves of some defunct economist' (*General Theory*, p. 383).

The object of a third element of Schumpeter's exposition of the economics of capitalist development, his combat against the theories of the Vanishing Investment Opportunity as a reason of capitalist decline, has hardly survived the publishing date of the book. He was of course totally right in rejecting this thesis, a predecessor of many equally misconstructed attempts to show the limits of capitalist development. And he goes to considerable length in doing so (*CSD*, Chapter X, pp. 111–120). It would need no further re-examination, were it not for a point which deserves some attention. It appears that Schumpeter's appreciation of Keynesian economics was unnecessarily lowered by the propagation of the investment doctrine in question, especially by some important American Keynesians. It has already been mentioned above that Keynesian fears of over-saving were understood by Schumpeter as rooting in this doctrine. And this misunderstanding, among others, may be seen in *Capitalism, Socialism and Democracy* to have been a major reason for Schumpeter's differences with Keynes. There are many references in the economic literature of the past 30 years registering astonishment and regret at the lack of understanding between the two and at the fact that Schumpeter sadly failed to gauge what would now seem to have been the true perspectives of the 'Keynesian revolution' (or, for that matter, of the New Deal) and other intellectual and political phenomena that in fact protected and perhaps critically supported the 'capitalist order' rather than demolishing it. But perhaps one should be careful lest one exaggerate the differences between great contemporaries. Later in the book, when discussing the application of Keynes's views to fiscal policy, Schumpeter does concede his agreement with 'deficit financing' 'whenever there is a danger, either from causes inherent in the business cycle mechanism or from any other, of a "downward cumulative process"' (*CSD*, p. 397), even though he qualifies that 'the true objection is not against income-generating government expenditure in emergencies once they have arisen, but to policies that create the emergencies in which such expenditure imposes itself' (*CSD*, pp. 397–398). This indeed opens a door through which many economists have passed. Perhaps we may speculate that, had Schumpeter lived to observe economic developments during the generation following the appearance of his last book, he would not have underestimated the remarkable adaptability of capitalism as much as he seemed to do in that book.

There remains for comment a statistical matter, in retrospect of some interest. Schumpeter takes as the statistical measure of success of the capitalist economy the average annual increase in 'real available output' (*CSD*, p. 64) (i.e., total output less a correction for something close to capital goods replacement) for 1870 to 1930. This works out at some 2 per cent, the rate for industrial output alone being considerably larger. This estimate—rough but not inadequate for the purpose—is not out of line with the more recent, improved ones by Sir Arthur Lewis (1978). Schumpeter accepts a continuing '2 per cent capitalism' as a creditable performance for the future. Much of his then following discussion of 'plausible capitalism' of the future considers a situation where the 1870 to 1930 performance is repeated as a result of the continuance of the capitalist system of selection of successful private entrepreneurs and despite the monopolistic market forms characteristic of it, in the manner summarized further above, and despite what social costs may be incurred by such a continuance. This discussion leads him to a conclusion which would seem capable of rather wider application than he concedes to it. It is worth quoting: 'The indictment stands that in the past—say, roughly, to the end of the nineteenth century—the capitalist order was not only unwilling but also quite incapable of guaranteeing . . .' that 'the private life of the unemployed [was] not seriously affected by their unemployment.' 'But since it will be able to do so if it keeps up its past performance for another half century this indictment would in that case enter the limbo filled by the sorry specters of child labor and sixteen-hour working days and five persons living in one room, which it is quite proper to emphasize when we are talking about the past social cost of capitalist achievement but which are not necessarily relevant to the balance of alternatives for the future' (*CSD*, p. 70) i.e., after 1946. Would not this 'limbo' by now have room also for other social costs of further capitalist progress since, such as unacceptable income inequalities, pollution of all sorts, inadequate health, poor and aged care? In fact, Schumpeter concedes almost as much on the next page. And had he lived to witness the explosion of output in the 25 years after his book was published, his conclusion would almost surely have been strengthened and extended. In fact, would not that 'limbo' have room even for some of the phenomena he adduces later in the book as the causes of capitalist self-destruction?

It remains unfortunately mere speculation to guess Schumpeter's reaction to the astonishing statistics presented (e.g., by David Moravetz, 1977). The growth rate of *per capita* gross national product (GNP) for the developed countries (OEEC members, except Greece, Portugal, Spain and Turkey) is there (p. 13) shown to have been a full 3.2 per cent per annum. OEEC population grew in these years by about 1 per cent p.a. This was, thus, a period of 4 per cent capitalism, while at the same time the resources were made available to drive the development of the less-developed world (excluding China) upwards by 3 per cent p.a. If GNP figures show the success of capitalism, it had never been more successful; this result could not have left Schumpeter's imagination untouched.

Schumpeter's contribution to the 'theory of the future for which we are slowly and laboriously accumulating stones and mortar, statistical facts and functional equations' (*CSD*, p. 43) carries him far beyond economics. 'Innovations' and the 'entrepreneur' which had, in his hands, become powerful levers to break out of the statics of the Walras-Pareto system became the fulcrum for an attempt to draw a large canvas setting out the forces that shaped Western culture. It leads him to examine 'the cultural complement of the capitalist economy . . . its socio-psychological *superstructure*, if we wish to speak the Marxian language . . . the mentality that is characteristic of capitalist society and in particular the bourgeois class' (*CSD*, p. 121). His view of the growth and meaning of capitalism is summed up in his last public address ('The March into Socialism', 1949): 'Capitalism . . . means a scheme of values, an attitude towards life, a civilization of inequality and of the family fortune' (*CSD*, p. 425). In Chapter XI of the book this broad claim is laid out in some detail, though in 'desperate brevity'. The three following chapters contain the vision of the rise and decline of capitalism. In this exposition a variety of 'theories', more or less self-contained analyses, is offered whose analytical content seems to me more durable than that of the vision, as a re-reading would show.

The first fundamental article of Schumpeter's vision is this: 'Not only the modern mechanized plant and the volume of the output that pours forth from it, not only modern technology and economic organization, but all the features and achievements of modern civilization are, directly or indirectly, the product of the capitalist process. They must be included in any balance sheet of it and in any verdict about its deeds and misdeeds' (*CSD*, p. 125). The second article is that '. . . there is inherent in the capitalist system a tendency towards self-destruction which, in its earlier stages, may well assert itself in the form of a tendency toward retardation of progress' (*CSD*, p. 162). No estimate is offered when, in historical time, these tendencies will become visible, though of the arrival of the latter of the two, the decline, Schumpeter was, at the time of his writing, sure enough. Between these two articles of his vision lies the chain of his interpretations on which we may focus the further re-reading of his book.

In an almost Marxian 'standing upon its head', this time not of Hegelian, but of Max Weberian doctrine, and after some observations on the anthropology of primitive, pre-capitalist society, he begins by relating economic behavioural patterns as the prime causal element to 'rational attitudes' and 'individualism'. 'I have no hesitation in saying that all logic is derived from the pattern of economic decision . . . that the economic pattern is the matrix of logic' (*CSD*, pp. 122–123). 'The inexorable definiteness, the quantitative character that distinguishes the economic from other spheres of human action' (*CSD*, p. 123) engenders the 'rational habit'. 'Capitalism develops rationality', more in particular via its exaltation of the 'money unit' as embodied in the 'towering monument' of the invention of double-entry bookkeeping (*ibid.*). In a flight so rapid and high that it reduces the reader's supply of historical oxygen, we are led to: 'the rugged individualism of Galileo was the individualism of the rising capitalist class' (*CSD*, p. 124), and introduced to the early 'entrepreneurs'—'the type immortalized by such men as Vinci, Alberti, Cellini, even Dürer' (*ibid.*), entrepreneurs who a little later became businessmen proper: Jacob Fugger, Agostino Chigi. But beyond this, the growth of 'rational science' (*CSD*, p. 123), 'modern medicine and hygiene' are presented as 'byproducts of the capitalist process just as modern education' (*CSD*, p. 124). And 'there is the capitalist art and the capitalist style of life': Giotto–Masaccio–Vinci–Michelangelo–Greco, and Cézanne, Van Gogh, Picasso and Matisse' (*CSD*, p. 126), and 'the capitalist novel' (e.g., Goncourt). And finally, 'whatever democracy there was, outside of peasant communities, developed historically in the wake of both modern and ancient capitalism' (*CSD*, p. 126).

I have neither the competence nor the space here to examine the detail of this breathtaking sweep of ideas. Surely, however, this is economic interpretation of history with a vengeance, though considerably refined from the Marxian variety. As such, it is open to the objection of confusing perhaps necessary with sufficient conditions of cultural development, and to the accusation of neglect of all the many serious problems of the growth and interaction of ideas which have always confronted historical investigation. It is one thing to say that the necessity to solve economic problems stimulated the exercise of man's power of logical thinking; it is quite another to say that the development of man's logical thinking depends in any causal sense on his economic situation. The difference cannot really be dissimulated by a phrase such as 'matrix'. Geometry owes its name to the stimulus it received from the need of measuring areas of land, but it would be nothing short of disingenuous to declare agriculture or irrigation the 'matrix' of the Euclidian system. Nor would it be less deplorable to explain the decay of Kantian philosophy in the 19th century by the commercialization and industrialization of Europe, or by the autocratic corruption of the Prussian civil service—although such things have of course been done. The implied criticism is neither easy to make nor painless vis-à-vis an author of undeniable erudition. But it does appear that the seemingly wholesale inversion of cause and effect indefensibly overloads the cost–benefit analysis of capitalism on the benefit side. To be sure, more restrained passages such as that the Renaissance created 'the social space for a new class that stood upon industrial achievement in the economic field' (*CSD*, p. 124) re-fasten the reader's seatbelt; but there is no doubt about Schumpeter's meaning. What has always been a part of the book that strained credulity does no less so on being reread.

It is not that Schumpeter's theses re-emphasize what has been treated and established in the many historical and sociological investigations before and after Max Weber: that there have been innumerable and significant inter-actions between Western intellectual and cultural developments from the late Middle Ages through the 18th century, that from the Italian Renaissance through the French Revolution the crescendo of intellectual, cultural and social individualism charged the capitalist mentality and society that are represented by the Schumpeterian 'entrepreneur', while concurrently the rapid economic growth established the material basis for that crescendo. It is the claim that the 'capitalist order' is the *cause* and the individualist art, science and society are the *effect*, which is quite unacceptable, or even the claim that outside capitalism these developments would be, or would have been impossible. Of course, it would be correct, but also trite, to say that if one were to take one major element out of the history of the last 500 to 600 years that history would not have happened. It would also be correct, but equally unenlightening, to say that without capitalism the future would not con-tinue the pattern of the past, however glorious or otherwise that has been.

That Schumpeter meant to say very much more than this is surprising, in particular in view of the characteristics and motivations which he attributes to the 'entrepreneur', both in the book under review and in the *Theory of Economic Development*: 'leadership', the ability to break through traditional patterns, utter rationality and utilitarianism ('the brain that was first in a pos-ition and had cause to bring ideals and beefsteak on a common denomi-nator'—Chapter 2 of *Theory of Economic Development*), the 'pathbreaker of modern man', the 'vehicle of reorganization of economic life' (*ibid.*), the will to win (the game that is 'more like poker than roulette'), the joy of creating, the urge for power and the ascetic businessman. If, indeed, all these elements of character can be found in one and the same type of man, can there be any doubt that their mentality and motivation grew on the soil that had been pre-pared during a long intellectual history which was not of their creation? Capitalism and capitalists are more its product and less its cause. It remains difficult, I am afraid, even after a benign re-reading of his book, to defend Schumpeter against the accusation of introducing, in the shape of the 'entre-preneur', a social miracle in the precise sense of the word: an event beyond the laws of nature and society. This does not by any means imply that he attempted a glorification of the entrepreneur, against which accusation he rightly defended himself indignantly. His admiration for the 'bourgeoisie' was too far from total. But it does mean the quite unnecessary introduction into an otherwise most productive hypothesis of a social mysticism.

During the highly condensed run through his sociologico-economic inter-pretation of the history of capitalism Schumpeter dwells, equally briefly, on a subject to which he had made a major contribution some 30 years before the publication of *Capitalism, Socialism and Democracy*: his analysis of imperialism, relevant here because of its connection with his analysis of capitalism. It deserves being singled out for comment because it represents, it seems to me, one of Schumpeter's lasting contributions to sociology, remarkable when it was first propounded (1919) and if anything even more relevant now. It is sharply different from the tortured Marxian—post-Marx—interpretation, and of a scientific quality equal to the best of Max Weber's work. It focuses on a sharp definition of the phenomenon, setting it apart from other types of national politico-military expansion which are still often confused with it: 'Imperialism is the disposition of a state to objectless violent expansion without definable limits' in his earlier work ('Zur Soziologie der Imperialismen', 1919). This definition very appropriately, by emphasizing the absence of limited objectives, excludes the economic interpretation which continues to be used with an abandon that dulls fruitful analysis. Schumpeter had already shown, in his earlier article, that the definition properly separates out the characteristic historical cases from the ancient Assyrian through the Arab case and that of the expansion of the Salic Franks to Louis XIV and Catherine the Great. It would equally fit certain phases of national-socialist and soviet expansion. In particular, he emphasizes the pseudo-religious impulses that are among the major motives of typical imperialists and gives their expansionist lunges their peculiar strength. What interests here—this is not the place for a more detailed discussion—is his conclusion: a review of the historical facts shows that far from being something like 'the last stage of capitalism', imperialism is a thoroughly non-capitalist phenomenon. What types of it are found to have been contemporaneous with capitalist societies are as a rule the activities of atavistic remnants of pre-capitalist groups or societies, or the recrudescences of non- or anti-capitalist religio-social phenomena, be they called (pseudo-)religious, nationalist, national-socialist, fascist or quasi-socialist 'liberation' movements, or mixtures of some or all of these. 'The industrial and commercial bourgeoisie is fundamentally pacifist' (*CSD*, p. 128), interpretations of, to name but one, Paul M. Sweezy (1942 and 1946), among many neo-Marxist versions to the contrary notwithstanding.

This does not mean that members of the capitalist societies (or, for that matter, of others) do not benefit from imperialist ventures, and therefore acquire an interest in them and even support them. But 'the more completely capitalist the structure and attitude of a nation, the more pacifist—and the more prone to count the costs of war—we observe it to be' (*CSD*, pp. 128–129). It also does not mean that the bourgeois class, to use Schumpeter's term, betrays a disinclination to exercise political influence or influence on foreign policy in particular; clearly this has not been the case. But an economic interpretation of foreign policy has always turned out to be a much more complicated enterprise than non- or anti-capitalist writers frequently think. It would, in this context, be well to heed Schumpeter's advice not to overestimate the influence of capitalists on aggressive foreign policy—e.g., that of the houses of Fugger and Chigi on the policies of Charles V and of Pope Leo X—or, to cite a fascinating more recent example, that of the house of Bleichröder on Bismarck's (see Fritz Stern, 1977). As mentioned, this 'theory' was much more fully developed in Schumpeter's imperialisms article which contains a splendid *histoire raisonnée* of the British case of the second half of the last century, much worth re-reading after some 60 years.

The present practical relevance of this analysis is that its most popular antagonist, the neo-Marxian interpretation, leads to a dangerous misdiagnosis which in turn tends to condemn to failure anti-imperialist policies designed on it as a basis. The international events preceding the 1939–45 war should still be close enough to demonstrate this. In particular, this misinterpretation of the religious—or better, the religionist (the deification of non-religious objects)—roots of imperialism leads to a nearly fatal underestimation of its strength, which has much to do with Western reactions of bewilderment in the face of 'erratic' actions of political expansion. Specifically, economic counter-measures will almost certainly miss their aim totally. This applies also to cases in the less-developed countries: economic development does not by itself produce non-aggression. Schumpeter's analysis provides the basis for avoiding this mistake, though his expectation (in his 1919 essay) that further progress of the 'capitalist order' could cut the ground from under imperialist recrudescences turned out to be too optimistic. Twenty years later he was far less sanguine.

This element in Schumpeter's interpretation of capitalism—a 'theory' in his sense—is perhaps, again, dated. But popularity need not increase with age, and it is well worth a careful re-reading.

So much, however limited it is, for Schumpeter's diagnosis of the rise and nature of capitalism. How, then, does he see the self-destruction of the 'capitalist order'?

From all appearances, the later 1970s and the beginning of the 1980s seem to be a historical time propitious to visions of breakdown, or at least of crisis, of the socio-economic order. Partly as a belated reaction to the events of the 1960s, the atmosphere is again dense with diagnoses, and of efforts to explain them, of 'crisis', 'limits', 'contradictions' of capitalism, of the 'welfare state', of 'growth', of rationalism and democracy, of something like despair in effective social and economic policy—in short, of many of the phenomena which Schumpeter associates with the later stages of the 'capitalist order'. And Schumpeter's vision seems to enjoy a modest revival of favour, to wit e.g. Professor Tibor Scitovsky's Ely Lecture at the 1979 annual meeting of the American Economic Association, which felt impelled to devote considerable programme space to these various crises. It is perhaps well to remember—as has been frequently observed, not least by Schumpeter himself—that, like bouts of religious revivalism, such *pompes funèbres* for the social order are a cyclical phenomenon not unrelated to economic cycles, as for example after 1873, 1929, and again after the cessation of the rapid expansion of 1950 to 1975. As their human objects, they 'have their exits and their entrances', that is, their own Kondratieffs, though some such minor cycles as the Juglars and Kitchins as in the 1960s can also be observed.

It is wise, therefore, to heed Professor Albert O. Hirschmann's (1979) advice to beware of what he calls, with something less than his customary elegance, the 'structuralist (or fundamentalist) fallacy': not all defects, however painful and persistent, are defects of basic structure. It is, however, a mark of distinction that Schumpeter's vision reaches beyond these cyclical catastrophes; it is meant to be the final one, however gradual. It is true that, as I have indicated above, the spectacular economic development during the generation after 1950 might well have moderated Schumpeter's views, had he lived to experience it, but since they are based on a much larger historical sweep of events than the 1930s, this is doubtful.

His view is that the same powerful force of capitalist rationalism that turned the late middle ages into the increasingly bourgeois world where the 'entrepreneur' eclipsed lords, princes and bishops will in the end erode itself: 'in breaking down the precapitalist framework of society, capitalism . . . broke not only barriers that impeded its progress but also the flying buttresses that prevented its collapse' (*CSD*, p. 139). The breakdown, then, does not occur for economic reasons. The capitalist economy is (dynamically) cyclical; this explains booms and depressions, and severe ones when the nadirs of long- and short-term cycles coincide. But it does not by itself break down as long as the 'framework' subsists. Here lies one of Schumpeter's sharp differences with Marx. This interpretation rests on three principal developments.

1. The rise of large-scale corporations, however instrumental in the capitalist progress, depersonalizes and automatizes what had initially been the functions of the 'entrepreneur': 'innovation is being reduced to routine' (*CSD*, p. 132), 'so many things can be strictly calculated that had of old to be visualized in a flash of genius' (*ibid.*); 'rationalized and specialized office work will eventually blot out personality; the calculable result, the "vision"' (*CSD*, p. 133). The executives of fully developed large-scale enterprises, 'the perfectly bureaucratized great industrial unit' (*CSD*, p. 134), will in the end become indistinguishable from the managers of departments of the socialist ministry of production. The 'entrepreneur' is ousted and the bourgeoisie expropriated into helpless stockholders, the strong forces of competition from innova-

tion, the 'gales of creative destruction', become exhausted. 'The true pacemakers of socialism were not the intellectuals or the agitators who preached it, but the Vanderbilts, Carnegies and Rockefellers' (*ibid.*). In the final result Schumpeter's vision ends, however different on the way there, indistinguishable from Marx's.

Bourgeois rationalism, on the strength of which the 'entrepreneur' defeated his predecessors as the *classe dirigente*, in the end demolishes its own hero. The teachings of the intellectuals and the doings of the capitalists themselves are the instruments of this destruction. Without the support of the 'flying buttresses' of pre-capitalist remnants, the bourgeois, essentially passive, pacifist and docile, succumbs. '[A] genius in the business office may be, and often is, utterly unable to say boo to a goose—both in the drawing room and on the platform' (*CSD*, p. 138). He cannot rule, 'there is surely no trace of any mystic glamor about [the industrialist and the merchant] which is what counts in the ruling of men. The stock exchange is a poor substitute for the Holy Grail' (*CSD*, p. 139). He is defenceless as the former ruling classes that served as the protectors of the 'capitalist order' join the bourgeoisie and its passivity and depersonalization.

This is a dramatic scenario and, at first sight almost despite itself, an appealing one. But this construction raises many questions. To begin with, this strand of the interpretation would seem to confirm a criticism made earlier: if indeed the Schumpeterian 'entrepreneur' is a social miracle, it would not be surprising—could this social type really exist—that this mystique fell victim to advancing rationalism, especially if this complex of ideas is not really his creation. Since the executor is in reality no such entity, however, he could also be more resistant to the rationalist attack. The latterday capitalist manager, or managing team, is in fact no apparatchik of Barone's ministry of production. He can go into bankruptcy other than according to plan, and he must stand the competition from other, new managers—however much his freedom of action has been circumscribed by governmental regulations of often questionable and inimical design and by new techniques of labour union co-determination of various degrees. In fact, he has adapted himself to his changed social environment, and 'creative destruction' has not disappeared, even though it may take place within large-scale enterprises more than between them, and however much it may have come to be hedged about by newly devised preservatives, or insufficiently promoted by adequately designed 'adjustment assistance'.

If in fact capitalism as an economic order is adequately described by Schumpeter's formula of innovations plus credit creation and private property—and given his meaning of these terms, this can hardly be questioned—there is no evidence that Peter Drucker's modern corporation cannot carry on where the individual entrepreneur of the 19th century began. Must the capitalist economic explosion stop when what Schumpeter calls the 'capitalist civilization' changes under the impact of accelerating advances in the exact sciences, the explosion of standards of living, spreading social legislation and the spread of highly organized and specialized management? Can capitalism, which has so far shown an impressive capacity for absorption and adjustment, be bent out of its basic shape just at the threshold of such developments as the electronic and genetic revolutions? Do not precisely these two scientific breakthroughs alone give enormous scope to a new, vast and potent wave of innovations produced by what in fact is a new wave of 20th–21st-century managers who indeed do show some of the adventurous characteristic of the 'entrepreneur'? Why should the new 'gales of creative destruction' which have by now, painfully, clearly begun, have to fit the mould either of a 19th-century bourgeoisie or the 20th-century apparatchik? Again, is it really necessary for the 'rulers of men' to possess that 'mystic glamor'? Schumpeter did not live to witness the turbulent developments in the world of the developing countries. Much, it would seem, can be learnt from this. It is difficult to fit them into the capitalist–socialist pattern. As in the United States, there is little 'mystic glamor' to be found there, nor much of the symbiosis of inherited protective strata and the new bourgeoisie. But perhaps the spreading of reversions of economic policies from early socialist attempts to near-capitalist forms indicates how strong, albeit in much changed form, the rules of the capitalist game are.

And finally, would we not, accepting Schumpeter's self-destruction vision, force ourselves into the shackles of an evolutionist dogma similar to the Marxian? Would not that carry with it the fatal danger of blinding us to the future, just as Marxian doctrine became totally unable to fit European development after 1870, after 1918 and after 1933, into its scheme except at the cost of perfectly ludicrous contortions of interpretation? 'Structural' dogmatics, much as they would have been against Schumpeter's intellectual nature, may nevertheless attach themselves to his 'vision'. A misdiagnosis of current developments would follow, and so would mistaken policies—either, when conservative, inappropriately preservative of the 'capitalist engine', or, when reformative, inappropriately promotive of the expected socialism. Much of Schumpeter's Chapter XXVII, though by no means all of it, carries the seeds of such dogmatizing growths, *malgré soi*.

If this were misunderstanding Schumpeter, one is driven to the alternative conclusion that the social sciences—even economics—have simply not yet reached the capacity of providing a scientific basis for the comprehensive prognoses that he loved. We shall have to continue to attack their problems piece by perhaps exasperating piece, as long as scientifically supportable long-term vistas, however tempting, escape us. What is valuable in the sociology of the entrepreneur and his demise served the wholesome purpose of putting the advances of economics, from Walras to post-Keynes, into perspective; perhaps we should leave it at that.

2. A second element of Schumpeter's analysis is the most interesting doctrine of the 'Destruction of the Protective Strata' of capitalism (*CSD*, p. 134ff.). The rise of the national state in continental Europe of the late 17th and early 18th centuries was the success of the economic and political alliance between the monarch and the increasingly capitalist bourgeoisie. In fact, in his early essay, 'Die Krise des Steuerstaates' (1918), Schumpeter had made it a point to show that no 'tax state' could exist except in a capitalist society. In *Capitalism, Socialism and Democracy* he holds, in addition, that in this process the destruction of the pre-capitalist social structure was, certainly during the 19th century, incomplete. 'The steel frame of that structure still consisted of the human material of feudal society . . .' (*CSD*, p. 136), and it discharged the functions of a *classe dirigente* by manning the offices of state, the army and the civil service. 'With the utmost ease and grace the lords and knights metamorphosed themselves into courtiers, administrators, diplomats, politicians and into military officers of a type that had nothing to do with that of the medieval knight' (*CSD*, p. 137). This 'active symbiosis of two social strata' (*ibid.*) provided the capitalist bourgeoisie with the 'protective strata' without which 'the bourgeoisie is politically helpless and unable not only to lead its nation but even to take care of its particular class interests. Which amounts to saying that it needs a master' (*CSD*, p. 138). The English case of the 19th century serves as his paradigmatic example, and later on, when discussing the preconditions of successful democracy (another product of the 'capitalist order'—*CSD*, p. 289ff.), he attempts to show that the absence of this 'active symbiosis' à l'anglaise caused, for example, the collapse of the Weimar republic. Now his point is that the capitalist progress destroys the 'flying buttresses' of the *classe dirigente*, born to rule and then to furnish a disciplined bureaucracy. In the absence of an independent economic base, the nobility finds its place in the capitalist order or disappears. With the disappearance of the 'mystic glamor', it accepts bourgeois ideas, and there follows the conclusion that 'we might well wonder whether it is quite correct to look upon capitalism as a social form *sui generis* or, in fact, as anything but the last stage of the decomposition of what we have called feudalism' (*CSD*, p. 139).

There is much merit in this view which is really a sociology of bureaucracy as a class of administrators in a capitalist society but to a large extent removed from the systems of incentives of entrepreneurdom. In the absence of a workable 'protective stratum', or at least of the tradition inherited from such a stratum, the growing problems of public policy administration, domestic and especially foreign, will strain the efficiency of a capitalist society. The cases of the less-developed countries—which in a sense can serve as laboratory cases because of both their variety and the enormously increased speed with which social changes take place there—show this complex of phenomena both as policy problems and as objects of sociological investigation; but these avenues of inquiry cannot be followed up here.

As with many of Schumpeter's historical analyses, his doctrine finds its most fruitful application in the analysis of the English case. There can be little doubt that the English combination of capitalism and democracy has owed a considerable share of its success to an effective 'protective stratum' of the Schumpeterian kind. Something similar may be said about the success of capitalism on the European continent, in Germany, say, or Austria-Hungary. It would be equally interesting, but cannot be carried out here, to examine the applicability of Schumpeter's thesis to the development of democratic methods and forms in these two countries as well as in several others on the continent. Though they did not benefit from the long social and political evolution that took place in the United Kingdom, the very far reaching disappearance of the traditional aristocracy after the Second World War seems not to have done the type of damage to the political structure of continuing capitalism that Schumpeter might have expected. And it is most difficult to apply his analysis to the case of the United States. In response to the question implied here, Schumpeter might have replied that it is precisely in these countries, as well as in England after the second war, that the 'march into socialism' is most undeniable. After all, the preface to the second edition of the book, written in 1946, ends in 'For this is one of those situations in which optimism [about the future of capitalist civilization] is nothing but a form of defection' (*CSD*, p. 414, 5th Edition).

Again, we may ask whether this extreme pessimism would have survived the robust expansion of the years after 1950—on both counts, that of capitalism and that of democracy. To be sure, there were special circumstances—there always are; but when compared with the inter-war period, the record on both counts turns out to stand the comparison well. The disappearance of the older 'protective stratum' did not damage the 1950 to 1975 expansion, and civil servants have not turned into socialist apparatchiks or anti-capitalist ideologized functionaries or brought 'ideals and beefsteaks on the same denominator'. One may debate the progress of 'capitalist civilization' during the last 35 to 40 years, but one should not forget that intellectual and artistic achievements did not carry the characteristics of *fleurs du mal* any more than they did not only in Weimar Germany but also long before the First World War.

As in the case of Schumpeter's analysis of the entrepreneur, one is struck by his pessimistic conviction of the poverty of the future. The impression is strong that his view of the world in the later years of his life evinces a perhaps not wholly rational love–hate relationship to the 'bourgeois'. Of this, the innovating entrepreneur, the gale of creative destruction and the basically pacific burgher is one side, and the figure that cannot 'say boo to a goose', who 'needs a master' in the shape of a pleasantly decomposing feudalism, is the other. This, however, is a matter for personality psychology.

3. A third prominent element of Schumpeter's vision of the demise of capitalism is the figure of the intellectual. This social type antedates the beginnings of capitalism but, originating in the West in the monastery, was 'well in hand' until the arrival of capitalism 'let him loose and presented him with the printing press' (*CSD*, p. 147). Difficult to define precisely, the type varies from the Duke of Wellington's 'scribbling set' to generally the wielders of the 'power of the spoken and the written word', characterized by 'the absence of direct responsibility for practical affairs' (*CSD*, pp. 146–147). He is not solely the product of late capitalism: Schumpeter's examples range from Pietro Aretino, via Voltaire, Rousseau and John Wilkes to the modern journalist. There is little doubt about his dislike of the type, but then it is in the nature of the phenomenon that one of its groups accuses the other of heterodoxy and nefariousness. Nor is there doubt about Schumpeter's high estimate of the intellectual's role in the decline of capitalism; he appears as something of an anti-hero to the 'entrepreneur'; and as capitalism matured, the influence of the intellectual is depicted as growing, and there were more of him.

As the very success of the capitalist order reduces the function of the entrepreneur, 'evaporates the substance of property', destroys the protective strata and other supportive institutions such as the bourgeois family, 'the bourgeois finds to his amazement that the rationalist attitude does not stop at the credentials of kings and popes but goes on to attack private property and the whole scheme of bourgeois values. The bourgeois fortress thus becomes politically defenseless' (*CSD*, p. 143). The capitalist begins to be arraigned 'before judges who have the death sentence in their pockets' (*CSD*, p. 144)— the intellectuals. A rational defence fails to master the power of emotions, 'sub- or superrational impulses' (*ibid.*). And in this cultural struggle 'the role of the intellectual group consists primarily in stimulating, energizing, verbalizing and organizing this material and only secondarily in adding to it' (*CSD*, p. 153).

There is no doubt, from Schumpeter's examples, that intellectuals of the type he describes have existed and exist but, as in the case of the 'entrepreneur', his treatment of their origins and their impact raises a series of questions about the nature of this deus ex machina, or rather, diabolus ex machina. Again, Schumpeter's explanation focuses on the social origin of the intellectual rather than on the development of his ideas. Without serious discussion, they are taken as by nature inimical to 'capitalist civilization'. The implication of his exposition is that all social institutions—pre-capitalist, capitalist and presumably post-capitalist—are equally vulnerable to attack from the 'rationalist attitude' which itself is part of the capitalist evolution. Moreover, what is even more astonishing, it is this same attitude which is described as first aiding to 'create the social space' for bourgeois capitalism and then later on producing its destruction, or at least helping to destroy it. One must wonder what these ideas were, how they acquired their power of conviction and how they developed; but Schumpeter does not meet this query. He does not set out explicitly, let alone explain, what seems to be the implication of his 'sociology of the intellectual', that effective dominance of a society or civilization requires, in its dominant groups, a mystique that cannot withstand 'rationalist' critique and attack.

Instead, he points to the spread of universal education, especially higher education, 'no less inevitable than the development of the largest-scale industrial unit' (*CSD*, p. 152), academic unemployability and unemployment which feed the growing reservoir of 'intellectuals' who then engage in providing the ideologies for anti-capitalist groups. Schumpeter holds that there is a direct relationship between the rise of the intellectual and the decline of the civil service. The latter, like the former, were never capitalists themselves. 'Except for inhibitions due to professional training and experience, they [the bureaucracies] are therefore open to conversion by the modern intellectual with whom, through similar education, they have much in common' (*CSD*, p. 155). 'The tinge of gentility that in many cases used to raise a barrier has been fading away from the modern civil servant' (*ibid.*), and when the public administration expands rapidly 'much of the additional personnel required has to be taken from the intellectual group—witness this country' (*ibid.*). The bourgeois is overwhelmed by the onslaught. 'The only explanation for the meekness we observe is that the bourgeois order no longer makes sense to the bourgeois himself and that, when all is said and nothing is done, it does not really care' (*CSD*, p. 161).

It is hard to resist the conclusion that this is an overdrawn portrait of decline, of a piece with the growing melancholy for what Schumpeter felt to be a passing world. Commentary on the details of his sociology of the intellectual would require an examination of how well it fits, on the one hand, the periods known to Schumpeter: Edwardian England, fin-de-siècle Austria and Weimar Germany and, on the other—perhaps much more difficult—the period after the Second World War: Europe, especially Germany and France; and the United States, to say nothing about the less-developed countries. Two specific questions may be mentioned, however. Are, as a matter of fact, 'intellectuals' all and always anti-capitalist? The answer would require a treatise, and the result would by no means be an unqualified yes. To be sure, such results are open to argument, but to maintain Schumpeter's view would require the neglect of a considerable sector of the intellectual history of the last generation.

Second, Schumpeter's sociology of the intellectual raises again the question which any 'sociology of knowledge' fails to answer. It was raised above in the discussion of 'capitalist civilization' and poses itself here even more forcefully. People who think thoughts, have ideas and ideals—artistic, moral, religious—do so because they convince themselves of them—to be sure for good or for insufficient reasons—and not because they are academic unemployed and live in the later stages of capitalism (or any other social and economic system). That they should direct some of their thoughts to these systems in which they live is certainly no wonder. But what their ideas are does not depend on, is not explained by, their living in them, but on their reasoning, right or wrong as it may be. How is it to be explained, then, that the powerful rationalism that in Schumpeter's view was produced, not only materially supported, by the 'capitalist order' over the centuries can convince them that the bourgeois world makes no more sense, if that is in fact what it did? What are the reasons for accepting another—socialist, in Schumpeter's view—set of convictions? Economic activity is no more the 'matrix of logic' than successful capitalism is the 'matrix' of socialist ideas. The power of ideas is great, or weak, not because they find institutional support, but because they *convince*, for good or bad reasons.

When a 'vision' rests so strongly on the changes of a social 'framework' and when the ideas of elements of this framework—of the 'entrepreneur', the 'protective strata', the 'intellectual'—are of such importance in its changes, one must ask what reasons, beliefs, ideas there were that changed basic socially-relevant convictions. This Schumpeter does not do, and he thus weakens much of his argument, much of his prognosis. As it is, the Schumpeterian capitalism-destroying intellectual is as much a social, or intellectual if you will, miracle as his entrepreneur. The intellectual's ideas are inserted into the explanation of capitalist decline arbitrarily, without adequate cause or reason. The implied materialist relativism, or scepticism—i.e., the belief that the power which the holders of ideas acquire in their action on these ideas can be explained without regard to the reasons for their convictions, so that only the social positions of the ideologues in question matter—will not do. It is not enough to say that 'to realize the relative validity of one's convictions and yet to stand for them unflinchingly is what distinguishes a civilized man from a barbarian' (*CSD*, p. 243); this cannot be taken seriously for it would follow that one must 'realize the relative validity' of the conviction expressed in this sentence as well. The consequence of this doctrine is that the analyst underestimates the power of ideas and overestimates the effect on them of the social environment.

To sum up, the thesis of the demise of capitalism into socialism as Schumpeter presents it is defective because its three elements—the demise of the 'entrepreneur' and of the 'supporting strata' and the rise of the 'intellectual'—form too narrow a basis for it and are themselves incompletely explained. In fact, developments during the one and a half generations after the book was written would seem to show this, and at the same time provide possible elements for a modification of that thesis. They show that capitalism changes, has absorbed and digested changes in ideas and institutions, has even spread to new territories of considerable extension. It has changed into forms that, social sciences being what they are even now, were impossible to predict. This is so, even though Schumpeter's analysis produced innumerable suggestions and many 'theories', economic and sociological, which survive a critical re-reading of his book.

As large a part of *Capitalism, Socialism and Democracy* as is devoted to the analysis of capitalism is taken up by a discussion of socialism and democracy. Then there is a most interesting essay on the history of socialist parties, which will not be re-examined here, however, since it is largely illustrative of the argument in the rest of the book. As before, there is much close reasoning and a good deal of the *histoire raisonnée* at which Schumpeter excelled. In what follows, only some of the principal analyses are reviewed; they would also seem to be the ones that survive the passage of time and to recommend themselves to the reader of the 1980s as much as they did (or should have) to that of the 1940s.

To begin with, one of Schumpeter's great merits is that, in his discussion of a socialist economy and society, he insisted that the debate must accept the (theoretical) possibility of a socialist (i.e., a centrally planned) economy as efficient as the capitalist one can be judged to be by accepted standards of economic efficiency. In that sense, what he calls the 'socialist blueprint' can work as well as the capitalist—in fact, possibly rather better. This eliminates much of the malfocused debate and refocuses it on what really matters.

Defined as 'an institutional pattern in which the control over the means of production and over production itself is vested with a central authority' (*CSD*, p. 167), a socialist economy can be shown to be operable on analytically the same scheme as a capitalist (free) economy. The reasoning in support of this proposition, found already in V. Pareto's *Cours d'Economie Politique* (1897)—the much neglected predecessor of the *Manual*—was fully worked out in Enrico Barone's 'Il ministro della produzione nello stato collettivista' (1908). It is conclusively shown there, except for minor detail, and remains correct today, that it is possible 'to derive, from its data and from the rules of rational behavior, uniquely determined decisions as to what and how to produce . . . [that] those data and rules, under the circumstances of a

socialist economy, yield equations which are independent and compatible
... and sufficient in number to determine uniquely the unknowns of the
problem before the control board or ministry of production' (*CSD*, p. 172).
Barone's is nothing but the Walrasian system applied to a planned economy,
fully equivalent in form to one for the unplanned economy.

The advantages of this demonstration, later improved by the writings of
Oscar Lange and A.P. Lerner, are two. The first concerns the pure economics of the socialist–capitalist debate. The Pareto–Barone demonstration
sloughs off that debate all that part which concerns technical attempts to
show the impossibility in principle of a centrally-directed economy: too
little information, no precise directives for production managers, an unmanageable number of equations to solve, thus the need for supermen to run
the system, the theoretically unavoidable inefficiency and waste and beyond
that the technical indeterminacy of the system. At the time when Schumpeter wrote, these problems were much in the foreground of the debate, as
exemplified by the writings then of Lionel Robbins and F.A. Hayek, as
against the Lange–Lerner articles just mentioned. Demonstrations of the
theoretical impossibility of a centrally planned economy are simply wrong.
Schumpeter, in accepting the Pareto–Barone results, took a position which,
it would seem, has been largely accepted now that this branch of the debate
has died down: 'There is nothing wrong with the logic of socialism' (*CSD*,
p. 172). He carried the argument further. He shows that the task of the 'ministro della produzione' is lightened, and the efficiency of the system
enhanced, in comparison with that of an unplanned economy, because the
central direction, as long as it is effectively carried out, avoids the 'uncertainties about the reaction of one's [i.e., the individual firm's] actual and potential competitors and about how the general business situations are going to
shape' (*CSD*, p. 186): effective central planning would solve much of the
'monopoly problem'.

Moreover, Schumpeter's 'comparison of blueprints' (*CSD*, Chapter
XVII) favours the socialist alternative principally because it should be able to
avoid economic cycles, therefore unemployment and inflation, and because
there cannot be the phenomenon of 'government interference' (*CSD*, p. 197)
which he feels so much fetters capitalism. This point is a part of the other
side of the coin of which capitalist self-destruction is the one: 'socialization
means a step beyond big business on the way that has been chalked out by it
... socialist management may conceivably prove to be as superior to big-
business capitalism as big-business capitalism has proved to be to the kind of
competitive capitalism of which the English industry of a hundred years ago
was the prototype' (*CSD*, pp. 195–196). 'Modern capitalism relies on the
profit principle for its daily bread yet refuses to allow it to prevail. No such
conflict, consequently, no such wastes would exist in socialist societies'

(*ibid.*). Schumpeter emphasized, and this is of course a major qualification, that these analytical conclusions apply only to the strictly economic aspects of a socialist system, to what he calls its 'blueprint'. They therefore cannot be, and they are not in Schumpeter's book, the final verdict on that system. It is nevertheless worth keeping them in mind in order to separate aspects of the problem that require separate discussion. In this sense must be understood his final conclusion that 'it is quite possible that future generations will look upon arguments about the inferiority of the socialist plan as we look upon Adam Smith's argument about joint stock companies which, also, is not simply false' (*CSD*, p. 196); otherwise this stricture would seem to go rather far.

So much for the pure economics of the debate, and the Pareto–Barone demonstration. The other benefit which the socialism–capitalism debate may derive from it is that it forces that debate into much clearer focus. That can perhaps be shown best by beginning with what Schumpeter calls the 'Cultural Indeterminateness of Socialism' (*CSD*, p. 170). By this he means that, given no more than the definition of a socialist system, as quoted further above, such a system is indeterminate in respect of the wider social and cultural institutions that may accompany it. The possibilities are many and none of them would be incompatible with a socialist system—democratic or autocratic forms of government, rationalist and 'irreligious' culture or its opposite, pacific or imperialist external policies—so long as one does not specify what social groups at what stage of their political and cultural development will make the transition to socialist planning. To be sure, this thesis owes its origin in part to the fact that much more is known about the history of civilization that has accompanied capitalism than about that which may develop with socialism, and Schumpeter readily concedes this. Nevertheless, he maintains that cultural indeterminateness cannot be attributed to capitalism while it must be conceded to a socialist society.

In any event, the crux of the socialism debate lies in this area, as may be seen when 'cultural indeterminateness' is fitted into the Pareto–Barone scheme. Schumpeter does this only by implication when discussing the institutional and human elements required for an effective socialist system. That the 'ministro della produzione' controls the means of production is of course analytical shorthand, perfectly permissible for the purposes of the Pareto–Barone demonstration, but requiring elaboration. No central planner, however autocratic, is independent of his political environment. In practice, the 'ministro' is likely to be something like a Politburo, a politico-economic élite. Thus the distribution of incomes among the members of the planned economy (i.e., among that élite and their followers), and with this the directives to the socialist production managers, will be determined by the outcome of an unavoidable struggle for influence on the direction of the economy among the members of that élite group. What in an unplanned economy is settled by the contests among the owners of the means of production (including labour) in the markets for the means of production and their services is determined in the socialist alternative by, if you will, a political 'market' among the members of the Politburo. The means of influence that are 'traded' between them may be military, religious or quasi-religious (such as degrees of party orthodoxy, with all the exegesis that goes along with that), access to scientific knowledge or simply personal endowment and property as in an unplanned system. These means of influence are pitted against one another, and whatever the type and form of combat in this influence 'market' are—between the soldiers, the priests and the regional lords of all varieties, etc.—the distribution of power will directly determine economic results, as private ownership of the means of production and its distribution will in a capitalist economy—modified of course by the system of net taxation which even here is determined by a political 'market'. The 'cultural indeterminateness of socialism' leaves a wide range of possibilities. In the working of this system of political combat in the socialist society, in the form which in any given case the elimination of the 'cultural indeterminateness' takes, lies the problem of the comparison between the two alternative forms of society. The Pareto–Barone result solves the problem merely in part—the results of the struggle in the 'influence market' are in fact one of its sets of data.

The struggle among the élite for the direction of the economy, which replaces in a socialist economy the purely economic contest in the markets of the means of production and their services in a capitalist system, is bound to pervade the socialist society and determine incentives, political institutions and practices. Whatever possibilities there may be in a capitalist society to separate politics from economics, it is by its nature and organization impossible in a socialist scheme to do so. This is the real problem of the relative merits of the two, beyond the 'comparison of blueprints'. Whether, then, a socialist system leads to Hayekian 'serfdom' or to Marxian (or any other socialist) millennium, to Stalinist autocracy or democratic central direction, depends on the structure, composition and generally the stage of social development of the socialist society concerned. Had Schumpeter lived to observe the developments in recent decades in the newly independent developing countries, his stock of examples for the indeterminateness of socialist and quasi-socialist societies would have been considerably augmented.

In summary, then, the merit of Schumpeter's exposition is twofold: it separates out the purely economic analytics, and it shows by the 'cultural indeterminateness of socialism' the need to discuss the political influence struggle as an indispensable part of a socialist system. When all is said, this may not be original and it may even seem quite obvious. Having been said as early as it was, it is nevertheless a merit to have thus sharpened the focus of the discussion; it is good 'theory'.

The consequences which Schumpeter draws from this position, which I have taken the liberty of spinning out rather farther than he himself did, without, I think, doing violence to his meaning, however, are two. One concerns what he calls the 'human element' required by, or likely to be available to, a modern socialist society. The other emphasizes the decisive importance of the stage of capitalist development from which the transition to socialism, as he sees it, takes place.

After what has been said, one will not expect Schumpeter to subscribe to the proposition that either 'demigods' (to manage the detail of the 'socialist engine') or 'archangels' (people of an 'ethical level that men as they are cannot be expected to reach') are either needed or likely to be found as capitalism declines and the transition to socialism, as he sees it, is made (*CSD*, pp. 203–204). But he does expect that 'the socialist order presumably will command the moral allegiance which is being increasingly refused to capitalism' (*CSD*, p. 211). That is, regardless of what form the struggle for the control of the socialist plan may be expected to take, the transition from capitalist to socialist allegiance of the rank and file will be facilitated by the decline of general belief in capitalist systems and the accompanying adherence to a system of rewards of a socialist nature. An effective bureaucracy is 'an inevitable complement to modern economic development and it will be more than ever essential to a socialist commonwealth' (*CSD*, p. 206). As capitalist managers and the public civil service become more and more alike and as the civil service and the intellectuals approach one another in training and convictions as capitalism declines, he thinks there is a perfectly good chance that this essential element for a successful socialist plan will be in place at the transition. 'The conditions for moral acceptance of the socialist order of things and for a transfer of loyalties to it are likely to be met' 'at least in the case of socialism in the fullness of time; and there need be no commissars to thwart and to insult'. 'Rational treatment of the ex-bourgeois elements with a view to securing a maximum performance from them will not require anything that is not just as necessary in the case of managerial personnel of any other extraction' (*CSD*, p. 207).

Profit incentives will, in the later development of capitalism itself, be replaced by the strengthening belief in the new system. In fact, 'one of the chief merits of the socialist order consists in the fact that it shows up the nature of economic phenomena with unmistakable clearness whereas in the capitalist order their faces are covered by the mask of the profit interest' (*CSD*, p. 211). In a socialist society 'nobody could possibly doubt that what a nation gets out of international trade is the imports and that exports are the sacrifice that must be undergone in order to procure the imports, whereas in commercial society this commonsense view is as a rule hidden from the man in the street who therefore cheerfully supports policies that are to his disadvantage' (*CSD*, pp. 211–212). Everybody will understand that it is necessary to work hard, and 'nobody will get away with nonsense about saving' (*ibid.*). Strikes would be 'nothing else but antisocial attacks on the nation's welfare... There would no longer be ... any well-meaning bourgeois of both sexes who think it frightfully exciting to applaud strikers and strike leaders' (*ibid.*).

The re-reader of the book reads these passages with increasing scepsis and astonishment. To be sure, lest he should fear that our author has got lost in the mirage of an economist's paradise, they are followed by more realist sections on the Soviet example; but even here, one's doubt about these extreme reaches of Schumpeter's vision is not removed. It is, after all, a very strong statement to make that 'socialism might be the only means of restoring social discipline' (*CSD*, p. 215). No doubt, 'the socialist management will have at its disposal many more tools of authoritarian discipline than any capitalist management can ever have again' (*ibid.*). That it operates in 'a society that once more believes in its own standards' (*ibid.*) is more doubtful than that 'economic necessities will no longer be a laughing matter. Attempts at paralysing operations and at setting people against their work will amount to attacking the government. And it can reasonably be expected to react to this' (*CSD*, p. 215). The re-establishment of 'social discipline', as Schumpeter describes it in these pages, may not be the beneficial result of re-establishing society's belief in itself so much as a form of settling the political combat in the Politburo which would claim less sympathy from us than we would be prepared to give other forms of reaching the same end. The loss of social discipline of the kind that Schumpeter's words seem to indicate he means, if indeed there has been such loss in late capitalism, may be less the precursor of capitalism's demise than a price for its robust continuation. From his pessimism over the development of late capitalism, it seems, Schumpeter came increasingly to believe that the 'cultural indeterminateness' of the society which he saw taking the place of capitalism had narrowed much more than his more abstract analysis earlier on implied. Nevertheless, the book here at issue shows less desperation than Schumpeter had given way to in his address to his students in Bonn (1932) on the occasion of taking leave for Harvard University.[4] Pessimism at times limits the imagination, and at worst leads to the non sequitur of a *va banque*.

The sociology of the bureaucracy is clearly of considerable importance. Schumpeter's contribution, the emphasis on the role of the 'protecting

---

[4] See his evaluation of possibilities for young economists in the coming national-socialist regime in Germany in 'Das Woher und Wohin unserer Wissenschaft' (1932).

strata' in a capitalist society and on the growing acceptance of quasi-socialist organization and beliefs in its later stages, deserves consideration. So does his attempt to gauge its character in a socialist order. But it is unlikely that these parts of his analysis could have been written, and less so that they could be accepted, had they been written a generation later.

Finally, the sharp distinction which Schumpeter draws between transition from capitalism to socialism from a mature as against an immature stage is worth noting. The state of capitalist development reached at the point of transition, if and when such transition does occur, determines the character and quality of the ensuing socialist regime. It is the difference between the socialist system imposed, say, by the Russian revolution or by socialist regimes in developing countries and that which Schumpeter expected to be the result of a gradual decline from fully developed capitalism (i.e., 'in the fullness of time'). In the first case, there is no avoiding the brutalities that have in fact taken place; in the latter there should, he thinks, be a chance for the gradual readying of 'things and souls' for the transition. And then Schumpeter singles out an intriguing third case: England as the example of the gradual introduction of 'socialist policy before the act' (of the actual step into socialism). In the pages filled by his interpretation of this case (further expanded in the purely historical last Part of the book) he writes a highly imaginative, almost loving, piece on England and its adaptive social system, as seen in 1938. 'It assimilated Disraeli who elsewhere would have become another Lassalle. It would have, if necessary, assimilated Trotsky himself or rather, as in that case he would assuredly have been, the Earl of Prinkipio, K.G.' (*CSD*, p. 229). The preface to the third English edition of the book continues this essay, now already less sanguine, as we assuredly would have to be now.

Almost 70 pages of the book are devoted to a discussion of socialism and democracy; after what has been said above, I may be permitted to be brief.

Schumpeter's views on democracy had undergone considerable change. In an essay some 20 years before *Capitalism, Socialism and Democracy*, on socialist possibilities after the First World War ('Sozialistische Möglichkeiten von heute', 1921–2), he took an extremely critical position: 'The realization that real democracy would mean not only getting stuck in the mire of sub-mediocrity, but generally being incapable of action, has of course been an age-old axiom for all leading groups and individuals' (my translation), and he cites with approval G. Sorel's phrase of the 'degenerazione in democrazia' (p. 328, footnote). This is replaced by a much more positive treatment in Part IV of *CSD*.

The question he proposed to examine is the relationship between socialist orders and democracy. The answer is arrived at in three steps which may be briefly summarized. The first is a brief inspection of the position taken by the socialist parties in Europe and the United States towards democracy. And this, detailed later on in the historical part of the book, is summed up in: 'As regards democracy, socialist parties are presumably no more opportunists than are any others; they simply espouse democracy if, as and when it serves their ideals and interests and not otherwise' (*CSD*, p. 240). That is, there is no evidence from the history of such parties that they will necessarily and in all situations adhere to democratic political forms, and there is much that they will not, when they do not live in an environment in which the espousing of non-democratic political methods would threaten their destruction. The second step extends through an examination of the 'classical' theory of democracy (i.e., that which developed in the 17th and 18th centuries), and generalizes the conclusion of the first step: 'Democracy is a political *method* . . . and hence incapable of being an end in itself' (*CSD*, p. 242). In particular, the formulation which identifies democracy with the 'rule of the people' fails to yield a workable definition and theory because of the ambiguity of the two terms involved. No autocrat is entirely undemocratic and no democracy is entirely unautocratic. And 'the People' has historically meant all the varied things the people decided it to mean. A separate chapter (*CSD*, pp. 250–268) in which the 'classical' theory is examined in some detail leads to the conclusion that 'democracy, when motivated in this way' (i.e., in the quasi-religious sense that, e.g., 'the voice of the people is the voice of God'), 'ceases to be a mere method that can be discussed rationally like a steam engine or a disinfectant'.

One may debate whether this is an original conclusion, and of course it does not fully settle the matter of how the 'classical' theory originated and why it has subsisted far beyond the 18th century, after 'later historical, sociological, biological, psychological and economic analysis proved destructive' both to the utilitarian version of it and to the political theory for which it provided the basis. For it leaves unanswered the question why it was that ethico–religious ideas were attached to this rather than to other forms of political method. But Schumpeter's examination serves the important purpose of separating a religionist confusion from the empirical sociological analysis of democracy as a social empirical phenomenon.

The third step in Schumpeter's inquiry begins with a realistic definition of democracy, derived from his historical and ideological considerations. The phenomenon is described as follows: 'the democratic method is that institutional arrangement for arriving at political decisions in which individuals acquire the power to decide by means of a competitive struggle for the people's vote' (*CSD*, p. 269). It is a description which provides a fruitful starting point for a series of empirical analyses on which Schumpeter offers suggestions and notes, such as that of political leadership, political parties, individual political 'volition' and of individual freedom as an empirical phenomenon, a catalogue of research listed but not carried out in the book. Inevitably, there are notes on the application of this theory to the workings of British parliamentarianism.

The focus of these chapters, however, is on the possibility of democratic socialism. The result is not surprising when one realizes that both socialism and democracy, as Schumpeter defines them, are characterized by what was earlier called 'cultural indeterminateness'. 'Between socialism as we defined it and democracy as we defined it there is no necessary relation... At the same time, there is no incompatibility' (*CSD*, p. 284). That is, provided the conditions are met, in any given situation, which make a success of both socialism and democracy possible—in fact, they overlap in part. In respect of democracy, they include not only political human material of 'sufficiently high quality' (*CSD*, p. 290)—we meet again what earlier on were called the 'supporting strata', then of capitalism now of democracy, the (English) aristocrat turned politician or civil servant—a not too far extended 'effective range of political decision' (*CSD*, p. 291); a 'well trained bureaucracy of good standing and tradition, endowed with a strong sense of duty and no less strong *esprit de corps*' (*CSD*, p. 293); 'democratic self-control' (i.e., public respect among voters and politicians, not only for decisions of parliament, but also for one another); and finally 'a large measure of tolerance for difference of opinion' (*CSD*, p. 295).

These are high and limiting standards, and Schumpeter believes that they were in fact met only at the apogee of capitalism where 'the bourgeoisie produced individuals who made a success of leadership upon entering a political class of non-bourgeois origin' (*CSD*, p. 298). The decline of capitalism also threatens the effectiveness of democracy. However, 'though the ideology of classical socialism is the offspring of bourgeois ideology' (*CSD*, p. 298), the maintenance of democratic forms in a socialist society would be a hopeless task except in the case of a society of capitalist maturity with the 'ability to establish the socialist order in a democratic way' (*CSD*, p. 301). Since, however, 'after all, effective management of the capitalist economy means dictatorship not *of* but *over* the proletariat in the factory' (*CSD*, p. 302), the maintenance of democratic government may prove 'extremely delicate even when the transition takes place from mature capitalism. So that, as a matter of practical necessity, socialist democracy may eventually turn out to be more of a sham than capitalist democracy ever was' (*CSD*, p. 302).

With this sentence, in which pessimism and realism meet, the analytical part of the book ends. A remarkable train of ideas: a realist definition and theory of democracy, formal enough, as it has to be, to meet any economic organization of society, applied to highly stylized situations, past conclusions that at times threaten to beg the question asked, and finishing with a final conclusion that almost demolishes the argument—a tour de force within a tour de force.

The impression with which the book leaves this re-reader is clearly of two main parts. There is the grand 'vision' of the capitalist–socialist process, explained from a set of consistently applied ideas and studded with innumerable historical vignettes and fascinating insights but, however stimulating in its development, unconvincing in the end. And there is a considerable number of hypotheses, 'theories' in the author's terminology, trenchant, precise and permanently added to the arsenal of economic and sociological scientific tools. It is in fact a document reflective of the state of the science: remarkable progress towards the explanation of individual problems but yet unable to provide an explanation of the development of society in the width and over the long spans of time that the 'vision' holds out as the eventual goal. Of the characteristics that once disturbed the early reader, there remain the traces of a strange—or perhaps not so strange—mixture of philosophical relativism and romanticism side by side with occasional expressions of strong value opinions; but one may wish to put that down to tensely stretched tolerance rather than understandable predilection.

REFERENCES

Barone, E. (1908) Il ministro della produzione nello stato collettivista. *Giornale degli Economisti,* **II.**

Hirschmann, A.O. (1979) *The Welfare State in Trouble: System Crisis or Growing Pains?* Paper presented to the American Economic Association annual meeting at New York, December.

Keynes, J.M. (1936) *The General Theory of Employment, Interest and Money.* London: Macmillan.

Lewis, Sir W.A. (1978) *Growth and Fluctuations, 1880–1913.* London: George Allen & Unwin.

Moravetz, D. (1977) *Twenty-five Years of Economic Development 1950–1975.* Washington: The World Bank.

Pareto, V. (1896/7) *Cours d'Economie Politique.* Lausanne: Rouge.

Schumpeter, J.A. (1918) Die Krise des Steuerstaates. *In Zeitfragen aus dem Gebriet der Soziologie.* Republished in *Joseph A. Schumpeter. Aufsätze zur Soziologie* (Ed.) Schneider, E. & Spiethoff, A. (1953) Tübingen: J.C.B. Mohr (Paul Siebeck).

Schumpeter, J.A. (1919) Zur Soziologie der Imperialismen. *Archiv für Sozialwissenschaft und Sozialpolitik,* **46,** 1–39.

Schumpeter, J.A. (1921/2) Sozialistische Möglichkeiten von heute. *Archiv für Sozialwissenschaft und Sozialpolitik,* **48,** 305–360.

Schumpeter, J.A. (1912) *Theorie der wirtschaftlichen Entwicklung, Eine Untersuchung über Unternehmergewinn, Kapital, Kredit, Zins und den Konjunkturzyklus, zweite Auflage.* München and Leipzig: Verlag von Duncker und Humblot. 2nd Edition, 1926. English translation (1934) *The Theory of Economic Development,* Cambridge, MA: Harvard University Press.

Schumpeter, J.A. (1926) Gustav von Schmoller und die Probleme von heute. In *Schmollers Jahrbuch für Gesetzgebung, Verwaltung und Volkswirtschaft,* 50 Jahrgang, pp. 337–388.

Schumpeter, J.A. (1932) Das Woher und Wohin unserer Wissenschaft. Published in *Joseph A. Schumpeter. Aufsätze zur ökonomischen Theorie* (Ed.) Schneider, E & Spiethoff, A. (1952), pp. 598–608. Tübingen: J.C.B. Mohr (Paul Siebeck).

Schumpeter, J.A. (1939) *Business Cycles: A Theoretical, Historical and Statistical Analysis of the Capitalist Process* (2 Volumes). New York: McGraw-Hill.

Schumpeter, J.A. (1946) John Maynard Keynes, 1883–1948. *American Economic Review*, September. Reprinted (1948) as Chapter X in *The New Economics* (Ed.) Harris, S.E., pp. 91–92. New York.

Schumpeter, J.A. (1949) *The March into Socialism.* Address to the American Economic Association annual meeting at New York, December. Published in *American Economic Review* (May 1950), pp. 446–456. Printed in the 3rd and later editions of *Capitalism, Socialism and Democracy.*

Schumpeter, J.A. (1951) *Ten Great Economists.* New York: Oxford University Press.

Stern, F. (1977) *Gold and Iron: Bismarck, Bleichröder and the Building of the German Empire.* New York: Random House.

Sweezy, P.M. (1942 and 1946) *The Theory of Capitalist Development.* Chapters XVII and XVIII. Cambridge, MA: Harvard University Press.

Index

203